A Compendium of Laws on Banking in Uganda

Fountain Publishers

Fountain Publishers Ltd
P.O. Box 488
Kampala, Uganda
Email: fountain@starcom.co.ug
Website: www.fountainpublishers.co.ug

Distributed in Europe, North America and Australia by African Books Collective (ABC), The Jam Factory, 27 Park End St, Oxford OX1 1HU, United Kingdom. Tel: 44(0) 1865-726686, Fax:1865-793298

First published 2005

ISBN 9970 02 361 6

Cataloguing-in-Publishing Data

A Compendium of Laws on Banking in Uganda. Compiled by Fountain Publishers, Kampala, Fountain 2005
__ p. __ cm

ISBN 9970 02 361 6
1. Banking Law – Uganda.

346.6761/082

CONTENTS

Acknowledgement

This compendium of laws on banking in Uganda has been put together by Alex Buri and Joseph Kyazze.

Publisher's Note

This compendium of laws on banking in Uganda is an important collection that will benefit all students of business law and other related subjects. It may also be used by lawyers and buniess peope operating in Uganda. This is the first time that all laws relating to business have been put together in one collection for ease of reference. This collection contains The Financial Institutions Act, The Bank of Uganda Act, The Bills of Exchange Act, The Evidence (Banker's Books) Act, The Bankruptcy Act, The Stamps Act, The Money-Lender's Act.

CHAPTER 54

THE FINANCIAL INSTITUTIONS ACT

Arrangement of Sections

Section

PART I – PRELIMINARY

PART II – LICENSING

PART III – CAPITAL REQUIREMENTS

PART IV – RESTRICTIONS AND PROHIBITIONS ON FINANCIAL INSTITUTIONS

Part V – Supervision

Part VI – Liquidation, Seizure and Re-organisation

Part VII – The Deposit Protection Fund

Part VIII – Miscellaneous

Section

CHAPTER 54

THE FINANCIAL INSTITUTIONS ACT

An Act to amend and consolidate the law relating to the regulation and control of financial institutions and to provide for related matters.

Commencement: 14th May, 1993.

PART I – PRELIMINARY.

1. Interpretation.

In this Act, unless the context otherwise requires.

(a) "bank" means any company licensed to carry on banking business as its principal business and includes all branches and offices of that company in Uganda;

(b) "banking business" means the business carried on as a principal business of –

(i) accepting deposits of money from the public repayable on demand or at the expiry of a fixed period or after notice.

(ii) employing such deposits wholly or partly by lending or any other means for the account and at the risk of the person accepting such deposits; and

(iii) presenting to another bank, for payment, cheques, drafts or orders received from customers in the capacity of a banker.

(c) "board" means the Board of the Central Bank;

(d) "building society" means a society formed for the purpose of raising by the subscriptions of members a stock or fund from which to make advances to members and registered in accordance with the provisions of the Building Societies Act;

(e) "Central Bank" means the Bank of Uganda established under the Bank of Uganda Act;

(f) "company" means a company incorporated or registered under the Companies Act and includes –

(i) the Uganda Commercial Bank Established by the Uganda Commercial Bank Act.

(ii) the Co-operative Bank Limited registered under the Co-operative Societies Act;

(iii) the Uganda Development Bank established under the Uganda Development Bank Act;

(iv) a building society duly incorporated under the Building Societies Act; and

(v) any institution classified as a financial institution under this Act;

(g) "core capital" means permanent shareholders' equipment in the form of issued and fully paid-up shares plus all disclosed reserves, less good will or any other intangible assets;

(h) "credit institutions" means any company licensed to carry on credit institution business as its principal business, and any other body specified by the Central Bank, to be a credit institution for the purposes of this Act, and includes all branches and offices of that company or body in Uganda;

(i) "credit institution business" means the business of accepting deposits of money from the public repayable after a fixed period or after notice and of employing such deposits wholly or partly by lending or any other means for the account and at the risk of the person accepting the deposits;

(j) "demand deposits" means deposits which are repayable on demand and are withdrawable by cheque, draft, order or by other means;

(k) "demand liabilities" means the total deposit liabilities of a bank or credit institution which are denominated in any currency and payable upon demand;

(l) "disclosed reserves" includes all reserves created or increased through share premiums, retained profits (after deducting all expenses, provisions, taxation, and dividends) and general reserves if such disclosed reserves are permanent and unencumbered and thus able to absorb losses;

(m) "draft" means a bankers' draft payable on demand drawn by or on behalf of a bank upon itself whether payable at the head office or some other office of the bank;

(n) "financial institution" includes a bank, credit institution, a building society, and any institution which by Statutory Instrument, is classified as a financial institution by the Central Bank;

(o) "foreign company" means a company not being a local company;

(p) "licence" means a licence issued under section 6;

(q) "licensed" means licensed under this Act;

(r) "local company" means a company registered or incorporated under the Companies Act in which the majority shares and actual controlling interest are held by citizens of Uganda.

(s) "Minister" means the Minister responsible for finance;

(t) "off balance sheet items" means all items not shown on the balance sheet but which constitute credit risk; and such risks include guarantees, acceptances, performance bonds, letters of credit, and other off balance sheet items deemed to constitute credit risk by the Central Bank;

(u) "officer" includes a person who carries out or is empowered to carry out functions relating to the direction of a financial institution;

(v) "order" when used in conjunction with the word "cheque" or "draft", means an unconditional order in writing constituting a bill of exchange as defined in the Bills of Exchange Act;

(w) "supplementary capital" means general provisions which are held against future and presently unidentified losses that are freely available to meet losses which subsequently materialize, and revaluation reserves on banking premises which arise periodically from independent valuation of such premises, and any other form of capital as may be determined from time to time by the Central Bank;

(x) "time deposits" means deposits repayable after a fixed period or after notice and includes saving deposits;

(y) "time liabilities" means deposit liabilities other than demand liabilities of a financial institution which are denominated in any currency and are subject to payment after a fixed period of time or after notice;

(z) "total capital" means the sum of core capital and supplementary capital;

(aa) "unsecured advances or unsecured credit facilities" means advance or credit facilities made without security, or in respect of any advance or credit facility made with security or any part of it which at any time exceeds the market value of the assets constituting that security, or where the Central Bank is satisfied that there is no established market value, on the basis of a valuation approved by the Central Bank.

2. Application of the Act

(1) This Act shall apply to a financial institution defined in section 1.

(2) Notwithstanding the general effect of subsection (1) of this section Parts II, IV, V, VI and sections 11, 12, 14, 33, 34, 35, 37, 40, 41 and 49 are the provisions of this Act which shall apply to a building society.

(3) This Act shall not apply to a co-operative society registered under the Co-operative Societies Act except save a co-operative society established for the purpose of deposits from the public.

PART II – LICENSING.

3. Licensing of financial institutions.

(1) A person shall not transact banking business, credit institution business, or building societies business without a valid licence granted for that purpose under this Act.

(2) No person shall be granted a licence unless it is a company within the meaning of this Act.

4. Application for a licence.

(1) A company proposing to transact banking, building societies or credit institution business shall apply, in writing, to the Central Bank for a licence under this Act and that application shall be considered by the Board.

(2) The application referred to in subsection (1) of this section shall contain the following information –

(a) the name and address of –

(i) the proposed financial institution;

(ii) the directors;

(iii) the shareholders;

(b) nationality of directors;

(c) nationality and shareholding of any shareholder;

(d) proposed location where the financial institution is going to operate from;

(e) the estimated number of persons to be employed;

(f) the qualifications, experience, nationality and other relevant particulars of the proposed management and staff;

(g) the capital structure and earning prospects of the financial institution;
(h) business, financial plans and earnings forecasts for at least three years;
(i) any other information relating to the viability of the financial institution or other matters as the applicant considers relevant to his or her application.

(3) An application under subsection (1) of this section shall be accompanied by a Memorandum and Articles of Association or rules, and a certificate of incorporation.

(4) Where an application under subsection (1) of this section does not provide all the relevant information or if clarification is necessary, the applicant may be called upon to provide that information or clarification to complete the application.

5. Factors to be considered when granting a licence.

(1) The Central Bank shall, in considering an application for a licence under section 4 of this Act, require to be satisfied to –
(a) the financial condition and history of the applicant;
(b) the nature of the business of the applicant;
(c) the competence and integrity of the proposed management;
(d) the adequacy of the applicant's capital structure, earning prospects, business plans, financial plans;
(e) the convenience and needs of the community to be served;
(f) whether public interest will be served by the granting of the licence.

6. Processing of applications.

(1) The Central Bank shall within six months, after receipt of an application, or of the additional information or clarification referred to in subsection (4) of section 4 investigate and prepare a detailed report in respect of each application.

(2) The Central Bank shall, for the purpose of considering and making a report on the application under this section appoint a committee of three or more members of the Board who shall report, in writing, their recommendations to the Board.

(3) The Central Bank shall within fourteen days after the period referred to in subsection (1) of this section consider the application and the report, and shall grant the licence if it is satisfied that the application is in accordance with this Act.

(4) The Central Bank shall within seven days after its decision under subsection (3) –
(a) inform the applicant of its decision in writing; and
(b) in the event of refusal to grant a licence the aggrieved applicant may appeal to the Minister who shall deal with the appeal in consultation with the Central Bank.

(5) Where the Central Bank grants the licence it may grant it upon such conditions as are necessary.

7. Licence fee.

The applicant shall, upon being granted a licence under this Act, pay a fee to be prescribed by the Central Bank and the holder of the licence shall thereafter pay a fee to be prescribed by the Central Bank on or before each anniversary of the granting of the licence.

8. Duration of licence, etc.

(1) A licence granted under section 6 shall remain in force until revoked.

(2) A licence granted under section 6 shall be kept displayed in a conspicuous place in the premises in which the financial institution carries on its lawful business, and copies of it shall be similarly displayed in each of its branch offices.

9. Failure to commence operations.

A licensed financial institution which fails to commence operations within twelve months from the date of issue of the licence shall have its licence revoked.

10. Revocation of licence.

The Central Bank may, at any time, in consultation with the Minister, revoke a licence of a financial institution if it is satisfied that the financial institution –

(a) has ceased to carry on business;

(b) has been declared insolvent;

(c) has gone into liquidation;

(d) has been wound up;

(e) has been dissolved;

(f) is carrying on business in a manner detrimental to the interests of depositors;

(g) has failed to comply with any condition stipulated by the Central Bank under subsection (5) of section 6.

PART III – CAPITAL REQUIREMENTS.

11. Minimum capital requirements for financial institutions.

(1) A local person proposing to transact banking business in Uganda shall have a minimum paid-up capital of not less than five hundred million shillings invested in such assets in Uganda as the Central Bank may approve.

(2) A foreign person proposing to transact banking business in Uganda shall have a minimum paid-up capital of not less than one billion shillings invested in such assets in Uganda as the Central Bank may approve.

(3) A person proposing to transact credit institution business shall, in the case of –

- (a) a local person, have a minimum paid-up capital of not less than three hundred million shillings; and
- (b) a foreign person, have a minimum paid-up capital of not less than five hundred million shillings, invested in such assets in Uganda as the Central Bank many approve.

(4) A person proposing to transact building societies business shall have a minimum paid-up capital of not less than three hundred million shillings invested in such assets in Uganda as the Central Bank may approve.

(5) A financial institution in existence immediately before the commencement of this Act shall be given a period of three years in which to build up its capital to the minimum level stipulated in this section.

12. Ongoing capital adequacy requirements.

(1) A financial institution shall at all times maintain –

(a) a core capital of not less than four per cent of total risk adjusted assets plus risk adjusted off balance sheet items as may be determined by the Central Bank by Statutory Instruments;

(b) a total capital of not less than eight per cent of its total risk adjusted assets plus risk adjusted off balance sheet items as may be determined by the Central Bank by Statutory Instrument.

(2) A financial institution in existence immediately before the commencement of this Act shall be given a period of three years in which to build up its capital to the level stipulated under this section,

13. Review of minimum capital requirements.

The Central Bank may, with the approval of the Minister, from time to time, review the minimum capital requirements by Statutory Instrument as circumstances warrant.

14. Minimum holdings of liquid assets.

(1) A financial institution shall maintain a minimum holding of liquid assets, as determined by the Central Bank in accordance with subsection (2) of this section.

(2) A minimum holding of liquid assets under this section shall be expressed as a proportion of the demand and time liabilities of a financial institution not exceeding 30 percent of those demand and time liabilities, but –

- (a) different proportions may be determined for demand liabilities and time liabilities and for various types of financial institutions; and
- (b) demand or time liabilities due by a financial institution to its head office or to any bank situated outside Uganda may, at the discretion of the Central Bank, be included wholly or in part.

(3) The Central Bank shall allow reasonable time after a minimum holding is prescribed or increased under subsection (1) of this section to enable the financial institutions comply with the requirement.

(4) A financial institution which contravenes this section is liable to pay, on being called upon to do so by the Central Bank, a fine not exceeding one-tenth of 1 percent of the amount of the deficiency for every day on which the deficiency continues.

(5) For the purposes of this section "liquid assets" means all or any of the following–

- (a) notes and coins which are legal tender in Uganda and any other currency prescribed by the Central Bank;
- (b) balances held at the Central Bank including any balances in accordance with the Bank of Uganda Act;
- (c) balances at banks in Uganda other than the Central Bank and other monies at call;
- (d) Uganda Treasury Bills maturing within a period not exceeding 91 days;
- (e) Uganda Government Stock maturing within a period not exceeding five years;

(f) balances at banks abroad withdrawable on demand and money at call abroad. Provided that balances and money at call are in currencies which are freely negotiable and transferable in international exchange markets consistent with the articles of agreement of the International Monetary Fund;

(g) commercial bills and promissory notes which are eligible for discount by the Central Bank under the Bank of Uganda Act;

(h) any other asset approved by the Central Bank.

15. Computing of minimum amount of liquid assets.

(1) The Central Bank shall prescribe the minimum amount of liquid assets to be held by financial institutions, including the off-setting of general or specified liquid assets against demand and time liabilities.

(2) In computing the minimum amount of liquid assets to be held by a financial institution operating in Uganda and elsewhere, all offices or branches of that financial institution in Uganda shall be deemed to constitute one financial institution.

16. Control of the foreign exchange holdings.

The Central Bank may fix or prescribe manner of determination of the maximum working balances which financial institutions may respectively hold in foreign currencies generally or in any specified foreign currency and may, at any time, require any financial institution to sell to the Central Bank all or any specified part of the surplus in excess of such maximum amount.

PART IV – RESTRICTIONS AND PROHIBITIONS ON FINANCIAL INSTITUTIONS.

17. Advances, credits and guarantees.

(1) A financial institution shall not, without the prior approval of the Central Bank –

(a) grant any advance of credit facility against security of its own shares or those of a company affiliated to it:

(b) grant or permit to be outstanding advances or credit facilities which in the aggregate exceed 25 percent of its core capital to any of its directors or of their immediate families or business enterprises in which they have substantial interests whether such advances or facilities are obtained by its directors jointly or severally;

(c) grant or permit to be outstanding in respect of any one of its officers or employees unsecured advances or unsecured credit facilities which in the aggregate exceed one year's emolument of such officer or employee;

(d) grant to a single person any advance or credit facility which is more than 25 percent of its core capital.

(2) For the purposes of this section, advances or credit facilities made to several persons sharing a common interest shall be deemed by the Central Bank to be a single advance or credit facility for purposes of applying this provision.

18. Trade, investments and immovable property.

(1) A financial institution shall not –

(a) engage on its own account, alone or with others, in wholesale or retail trade, including import or export trade except in the course of the satisfaction of debts due to it in which case all interests in such trade shall be disposed of at the earliest moment suitable to that financial institution;

(b) acquire or hold any part of the share capital of, or make any other capital investment or otherwise have a direct interest in any commercial, agricultural, industrial or other undertaking exceeding 25 percent of its core capital; except such shareholding, capital investment, or interest as the financial institution may acquire in the course of the satisfaction of debts due to it, which shall be disposed of at the earliest moment suitable to that financial institution; but any shareholding approved by the Central Bank in any corporation set up for the purpose of promoting development in Uganda, shall not be included in any of the said percentage;

(c) purchase or acquire any immovable property or any right on it except as may be reasonably necessary for the purpose of conducting its business or of housing or providing amenities for its staff but this paragraph shall not prevent a financial institution –

(i) from letting part of any building which is used for the purpose of conducting its business; or

(ii) from securing a debt on any immovable property and in the event of default in payment of such debt, from holding such immovable property for realisation at the earliest moment suitable to that financial institution.

(2) Notwithstanding subsection (1) of this section, the Central Bank may permit a financial institution to engage in a commercial, agricultural, industrial or other undertaking upon such conditions as it may deem fit, provided that such undertaking is not likely to impair the viability and efficiency of the financial institution.

19. Dividends.

(1) A financial institution shall not at any time pay any dividend or make any transfer from profits or capital if the payments result in the financial institution not meeting the requirements of section 12 .

(2) A financial institution in existence before the commencement of this Act, which fails to meet the requirement of section 12 shall not pay any dividend in excess of twenty per cent of its net profit until such time as that financial institution complies with section 12.

(3) A financial institution which contravenes this section commits an offence and is liable on conviction to a fine of ten per cent of the dividends paid out contrary to this section.

PART V– SUPERVISION.

20. Accounts.

(1) A financial institution shall keep accounts and records which–
  (a) show a clear and correct state of its affairs;
  (b) explain its transactions and financial position to enable the Central Bank to determine whether the financial institution has complied with this Act.

(2) A financial institution shall preserve the accounts and records referred to in this section for a period of not less than ten years.

21. Books and accounts to be kept in English.

All entries in any books and all accounts to be kept by a financial institution shall be kept and recorded in the English language using the system of numerals employed in Government accounts.

22. Appointment of an auditor by a financial institution.

(1) A financial institution shall appoint annually a person qualified as an auditor under the Companies Act and approved by the Central Bank whose duty shall be to make a report upon the annual balance sheet and accounts of the financial institution.

(2) A financial institution shall ensure that a report made under this section is submitted to the Central Bank within a period of four months after the close of its financial year.

(3) A financial institution which contravenes subsection (2) of this section commits an offence and is liable to a fine prescribed by the Central Bank under section 47.

23. Appointment of an auditor by the Central Bank

Where a financial institution fails to appoint an auditor under section 22 or fails to fill a vacancy for such auditor where the Central Bank is not satisfied with the audit report in respect of a financial institution, the Central Bank may appoint an auditor for, and shall fix the remuneration to be paid to the auditor by that financial institution.

24. Accessibility to books, etc.

An auditor appointed under section 22 or 23 shall have a right of access at all times to such books, accounts, vouchers, and securities of the financial institution and shall be entitled to receive from the officers, and staff of the financial institution such information and explanations as he or she may require to perform his or her duties.

25. Responsibilities of the auditor to the Central Bank.

(1) The Central Bank if dissatisfied with the results of the audit may reject it and call for a new audit at the expense of the financial institution concerned.

(2) Before annual accounts are finalised, dividends paid, and the capital requirements of sections 11 and 12 are met, the Central Bank must be satisfied that –
  (a) provisions for bad debts are sufficient; and

(b) a proper policy of non-accrual is in place and being enforced.

(3) External audits are to be prepared in accordance with generally accepted accounting standards and such other regulations, directives, policies or guidelines as the Central Bank may issue.

(4) The Central Bank may impose any or all of the following duties on an external auditor –

(a) a duty to submit such additional information in relation to his audit as the Central Bank considers necessary;

(b) a duty to carry out any other investigation or establish any procedure in any particular case;

(c) a duty to verify the accuracy of returns and other reports submitted to the Central Bank;

(d) a duty to submit a report to the Central Bank on the matters referred to in paragraphs *(a)*, *(b)* and (c) and the financial institution concerned shall remunerate the auditor in respect of his or her discharge of all or any of these additional duties.

(5) The Central Bank if it considers it necessary, may arrange, from time to time trilateral meetings with each financial institution and its auditors, to discuss matters relevant to the Central Bank's supervisory responsibilities which have arisen in the course of the statutory audit of that financial institution, including relevant aspects of its business, its accounting and internal control systems, and its annual balance sheet and profit and loss accounts.

(6) The Central Bank may, if it considers it desirable or necessary in the interest of depositors, arrange from time to time, bilateral meetings with the auditors of financial institutions.

(7) No duty or confidentiality to which an auditor may be subject shall be regarded as contravened by reason of the auditor's communication in good faith with the Central Bank, whether in response to a request by it or not, and this includes any information or opinion which is relevant to the Central Bank's functions under this Act.

26. Information to be furnished by financial institutions.

(1) A financial institution shall furnish to the Central Bank at such times in such form as the Central Bank may prescribe all information and data of its operations in Uganda including periodic returns called for by the Central Bank and the audited balance sheet and profit and loss account and those of any company or body affiliated to it which the Central Bank may require for the proper discharge of its functions under this Act.

(2) A Financial Institution shall prepare and cause to be submitted to the Central Bank an audited balance sheet within a period of four months after the end of its financial year.

(3) A Financial Institution shall exhibit throughout the year, in a conspicuous place in each of its offices and branches with a copy of its last audited balance sheet with full and correct names of all persons who are directors of the financial institution and a copy of the balance sheet shall be published in a local newspaper of general circulation.

(4) The Central Bank may publish in whole or in part at such time as it may determine any information or data furnished under subsection (1) of this section, except that no information or data shall be published which might disclose the affairs of a financial institution or of a customer of a financial institution unless the consent of the financial institution or customer has been obtained.

(5) A Financial Institution which fails to comply with subsection (1) of this section is liable to a fine of 0.5 percentum of the total deposit liabilities of the financial institution for each month in default.

27. Inspection of financial institutions.

(1) The Central Bank may, periodically or at any time at its discretion cause an inspection to be made by an officer of the Central Bank or other person appointed by the Central Bank, of any Financial Institution and of its books and accounts on the premises of such Financial Institution and shall supply to that Financial Institution a copy or the report on the inspection.

(2) It shall be the duty of a Financial Institution to produce to the officer making an inspection under subsection (1) of this section, all books, accounts and other documents as well as assets including cash, notes and securities held by a Financial Institution in its custody on power and to furnish that officer with such statements or information relating to the affairs of the Financial Institution as the officer may require of it within such reasonable time as that officer may specify.

(3) Any officer of a Financial Institution who fails to furnish any document in his custody or power as may be required under subsection (2) of this section commits on offence and is liable to a penalty fixed by the Central Bank from time to time by Statutory Instrument.

28. Powers of the Central Bank to issue order after inspection.

(1) If the Central Bank finds upon an inspection under section 27 of this Statute that the affairs of a financial institution are conducted in a manner detrimental to the interests of the depositors or prejudicial to the interests of the financial institution or in contravention of this Act or of any other written law, the Central Bank may without prejudice to any other course of action –

(a) require that financial institution to take the necessary measures to rectify the situation which measures may include signing an agreement between the directors and management of the financial institution and the Central Bank;

(b) appoint a competent person to advise the financial institution on the measures to be taken to rectify its situation and shall fix his remuneration which shall be paid by the financial institution;

(c) prohibit the declaration of dividends until the situation is rectified;

(d) withhold approvals on the establishment of new branches or other expansion of operations;

(e) initiate a legally binding cease and desist order of either temporary or indefinite duration requiring the financial institution and its management to stop the unacceptable practice or take affirmative action to rectify the undesirable situation;

(f) initiate the legal removal or suspension of a person from the management of the affairs of the financial institution;

(g) impose fines on a member of the management for contravention of this Act.

(2) The Central Bank may, upon representation made to it or on its own motion, modify or cancel any order issued under this section, and in so modifying or cancelling any order, may impose such conditions as are necessary subject to which the modification or cancellation shall have effect.

PART VI – LIQUIDATION, SEIZURE AND RE-ORGANISATION.

29. Liquidation.

(1) A financial institution may, with the approval of the Central Bank, voluntarily liquidate its operations.

(2) Subject to subsection (1) of this section a financial institution shall immediately cease all activities except those which are incidental to the orderly realisation, conservation and preservation of its assets and the settlement of its obligations.

(3) In case of a liquidation under this section –

(a) the liability of the shareholders for uncalled subscriptions to the capital stock of the financial institution shall continue until the end of the liquidation process;

(b) the depositors shall be entitled to first claim and thereafter all other creditors shall be ranked in accordance with the law relating to insolvent companies under the Companies Act;

(c) the Board of Directors of the financial institution shall, before paying creditors holding direct claims and with the approval of the Central Bank, make arrangements as are necessary to ensure a pro rata distribution among holders of claims that are likely to be reduced to judgement in a court.

(4) Where the Central Bank is satisfied that the assets of a financial institution which has voluntarily liquidated its operations under this section are not sufficient to discharge its obligations or that the completion of the liquidation of its operation is unduly delayed, the Central Bank may, if it deems it fit, take possession of the financial institution and take proceedings leading to compulsory liquidation in conformity with this Statute.

30. Seizure.

(1) The Central Bank may take possession of a financial institution –

(a) which is insolvent;

(b) which is conducting its business in a manner contrary to this Act.

(c) when the continuation of its activities is detrimental to the interests of depositors;

(d) that refuses to submit itself to inspection by the Central Bank as required by this Act or

(e) whose license has been revoked under section 10 of this Act.

(2) Where a financial institution is seized under this section the following shall apply –

(a) any term whether statutory, contractual or otherwise on the expiration of which a claim of right of the financial institution would expire or be extinguished, shall be extended six months from the date of seizure;

(b) any attachment or lien existing six months prior to seizure of the institution shall be vacated and no attachment or lien except a lien created by the Central Bank, shall attach any property or assets of the financial institution as long as the Central Bank continues to possess the financial institution; and

(c) any transfer of any asset of the financial institution made six months before the insolvency or seizure of the institution, with intent to effect a preference shall be void.

31. Management of seized financial institution.

(1) The Central Bank shall, upon possessing a financial institution under section 30, be vested with exclusive powers of management and control of the affairs of the financial institution.

(2) The powers referred to in subsection (1) of this section shall include power to –

(a) continue or discontinue its operations as a financial institution (notwithstanding the revocation of its licence).

(b) stop or limit the payment of its obligations;

(c) employ any necessary staff;

(d) execute any instrument in the name of the financial institution;

(e) initiate, defend and conduct in its name any action or proceeding to which the financial institution may be a party;

(f) re-organise or liquidate the financial institution in accordance with this Act; and

(g) do any other act which is necessary to enable the Central Bank carry out its obligations under this section.

(3) The Central Bank shall, as soon as possible after taking possession of a financial institution, make an inventory of the assets of the financial institution and shall transmit a copy of it to the Minister.

(4) Where, as a result of its inventory under this section the Central Bank determines that a financial institution is insolvent, the Central Bank may, in consultation with the Minister close the financial institution on account of its inability to meet its obligations to its depositors and other creditors.

32. Receiver.

(1) The Central Bank or an appointee of the Central Bank, upon a financial institution becoming insolvent, shall be the receiver of the financial institution.

(2) The Central Bank may, in carrying out its duties as receiver, either arrange a merger with another financial institution in which case the acquiring financial

institution will assume all recorded deposit liabilities of the insolvent financial institution or proceed with liquidation of the insolvent financial institution.

(3) The Central Bank, in making a decision under subsection (2) of this section, shall take into consideration –

(a) the estimated cost of the Central Bank with regard to shortfalls to be covered through acquisition of all deposit liabilities by the acquiring financial institution;

(b) the impact on and loss to depositors as a result of liquidation; and

(c) the overall impact on public confidence in and the stability of the financial sector in general as a result of acquisition or liquidation.

(4) Where the Central Bank arranges an acquisition under subsection (2) of this section it shall negotiate with the acquiring financial institution the terms and conditions of acquisition.

(5) Where the Central Bank decides to liquidate a financial institution it shall –

(a) realise the assets of the insolvent financial institution;

(b) enforce the individual liability of the shareholders and directors of the financial institution;

(c) wind up the affairs of the insolvent financial institution; and

(d) in winding up the affairs of the insolvent financial institution, eliminate the interests of shareholders and may purchase, sell or transfer assets in order to recover the maximum amount of a pro rata distribution to depositors and creditors of an insolvent financial institution.

PART VII – THE DEPOSIT PROTECTION FUND.

33. Establishment of the fund.

(1) There is established a Fund .in the Central Bank to be known as the Deposit Insurance Fund.

(2) The fund shall be managed and controlled by the Central Bank into which shall be paid all contributions and other payments required by this Part to be paid into the Fund and out of which shall be made the payment require by this Part to be made out of the Fund.

(3) The Minister may, from time to time in consultation with the Central Bank and by notice in the Gazette fix the size of the Fund sufficient to protect the interests of depositors to be made up by the contributions under section 34 and may authorize the Central Bank to borrow any such amount as it may require for temporary purposes of making up deficiency in the Fund pending collection of contributions.

(4) The Fund shall consist of –

(a) moneys contributed to the Fund by financial institutions under section 34;

(b) income credited to the Fund under subsection (5);

(c) money borrowed for purposes of the fund under subsection (3).

(5) The money constituting the Fund shall be placed in an account with the Central Bank to be invested in such manner as the Central Bank shall deem appropriate and any income from the investment shall be credited to the Fund.

(6) There shall be chargeable to the Fund the administrative expenses of the Central Bank, re-payment of money borrowed by the Fund and payments made in respect of protected deposits.

34. Contributors and contributions to the fund.

(1) Every financial institution shall be a contributor to the Fund and shall pay into the Fund such annual amount and at such times, as the Central Bank may determine.

(2) The Central Bank shall serve on a financial institution a notice specifying the amount and the period, which shall not be later than twenty-one days after the date of service of the notice, within which the amount shall be paid into the Fund by the financial institution.

(3) The amount of a contribution to the Fund under this section shall not be less than one per cent of the average of the financial institution total deposit liabilities during the period of twelve months prior to the date of the notice served under subsection (2) but the Minister may, after consultation with the Central Bank, by order, amend the minimum and maximum amounts of contributions prescribed by this subsection.

(4) A financial institution which for any reason fails to pay its contribution to the Fund within the periods specified in a notice issued under subsection (2) shall be liable to pay to the Fund a penalty interest charge not exceeding one half per cent of the unpaid amount for every day outside the notice period on which the amount remains unpaid.

(5) If it appears to the Central Bank that the affairs of a financial institution are being conducted in a manner detrimental to its own interests or to the interests of the depositors, the Central Bank may increase the contributions of that financial institution beyond the maximum set out under subsection (4) or terminate the protection of the deposits of that financial institution.

35. Protection of deposits and payments out of fund.

(1) The amount being the aggregate credit balance of any accounts maintained by a customer at a financial institution less any liability of the customer to the financial institution shall be a protected deposit to the extent determined by the Minister, from time to time, by order published in the Gazette.

(2) A customer of a financial institution may upon the financial institution becoming insolvent, lodge a claim with the Central Bank in such form as the Central Bank may approve for payment to him or her out of the Fund of any protected deposit which he or she would but for the insolvency have been paid had he or she demanded payment from the insolvent financial institution.

(3) The Central Bank may, before paying any claim lodged under subsection (2), require the claimant to furnish it with such documentary proof as may be proper to show that he or she is entitled to payment out of the Fund, and the Central Bank may decline to make any payment under this section to a person who, in the opinion of the Central Bank, had any responsibility for or may have profited directly or indirectly from the circumstances leading up to the financial institution becoming insolvent.

(4) Notwithstanding subsection (3), the Central Bank may carry out inspections under section 27 and ascertain the type, number and values of the protected deposits which, but for the insolvency would be payable by an insolvent financial institution.

(5) Upon payment of a protected deposit the Fund shall be entitled to receive from the financial institution or liquidator, as the case may be, an amount equal to the insolvency payment paid by the Fund on account of its subrogation to the claims of any customer or depositor.

(6) For the purposes of this section "customer" includes persons entitled to a deposit as trustees or persons holding any deposits jointly.

36. Power of the Central Bank to lend.

If the Central Bank considers it desirable to reduce risk or avert threatened loss to the Fund, the Central Bank may, on such terms and conditions as it may prescribe lend, place a deposit or issue a guarantee, or purchase the assets of a financial institution.

37. Annual report of the Central Bank's activities.

(1) The Central Bank shall, within three months after the close of each financial year, submit an annual report of its operations to the Minister.

(2) The financial year of the Fund shall be the same as the Central Bank's financial year.

PART VIII – MISCELLANEOUS.

38. Branches, etc.

(1) A financial institution shall not open a new place of business or change the location of an existing place of business or change its hours of business without the approval of the Central Bank.

(2) Before granting any approval under this section in respect of opening a new place of business or change of location to an existing place of business the Central Bank may require to be satisfied by an inspection of the financial institution or otherwise as to –

- (a) the history and financial condition of the financial institution;
- (b) the general character of its management;
- (c) adequacy of its capital structure and earning prospects;
- (d) the convenience and needs of the community to be served; and
- (e) whether public interest will be served by the opening of a new place of business or changing the location of the place or hours of business as the case may be.

(3) A financial institution shall not close an existing place of business unless it has given six months' notice to the Central Bank, or such shorter period of notice as the Central Bank may consider reasonable, of its intention to close the place of business.

(4) A financial institution which contravenes this section commits an offence and is liable to a fine fixed by the Central Bank, from time to time, by Statutory Instrument.

39. Mergers.

(1) A financial institution operating in Uganda shall not be merged or consolidated with or taken over by any other institution or individual and no interest in the capital of any financial institution with a voting share exceeding 10 percent shall be acquired by any other financial institution without the approval of the Central Bank.

(2) In considering any application for approval under this section, the Central Bank shall have power to call for the relevant information.

(3) A financial institution which contravenes subsection (1) of this section commits an offence and is liable to a fine of one million shillings for every day during which the offence continues; and any officer who contravenes this section commits an offence and is liable on conviction, to a fine of one hundred thousand shillings for every day during which the offence continues and in default of payment to imprisonment for a term of one year.

40. Restriction on transfer of shares.

(1) A person shall not transfer shares in a financial institution representing more than 15 percent of either capital stock or voting rights without the prior approval of the Central Bank.

(2) Where the Central Bank refuses to allow a person to transfer shares under this section, an appeal shall lie to the court.

(3) A financial institution shall as may be required by the Central Bank, make periodic returns in respect of persons holding more than fifteen per cent of the total shares of the financial institution.

41. Mortgages, liens.

For the avoidance of doubt a financial institution may accept lien on crops, animals or other chattels as collateral security for liens and overdrafts.

42. Unclaimed balances.

(1) Whenever any current or savings account has not been operated for a period of two years or a time or savings deposit account has not been operated for a period of two years after the date of maturity of the deposit, no withdrawals shall be allowed on such account except with the permission of two officers of the financial institution out of a number of signatories authorised to grant such permission.

(2) An account referred to in subsection (1) of this section shall be transferred to a separate register of dormant accounts in the books of the financial institution and a notice in writing of such action shall be given to the depositor at his or her last known address.

(3) Where any account which is transferable under subsection (2) of this section is subject to a service charge, the charge may continue to be levied up to the date on which the account has been transferred to the separate ledger of dormant accounts except that no charge shall be levied beyond two years.

(4) Where an account is transferred to a register of dormant accounts an advertisement shall be published after a period of ten years of such an account having been on the register of dormant accounts and thereafter after ten years and the cost of advertisement shall be charged on the respective accounts on a pro rata basis.

(5) Any account may be transferred out of the register of dormant accounts if the depositor, or if he or she is dead his or her legal representative, makes such a request.

(6) Unclaimed balances shall after a period of twenty years be employed by the Central Bank to off set costs of supervising financial institutions or as may be prescribed.

43. Disqualification of officers.

(1) A person –

(a) who has been a director or officer of, or directly responsible for the mismanagement of a financial institution leading to its being compulsorily wound up by a court;

(b) who has been convicted of an offence under section 47; or

(c) who is a bankrupt or suspends payment or compounds with his or her creditors, shall not without the express authorization of the Central Bank, act or continue to act as a director or officer, or be directly or indirectly involved in the management of a financial institution.

(2) A person who has been convicted of an offence involving dishonesty or fraud shall not act or continue to act in any way in the management of a financial institution.

44. Officers deemed public officers.

An officer or servant of a financial institution shall be deemed to be a person employed in the public service for the purposes of sections 87, 89, and 93 of the Penal Code Act

45. Obligation under the Companies Act, etc.

Nothing in this Act shall be deemed to relieve a financial institution from any of its obligation under the Companies Act or Building Societies Act.

46. Use of the word "bank"

(1) No person except a person licensed under this Act, without the consent of the Central Bank –

(a) use the word "bank" or any of its derivatives in any language or any other word indicating the transaction of banking business in the name or, description of title under which such person is transacting business;

(b) make or continue to make any representation indicating the transaction of banking business in any billhead, letter-paper, notice, advertising or in any manner whatsoever.

(2) No company shall carry on the business of banking unless it uses as part of its name the word "bank" or one of its derivatives.

(3) A person who contravenes this section commits an offence and is liable on conviction, to a fine of not less than fifty thousand shillings for every day during which the offence continues.

47. Examination of persons suspected of doing banking business, etc.

Whenever the Central Bank has reasonable grounds leading it to believe that any person is transacting banking or credit institution or building society business without a license, it shall have the power to examine the books of accounts and records of such person in order to ascertain whether or not such person has violated or is violating any provisions of this Act; and any refusal to submit such books, accounts and records shall be prima facie evidence of the fact of operation of banking or as the case may be credit institution business or building society business, without a licence.

48. Protection of the central bank, etc.

(1) No suit or other legal proceedings shall lie against the Central Bank or any officer of the central bank for anything which is done or is intended to be done in good faith pursuant to the provisions of this Act.

49. Declaration of bank holidays.

(1) The Minister may, at any time by Statutory Instrument, declare any day to be a bank holiday.

(2) A financial institution shall not transact any business with the public on a bank holiday.

(3) A bank holiday declared under subsection (1) of this section shall not necessarily be a public holiday and nothing in this section shall be deemed to affect the provisions of any law in force relating to public holidays.

50. Non-application of interpretation Act.

Sections 37 and 38 of the Interpretation Act, shall not apply to this Statute.

51. Regulations.

The Central Bank may in consultation with the Minister responsible for Finance make regulations –

(a) prescribing prudential norms on asset quality, including bad debt provisions and write-offs;

(b) providing for the licensing of financial institutions;

(c) providing for the minimum level of capital for financial institutions;

(d) providing for the computation of on-going capital adequacy requirements for financial institutions;

(e) providing for lending limits on credit extended to insiders;

(f) providing for the limitations for advances or credit facilities to a single borrower;

(g) providing for reporting requirements by financial institutions to the Central Bank;

(h) generally for giving effects to the provisions of this Act.

52. Offences and penalties.

(1) A person who carries on or is privy to the carrying on of the business of a financial institution which has been established contrary to this Act commits an offence and is liable on conviction, to a fine of not less than two million shillings or to imprisonment for a term of two years or both.

(2) A person convicted of an offence under subsection (1) of this section shall be disqualified from acquiring a licence under this Act for five years and thereafter shall not, without approval of the Central Bank, be issued with a licence.

(3) A person who, being a director, manager or officer of a financial institution –

(a) fails to take any reasonable steps to secure compliance with the requirements of this Act.

(b) makes any statement or gives any information which is false in answer to any request for information made under any provisions of this Act;

(c) is privy to the furnishing of any false information supplied under this Act, commits an offence and is liable on conviction to a fine or not less than one million shillings or to imprisonment for a term not exceeding two years or to both.

(4) A financial institution which fails to comply with an order issued by the Central Bank under this Statute commits an offence and is liable to a fine fixed by the Central Bank by the Statutory Instrument.

(5) A financial institution which contravenes any provision of this Act commits an offence and where no specific penalty is provided the financial institution is liable on conviction, to a penalty prescribed by the Central Bank by Statutory Instrument.

(6) Where a director or officer of a financial institution authorises or commits the contravention of any provision of this Act, he or she shall be personally liable to the penalty specified in relation to the contravention.

53. Act to take precedence over other Acts that relate to banking, etc.

For purposes of banking, credit institutions, and building societies business, this Act shall take precedence over any legislation relating to financial institutions and in case of conflict this Act shall prevail.

CHAPTER 51

THE BANK OF UGANDA ACT

Arrangement of Sections.

Section

PART I - INTEPRETATION.

PART II - ESTABLISHMENT OF THE BANK AND THE BOARD OF DIRECTORS.

Establishment of the bank

The board of directors

PART III - CAPITAL, RESERVE AND CURRENCY

PART IX – MISCELLANEOUS PROVISIONS

SCHEDULE

CHAPTER 51

THE BANK OF UGANDA ACT

An Act to amend and consolidate the Bank of Uganda Act for regulating the issuing of legal tender, maintaining external reserves and for promoting the stability of the currency and a sound financial structure conducive to a balanced and sustained rate of growth of the economy and for other purposes related to the above.

PART I – INTERPRETATION.

1. Interpretation

In this Act, unless the context otherwise requires –

(a) "Bank' means the Bank of Uganda established under section 2;

(b) "Board" means the Board of Directors established under section 7;

(c) "Executive Director" means a person appointed under section 28;

(d) "financial institution" includes a bank, credit institution, a building society and any institution classified as a financial institution by the Bank;

(e) "Fund" means the General Reserve Fund of the Bank established under section 15;

(f) "Governor" means the Governor of Bank of Uganda appointed under section 27;

(g) "Minister" means the Minister responsible for finance.

PART II – ESTABLISHMENT OF THE BANK AND THE BOARD OF DIRECTORS.

Establishment of the bank

2. Establishment of the bank.

(1) The Bank of Uganda established under the Bank of Uganda Act, 1966 continue as the Central Bank of Uganda.

(2) The Bank shall be a body corporate with perpetual succession and a common seal and may sue or be sued in its corporate name.

(3) The Bank may, subject to the limitations contained in this Act relating to the business which the Bank may carry on, purchase, hold, manage and dispose of real and movable property, and may enter into contracts that may be expedient.

3. The Seal of the bank.

(1) The seal of the Bank shall be authenticated by the signatures of the Governor and the Secretary to the Board.

(2) In the absence of the Governor, the Deputy Governor may sign in his or her place, and the person performing the functions of the Secretary may sign in the absence of the Secretary.

(3) A document issued by the Bank which document is sealed with the seal of the Bank and authenticated in the manner provided under this section shall be received and taken to be a true document without further proof unless the contrary is shown.

4. Functions of the bank.

(1) The functions of the Bank shall be to formulate and implement monetary policy directed to economic objectives of achieving and maintaining economic stability.

(2) Without prejudice to the generality of subsection (1) the bank shall –

(a) maintain monetary stability;
(b) maintain external assets reserve;
(c) issue currency notes and coins;
(d) be the banker to Government;
(e) act as financial adviser to Government and manager of public dept.;
(f) advise Government on monetary policy as is provided under sub-section (3) of section 32;
(g) where appropriate, act as an agent in financial matters for the Government;
(h) be the banker to financial institutions;
(i) be the clearing house for cheques and other financial instruments for financial institutions;
(j) supervise, regulate, control and discipline all financial institutions, and pension funds institutions;
(k) where appropriate, participate in the economic growth and development programmes.

5. Powers on the bank.

Subject to this Act, the Bank shall have all the powers pertaining to a legal person and may do all things necessary for better carrying out of its functions.

6. Head office.

The Bank shall have its head office in Kampala and may establish branches and appoint agents and correspondents in and out of Uganda as the Board may decide.

The Board of Directors

7. The board of directors.

(1) The governing body of the Bank shall be a Board of Directors consisting of: –

(a) the Governor, who shall be the Chairperson;
(b) the Deputy Governor who shall be the Deputy Chairperson;
(c) the Secretary to the Treasury; and
(d) not less than four nor more than six other Directors.

(2) The Directors referred to under paragraph (d) of subsection (1) shall be appointed by the Minister.

(3) A member of the Board may hold office for a period of four years and different members shall be appointed at different times so that the expiry date of the members shall fall at different times.

(4) A member of the Board appointed under subsection (2) shall be eligible for re-appointment.

(5) A Director may resign his or her office by writing under his or her hand addressed to the Minister which resignation shall take effect one month from the date of receipt of the letter of resignation by the Minister.

(6) If a member of the Board dies or resigns or otherwise vacates office before the expiry of the term for which he or she was appointed, the Minister may appoint another person in his office and the person so appointed shall hold office for the unexpired period of the term of office of the person in whose place he or she is appointed.

(7) Whenever for any sufficient reason the offices of the Governor and the Deputy Governor are vacant at the same time, the Minister shall, in consultation with the Board designate one of the Executive Directors to perform the duties of the Deputy Governor and attend meetings of the Board until the appointment of the Governor or Deputy Governor, but the executive director shall not for those purposes be, or be deemed to be a member of the Board.

(8) Whenever for any sufficient reason the Governor and Deputy Governor are absent at the same time, the Governor shall designate a senior officer to perform the executive functions of the Deputy Governor and attend meetings of the Board until the resumption of office by the Governor or the Deputy Governor and the Board shall appoint from among themselves a Chairperson for the period of absence of the Governor and Deputy Governor.

8. Qualifications of directors.

A person may be appointed a Director–

(a) if he or she is a citizen of Uganda; and

(b) if he or she has recognised qualification in economic financial, business or banking experience.

9. Disqualifications of Directors.

(1) No person shall be appointed or be a member of the Board who is or becomes a director or salaried officer of the Bank other than the Governor and the Deputy Governor.

(2) A member of the Board shall cease to hold office if –

- (a) he or she becomes of unsound mind or is incapable of carrying out the duties of his or her office;
- (b) he or she becomes bankrupt or suspends payment or compounds with his creditors;
- (c) he or she is convicted of an offence punishable by more than three months imprisonment or is convicted of an offence involving fraud or dishonesty;
- (d) he or she is convicted of an offence of abuse of office;

(e) in the case of a person having professional qualifications, he or she is disqualified or suspended from practising his or her profession by a competent authority or ceases to be a member of the profession otherwise than at his or her own request.

10. Duties and powers of the board.

The Board shall –

(a) be responsible for the general management of affairs of the Bank;

(b) ensure the functioning of the Bank and the implementations of its functions;

(c) formulate the policies of the Bank;

(d) do anything required to be done by the Bank under this Act; and

(e) do anything that is within, or incidental to the functions of the Bank.

11. Meetings of the board.

The procedure of the meetings of the Board shall be as is provided in the Schedule to this Act.

12. Remuneration of members.

Members of the Board and any person not being an employee of the Bank attending a meeting of the Board may be paid a remuneration or allowance as the Board may, in consultation with the Minister, determine.

13. Conditions of service of members.

The Board may make bye laws to regulate conditions of service of its members and the byelaws shall be submitted to the Minister for approval which approval shall be given in a period not exceeding thirty days from the date of submission of the proposed bye laws.

PART III – CAPITAL, RESERVE AND CURRENCY.

14. Authorised capital.

(1) The authorised capital of the Bank shall be thirty billion shillings, which shall be subscribed by the Government from time to time.

(2) The authorised capital may be increased by a resolution of the parliament to ensure adequacy to the operations of the Bank.

(3) The issued and paid up capital of the Bank shall be a minimum of twenty billion shillings.

(4) Where the capital of the Bank is impaired at any particular time the Government will furnish securities to the Bank to make good the impairment.

15. General Reserve Fund.

(1) There shall be a General Reserve Fund of the Bank which shall be determined by the Board from time to time.

(2) The Bank may, in consultation with the Minister transfer funds from the General Reserve Fund to the capital of the Bank.

16. Distribution of profits and loss.

(1) At the end of each financial year of the Bank, and after –

(a) *making good the authorized capital and Reserve Fund balance;*

(b) allowing for expenses of operation;

(c) making provision for bad and doubtful debts;

(d) making provision for depreciation of assets;

(e) contributing to any scheme or fund established under this Act;

(f) taking into consideration any other contingencies;

any net profits or losses from the Bank's operations shall be shared between the Bank and the Government in respective proportions of twenty five percent and seventy five percent.

(2) In determining the profits and loss at the end of each financial year, the accounts shall clearly distinguish profits or loss arising from the normal operations of the Bank and those resulting from profits or loss from exchange fluctuation.

(3) The Board may determine that the whole of the net profit of the Bank be paid into the Consolidated Fund if at the end of the financial year the amount of money in the General Reserve Fund is twice or more than the amount of the paid up Capital of the Bank.

(4) The Bank may, after consultation with the Minister, retain from money payable into the Consolidated Fund under this section any amount of money as the Board may determine, in satisfaction or reduction of any amount of money due to the Bank by the Government.

17. Unit of currency.

(1) The unit of currency shall be the shilling .

(2) All monetary obligations or transactions shall be expressed, recorded and settled in the shilling unless otherwise provided under any enactment or is lawfully agreed to between the parties to an agreement under any lawful obligation.

18. External value of the shilling.

(1) The Board shall in consultation with the Minister prescribe the framework for determining the external value of the shilling.

19. Auctioning of foreign currency.

The bank may buy and sell foreign currency –

(a) at rates determined by market conditions; and

(b) on terms that may be determined by the Board.

20. Right to issue notes and coins.

(1) The Bank shall, have the sole right to issue notes and coins and the Government or any person shall not issue currency notes, bank notes, coins, any documents or tokens payable to bearer on demand, being documents or tokens likely to be passed as legal tender.

(2) The Bank shall –

(a) arrange for the printing of notes and minting of coins;
(b) determine the denominations to be issued;
(c) issue and re-issue and exchange notes and coins at the Bank's offices and at the Bank's agencies established or appointed by the Bank;
(d) arrange for the custody of unissued stocks of currency and for the preparation, safe custody and destruction of plates and paper for the printing of notes and of dyes for the minting of coins.

21. Design of bank notes.

The Bank shall determine the design of the bank notes issued by it but no bank note shall bear in its design a portrait of a living person or any political symbol or word.

22. Denominations and form of bank notes and coins.

(1) The bank notes and coins issued by the Bank shall be in denominations of the shilling or fraction of the shilling expressed in cents as shall be determined by the Board with the approval of the Minister.
(2) Denominations issued by the Bank shall be in forms and designs and bear devices that shall be determined by the Board.
(3) The standard weight and composition of coins issued by the Bank and the remedy and variation shall be determined by the Board.

23. Legal tender.

(1) Notes issued by the Bank shall be legal tender at their face value.
(2) Coins issued by the Bank, if not tampered with shall be legal tender for payments up to an amount not exceeding –
  (a) one thousand shillings, in case of coins of denominations of not less than five shillings;
  (b) five hundred shillings in case of coins of a lower denomination; or
  (c) as may be prescribed by the Board, from time to time.
(3) On giving not less than fifteen days' notice in the Gazette, the Bank may call in any of its bank notes and coins on payment of the face value and any notes or coins with respect to which notice may have been given under this subsection shall, on the expiration of the notice cease to be legal tender.
(4) For the purpose of this Act, a coin shall be deemed to have been tampered with if the coin shall have been –
  (a) impaired, diminished or lightened otherwise than by fair wear and tear; or
  (b) defaced by stamping, engraving or piercing whether the coin shall or shall not have been diminished or lightened.

24. Fund of lost or imperfect bank notes and coins.

(1) No person shall be entitled to recover from the Bank the value of any lost, stolen, mutilated or imperfect bank note or any coin, which is tampered with.
(2) Subject to subsection (1) the circumstances in which and the conditions and limitations subject to which the value of any lost, stolen, mutilated or imperfect bank notes or coins tampered with may be refunded as of grace shall be within the absolute discretion of the Board.

25. Evidence of imitation of bank notes.

Where in any proceedings in any court of competent jurisdiction it is to be determined whether a document purporting to be a bank note is an imitation of a bank note, a certificate under the hand of the Governor or any officer of the Bank authorised by him certifying that he has examined the document which purports to be a bank note, stating the denomination, and the number of the bank note, and that the document is an imitation of a bank note and is not a note issued by the Bank, shall be received in evidence without further proof as conclusive evidence of the fact that that document is an imitation of a banknote.

26. Exemption from stamp duty.

The Bank shall not be liable to the payment of any stamp duty under the Stamps Act in respect of notes issued by it.

PART IV – OFFICERS AND STAFF.

27. The governor and deputy governor.

(1) There shall be a Governor who shall be a person of recognised financial or banking experience and shall be appointed by the President on the advice of the Cabinet.

(2) There shall be a Deputy Governor who shall be a person of recognised financial or banking experience and shall be appointed by the President acting on the advice of the Cabinet.

(3) The Governor and the Deputy Governor shall be appointed for a period of five years and shall be eligible for reappointment.

(4) The Governor and Deputy Governor shall not, while holding office of Governor or Deputy Governor occupy any other office or employment whether remunerated or not.

(5) Notwithstanding subsection (4) the Governor or Deputy Governor may –

- (a) become a trustee of any staff, pension, provident or superannuation fund or scheme;
- (b) with the approval of the Minister act as a member of any commission or committee appointed by the Governor to inquire into any matter affecting currency or banking or other matters;
- (c) with the consent of the Minister and the approval of the Board, become a director, governor or member of the board, by whatever name called, of any international bank or an international monetary authority to which the Government shall have adhered or given support or approval.

(6) The Governor and Deputy Governor shall be appointed on conditions specified in their letters of appointment.

(7) The Governor or Deputy Governor may resign his or her office by writing addressed to the Minister and the resignation shall take effect one month from the date of receipt of the letter of resignation by the Minister.

28. Appointment of employees.

(1) There shall be Executive Directors who shall be appointed by the Board and carry on supervisory functions over a number of departments as may be determined by the Board.

(2) There shall be Heads of departments of the Bank who shall be appointed by the Board.

(3) The Bank shall have other officers and employees as the Board may determine.

(4) Except as may otherwise be provided by bye laws of the Bank, all appointments of employees shall be made by the Board.

(5) Employees of the Bank shall be engaged on terms and conditions that shall be laid down by the Board.

(6) No salary, fee, wage, or other remuneration or allowance paid by the Bank shall be computed by reference to the net or other profits of the Bank.

(7) No employee of the Bank shall be liable –

(a) for any loss or damage suffered by the Bank unless that loss or damage was caused by his or her own default or wilful act;

(b) to any legal proceedings for anything which is done in good faith under this Act.

PART V – BANKING.

29. Credit and other operations.

(1) The Bank may –

(a) open accounts for and accept deposits from –

(i) the Government,

(ii) local governments,

(iii) funds, corporations and institutions controlled by the Government, and

(iv) financial institutions;

(b) buy, sell, discount and rediscount inland bills of exchange, promissory notes, treasury bills or other instruments;

(c) subject to the provisions of subsection (4) of this section, purchase and sell securities of the Government which have been publicly offered on issue which is being made to the public at the time of acquisition and such securities are to mature within a period of twenty years;

(d) grant advances to its customers specified under paragraph (a) for fixed periods not exceeding three months against publicly issued treasury bills of the Government maturing within ninety-three days;

(e) grant to financial institutions advances for fixed periods not exceeding three months, at a rate of interest not being less than 1 percent above the Bank's standard rediscount rate against promissory notes secured by the pledge with the Bank –

(i) securities of the Government which have been publicly offered for sale and are to mature within a period of twenty-five years, so however that any advance so secured shall not at any time exceed 75 percent of the market value of the security pledged and that the total amount of the securities held by the Bank, whether under the provisions of this sub-paragraph or otherwise, is within the limitations imposed under subsection (4) and that where in the opinion of the Bank there is no established market value for those securities the value shall be determined by the Bank; the securities referred to exclude such bonds issued for purposes of capitalisation of the Bank,

(ii) bills of exchange and promissory notes as are eligible for purchase, discount or rediscount by the Bank, so however that any advances so secured shall not at any time exceed 75 percent of the normal value of the instrument pledged;

(iii) warehouse warrants issued by lawfully formed general and bonded warehouses or their equivalent securing possession of goods;

(iv) required reserves held at the Bank.

(f) subject to subsection (4) grant to financial institutions medium and long term loans for periods not exceeding fifteen years upon such securities as the Board of Directors of the Bank may prescribe;

(g) guarantee loans granted by financial institutions not exceeding 20 percent of the core capital or as may be determined by the Board.

(2) The Bank may –

(a) issue demand drafts and effect other kinds of remittances payable at its own offices or at the offices of its agents or correspondents;

(b) purchase and sell gold coin or gold bullion;

(c) invest in securities of the Government for any amount, and to mature at any time, on behalf of staff funds and superannuation funds and other internal funds of the Bank;

(d) with the approval of the Minister and subject to subsection (4) subscribe to hold and sell shares of any corporation or company established for the purpose of facilitating the financing of economic development;

(e) maintain accounts with central and other banks and act as correspondent, banker or agent for any central or other bank or other monetary authority outside Uganda and for any international monetary authority established under Government auspices;

(f) accept from its customers for custody securities and other articles of value;

(g) undertake on behalf of customers specified under paragraph (1) (a) and correspondents the purchase, sale, collection and payment of securities, currencies and credit instruments within and without Uganda and the purchase and sale of gold.

(3) Subject to the provisions of this Act, the Bank shall not –

(a) engage in trade or otherwise have a direct interest in any commercial, agricultural, industrial or any other undertaking except such interest as the Bank may in any way acquire in the course of the satisfaction of debts due to it, which interest acquired shall be disposed of as soon as may be reasonably practicable;

(b) purchase the shares of any body corporate, incorporate including the shares of any financial institution;

(c) grant loans upon the security of any shares;

(d) grant unsecured advances or advances secured otherwise than as provided for under the provisions of paragraphs (d) and (e) of subsection (1) of this section but in the event of any debts due to the Bank becoming in the opinion of the Bank endangered, may secure such debts on any real or other property of the debtor and may acquire such property which shall be resold as soon as may be reasonably practical.

(4) At any particular date the total amount –

(a) of long term securities or loans referred to under paragraphs (c) and (f) of subsection (1);

(b) subscriptions under paragraph (d) of subsection (2); or

(c) any other long term loan than securities held under paragraph (c) of subsection (2), shall not exceed 20 percent of the corecapital of the Bank or such other percentage as the Board may determine.

(5) Without prejudice to any provision contained in this section the Bank may do all matters and things that are incidental or subsidiary to its functions under this Act.

(6) Notwithstanding anything contained in this section, the Bank may, with the approval of the Minister, establish a Credit Guarantee scheme, a Development Finance Fund, and any other scheme for development purposes not exceeding 10 percent of the core capital of the Bank.

(7) A scheme or Fund referred to under subsection (6) shall be established by a Statutory Instrument in which Instrument the structure and operations of the Scheme and other matters connected thereto shall be spelt out.

30. Publication of rediscount rates.

The Bank shall fix and make public at all times its standard rediscount rate and the Bank may determine different terms, conditions and rates of interest in respect to particular classes of transactions.

31. External reserve.

(1) The Bank shall maintain a reserve of external assets at least equal to four weeks import requirements of the country consisting of any or all of the following –

(a) gold coin or gold bullion;

(b) convertible foreign exchange in any of the following forms –

(i) demand or time deposits, money at call, notes and coins,

(ii) bills of exchange when they bear at least two signatures of which one is that of a commercial bank and which have a maturity not exceeding ninety days exclusive of days of grace,

(iii) marketable securities of, or guaranteed by foreign governments or international financial institutions;

(c) any external fund, facility or drawing rights inclusive of the reserve tranche purchase from the International Monetary Fund which the Minister, after due consultations with the Bank considers acceptable for inclusion.

(2) The Bank will advise the Minister whenever the target on reserves is likely to be violated for any reason and suggest remedial measures.

Part VI – Bank Relationship with Government.

32. Relationship with the Government.

(1) The Minister may direct the Bank to render advice to Government on financial or other related matters and the Bank shall advise and inform the Government through the Minister on any matter which is within its functions and powers under this Act.

(2) The Bank shall render services to Government as may be determined by the Minister.

(3) The Government shall seek advice from the Bank on monetary policy and it shall be the duty of the Bank to formulate such monetary policy and advise Government accordingly.

(4) The Government shall consult with the Bank from time to time on its domestic or foreign credit requirements or any relevant matter.

33. Temporary advances.

(1) The Bank may make temporary advances to the Government and local governments in respect of temporary deficiencies of recurrent revenue.

(2) The Treasury shall at the beginning of each financial year identify and submit to the Bank all its requirements for temporary advances for that year and the Bank shall subject to subsection (3) operate within that requirement.

(3) The total amount of advances made under subsection (1) shall not at any time exceed18 percent of the recurrent revenue of the Government.

(4) The Bank shall charge market rates of interest on any advance to the Government or local government unless the Board determines otherwise.

34. Report on advances.

(1) Where in the opinion of the Bank the limitations on Bank credit prescribed under subsection (3) of section 33 or the holding of securities is exceeded, the Bank shall make a report on the Bank's outstanding advances or holding of securities in terms of those sections, and the causes that have led to the breach of the limitations, together with any recommendation or remedy; and the Bank shall make further reports and recommendations to the Minister at intervals not exceeding six months until the situation has been rectified.

(2) At any time when the limitations on Bank Credits or the submitted requirement is exceeded, the powers of the Bank to grant additional financing shall cease until the situation has been rectified.

35. Development financing.

(1) The Bank may participate in development financing through –
- (a) the refinancing facilities to financial institutions;
- (b) the management of loans and grants for development projects through commercial banks;
- (c) closely supervising the outcome of the funds dispersed to commercial banks;

(2) For the avoidance of doubt the Bank shall not directly finance any development project with exception of development funds established under section 29 (6).

PART VII – BANK RELATIONSHIP WITH FINANCIAL INSTITUTIONS.

36. Clearing house.

(1) The Bank may provide facilities for clearing financial instruments generally on terms that may be determined by the Bank.

(2) The Bank may make regulations prescribing the procedure and other provisions for the participation in the clearing house and for the clearing of cheques and other credit instruments.

(3) The bank may allow a commercial bank to participate in the activities of the clearing house on the recommendation of the Uganda Bankers Association.

37. Co-operation with financial institutions.

The Bank shall in the discharge of its functions under this Act, seek the co-operation of and co-operate with financial institutions in order to –
- (a) to promote and maintain adequate and reasonable banking services for the public;
- (b) to ensure high standards of conduct and management throughout the banking system;
- (c) to promote such policies not being inconsistent with any provision of this Act; and
- (d) to provide facilities for the clearing of financial instruments for financial institutions generally on terms determined by it; and
- (e) to vet Directors of the financial institutions.

38. Minimum cash reserve balances.

(1) Subject to the provisions of this section, the Bank may prescribe for each bank or group of financial institutions the minimum cash reserve balances inclusive of vault cash which may be required to be maintained in the form of deposits at the Bank or any other method laid down by the Bank.

(2) The Bank may prescribe various ratios for different kinds of liabilities and shall prescribe the methods of computing the amount of cash reserve balances.

(3) The total amount of the cash reserve balances referred to in subsection (1) of this section shall not exceed 25 percent of the financial institution's deposits and other liabilities provided that within this overall limit the Bank may impose

incremental reserves up to 100 percent on any increase of any kind of liability from a date prescribed by the Bank.

(4) The Bank may impose on a financial institution which fails to maintain the minimum cash reserve balances required under this section a penalty not exceeding one tenth of 1 percent per day on the amount of the deficiency for each day during which the deficiency continues and the amount of any such penalty may be recovered by deduction from any balance of, or monies owing to the financial institution concerned or as a civil debt.

(5) For the purposes of this section the liabilities of a financial institution means its liabilities in Uganda whether these are payable within or without Uganda.

39. Control of credit and interest rates, etc.

(1) The Bank may, in consultation with the Minister, by statutory instrument, prescribe –

(a) the maximum amounts of investment, loans, advances and bills and promissory notes discounted whether applied in total or to any specified class or classes of such investments, loans, advances and bills and promissory notes discounted which each financial institution may have outstanding during the period that may be specified by the Bank;

(b) the purpose for which loans and advances may be granted and the class of business underlying investments and bills and promissory notes discounted;

(c) the maximum period of loans and advances and the type and minimum amount of security which shall be required; and the maximum tenor of bills and promissory notes discounted;

(d) the maximum or minimum rates of interest and other charges which in the transaction of their business financial institutions may pay on any type of deposit or other liability and impose on credit extended in any form;

(e) the maximum charges which in the transaction of their business financial institutions may impose on any banking transaction.

(2) Any prescription made under subsection (1) shall –

(a) have regard to commitments which financial institutions may have entered into with their customers at the time of the coming into force of the statutory instrument and shall take effect after the period of grace as the Bank may specify in the instrument;

(b) not discriminate between one financial institution and another.

(3) A financial institution which contravenes any prescription made under subsection (1) of this section shall be liable to pay, on being called upon to do so by the Bank a fine not exceeding one million shillings.

40. Financial institutions to furnish information.

(1) Every financial institution shall furnish to the Bank in a manner prescribed by statutory instrument all information that may be required by the Bank for the proper discharge of its functions.

(2) The Bank may publish in whole or in part information furnished to it under subsection (1) as the Board may determine.

(3) The Bank shall not publish or disclose any information regarding the affairs of a financial institution or of a customer of a financial institution unless the consent of the institution or the customer has been obtained.

41. Financial institutions as agents of the bank.

The Bank may appoint any financial institution as its agent for the issue, re-issue, exchange and withdrawal of notes and coins or for any other purpose on terms and conditions that may be agreed upon by the Bank and the institution appointed agent.

PART VIII – ACCOUNTS AND FINANCIAL STATEMENTS.

42. Bank's financial year.

The financial year of the Bank shall be the same as the financial year of the Government.

43. Audit.

The Accounts of the Bank shall be audited at least once every financial year, by the Auditor General or an auditor appointed by him or her to act on his or her behalf.

44. Returns.

(1) The Bank shall as soon as may be practicable, after the end of each quarter, make a quarterly return of its assets and liabilities and the return shall be published in the Gazette and a copy submitted to the Minister.

(2) The Bank may submit to the Minister, from time to time, information on the exercise and performance of its duties or on its assets and liabilities in a form that may be determined by the Board.

PART IX – MISCELLANEOUS PROVISIONS.

45. Declaration of Secrecy.

(1) The members of the Board, officers and employees of the Bank shall be bound by a declaration of secrecy and shall not, except as may reasonably be in the performance of their functions, disclose to any person any material information acquired in the performance of their functions unless called upon to give evidence in a court of competent jurisdiction or to fulfil other obligations imposed by law.

(2) Every former member of the Board, officer or employee of the Bank shall continue to be bound by the declaration of secrecy after the termination of service and shall not except with the prior written permission of the Bank disclose any material information acquired by him in that capacity, unless he or she is called upon to give evidence in a court of competent jurisdiction or to fulfil other obligations imposed by law.

(3) Where the Bank unreasonably withholds permission under this section, the aggrieved party may appeal to the High Court whose decision shall be final.

(4) Any person who contravenes the provision of this section commits an offence and shall be liable on conviction, to imprisonment for a term not exceeding five years or to a fine not exceeding five hundred thousand shillings or both such imprisonment and fine.

46. Exemption from tax.

The Bank shall be exempted from the payment of income tax and profits or capital gains tax in respect of its functions under this Act.

47. Prohibited names.

Unless a written consent from the Minister has been obtained, no financial institution shall register or be registered under any law in force by a name which includes the following words –

(a) Central;
(b) National;
(c) Uganda;
(d) Ugandan;
(e) Reserve;
(f) State; or
(g) Other equivalent word in any language.

48. Minister's powers of direction.

(1) The Minister may, after consultation with the Governor and subject to the provisions of this Act give directions of a general nature in writing, relating the financial and economic policy of the Bank.

(2) If after consultation with the Governor, the Minister is of the opinion that the policies being pursued by the Bank are not adequate for, or conducive to, the achievement of the functions of the Bank, the Minister may, with the approval of Cabinet, by directive in writing determine the specific policy to be adopted by the Bank and the Bank shall give effect to that policy while the directive remains in force.

(3) The Minister shall lay before parliament any directive issued under subsection (2) within fifteen sitting days after issuing that directive to the Bank.

49. Annual report.

(1) The Bank shall, not later than three months after the end of each financial year, present to the Minister a report generally on the activities and operations of the Bank during the preceding financial year and in particular –

(a) with regard to the procedures and policy of the Bank as the Bank considers may properly be given without detriment to the interests of the activities of the Bank;

(b) a copy of the audited accounts.

(2) The Minister shall lay before the Legislature the report received under subsection (1) within three months after the end of the financial year.

50. Bye laws.

The Board may, with the approval of the Minister, make bye-laws not inconsistent with this Statute regulating –

(a) the terms and conditions of service by the Board members;
(b) the structured establishment of the Bank;
(c) the terms and conditions of service for officers and employees of the Bank;
(d) retiring and other service benefits of the employees and officers of the Bank; or
(e) any other matter falling within the scope of its functions.

51. Offences and penalties.

(1) A person commits an offence and is liable on conviction, to a term of imprisonment not exceeding twelve months or to a fine not exceeding four hundred thousand shillings or to both the fine and imprisonment, who –
 (a) contravenes a provision of this Act;
 (b) knowingly makes an incorrect statement in a document submitted by him; or
 (c) knowingly makes a false reply to a question asked of him for the purpose of this Act.

(2) Where an offence is committed by a body of persons, every person who at the time of its commission was a director, manager or partner of that body shall be deemed to have committed the offence unless he proves –
 (a) that the offence was committed without his knowledge; and
 (b) that he took all reasonable steps to ensure compliance with the provisions of this Act.

52. Regulations.

The Minister may, after consultations with the Board, make regulations generally for the better carrying into effect the provisions of this Act.

Schedule **S.11.**

Meetings of the Board

1. The Governor shall preside at all meetings of the Board and in the absence of the Governor the Deputy Governor shall preside.
2. The Board shall meet for the discharge of its function as often as business requires and in any case the Board shall meet at least ten times in a year and the Governor may convene a meeting whenever two Directors request for a meeting.
3. The quorum at any meeting of the Board shall be by a simple majority including either the Governor or the Deputy Governor or a person presiding at the meeting.
4. A decision on a question proposed at any meeting of the Board shall be determined by a simple majority of the votes of the members present and voting and in the case of equality of votes the person presiding shall have a casting vote.

5. The Board shall cause to be kept minutes of all the proceedings of its meetings.
6. The Board may invite any number of persons to attend any of its meetings as consultant or adviser.
7. No act or proceedings of the Board shall be invalidated by reason only of the existence of a vacancy among the members of the Board.
8. All acts done by any person in good faith as a member of the Board, shall be valid notwithstanding any defect in his or her appointment.
9. In all other matters not provided for under this Statute the Board may regulate its own procedure.

CHAPTER 68

THE BILLS OF EXCHANGE ACT

Arrangement of Sections

Section

PART I – INTERPRETATION.

PART II – BILLS OF EXCHANGE.

Form and Interpretation

Capacity and Authority of Parties

The consideration for a bill

Negotiation of bills

General duties of the holder

Liabilities of parties

Discharge of bill

Part V – Supplementary.

Schedule.

CHAPTER 68

THE BILLS OF EXCHANGE ACT

Commencement: 15 August, 1933.

An Act Relating to Bills of Exchange, Cheques and Promissory Notes.

PART I – INTERPRETATION.

1. Interpretation.

In this Act unless the context otherwise requires –

(a) "acceptance" means an acceptance completed by delivery or notification;

(b) "action" includes counter-claim and set-off;

(c) "banker" includes a body of persons whether incorporated or not who carry on the business of banking;

(d) "bankrupt" includes any person whose estate is vested in a trustee or assignee under the law for the time being in force relating to bankruptcy;

(e) "bearer" means the person in possession of a bill or note which is payable to bearer;

(f) "bill" means bill of exchange, and "note" means promissory note;

(g) "delivery" means transfer of possession, actual or constructive, from one person to another;

(h) "endorsement" means an endorsement completed by delivery;

(i) "holder" means the payee or endorsee of a bill or note who is in possession of it, or the bearer thereof;

(j) "issue" means the first delivery of a bill or note, complete in form, to a person who takes it as a holder;

(k) "person" includes a body of persons whether incorporated or not;

(l) "value" means valuable consideration;

(m) "written" includes printed, and "writing" includes print.

PART II – BILLS OF EXCHANGE.

Form and interpretation

2. Bill of exchange defined.

(1) A bill of exchange is an unconditional order in writing, addressed by one person to another, signed by the person giving it, requiring the person to whom it is addressed to pay on demand or at a fixed or determinable future time a sum certain in money to or to the order of a specified person or to bearer.

(2) An instrument which does not comply with these conditions, or which orders any act to be done in addition to the payment of money, is not a bill of exchange.

(3) An order to pay out of a particular fund is not unconditional within the meaning of this section; but an unqualified order to pay, coupled with –

(a) an indication of a particular fund out of which the drawee is to reimburse himself or herself a particular account to be debited with the amount; or

(b) a statement of the transaction which gives rise to the bill, is unconditional.

(4) A bill is not invalid by reason –

(a) that it is not dated;

(b) that it does not specify the value given or that any value has been therefor;

(c) that it does not specify the place where it is drawn or the place where it is payable.

3. Inland and foreign bills.

(1) An inland bill is a bill which is or on the face of it purports to be –

(a) both drawn and payable within East Africa; or

(b) drawn within East Africa upon some person resident therein, and any other bill is a foreign bill.

(2) Unless the contrary appears on the face of the bill the holder may treat it as an inland bill.

4. Effect where different parties to bill are the same person.

(1) A bill may be drawn payable to, or to the order of the drawer, or it may be drawn payable to, or to the order of, the drawee.

(2) Where in a bill drawer and drawee are the same person, or where the drawee is a fictitious person or a person not having capacity to contract, the holder may treat the instrument, at his or her option, either as a bill of exchange or as a promissory note.

5. Address to drawee.

(1) The drawee must be named or otherwise indicated in a bill with reasonable certainty.

(2) A bill may be addressed to two or more drawees whether they are partners or not, but an order addressed to two drawees in the alternative or to two or more drawees in succession is not a bill of exchange.

6. Certainty required as to payee.

(1) Where a bill is not payable to bearer, the payee must be named or otherwise indicated in it with reasonable certainty.

(2) A bill may be made payable to two or more payees jointly, or it may be made payable in the alternative to one or two, or one or some of several payees. A bill may also be made payable to the holder of an office for the time being.

(3) Where the payee is a fictitious or non-existing person the bill may be treated as payable to bearer.

7. What bills are negotiable.

(1) When a bill contains words prohibiting transfer, or indicating an intention that it should not be transferable, it is valid as between the parties thereto, but is not negotiable.

(2) A negotiable bill may be payable either to order or to bearer.

(3) A bill is payable to bearer which is expressed to be so payable, or on which the only or last endorsement is an endorsement in blank.

(4) A bill is payable to order which is expressed to be so payable, or which is expressed to be payable to a particular person, and does not contain words prohibiting transfer or indicating an intention that it should not be transferable.

(5) Where a bill, either originally or by endorsement, is expressed to be payable to the order of a specified person, and not to him or her or his or her order, it is nevertheless payable to him or her or his or her order at his or her option.

8. Sum payable.

(1) The sum payable by a bill is a sum certain within the meaning of this Act, although it is required to be paid –

(a) with interest;

(b) by stated installments;

(c) by stated instalments, with a provision that upon default in payment of any installment the whole shall become due;

(d) according to an indicated rate of exchange or according to a rate of exchange to be ascertained as directed by the bill.

(2) Where the sum payable is expressed in words and also in figures, and there is discrepancy between the two, the sum denoted by the words is the amount payable.

(3) Where a bill is expressed to be payable with interest, unless the instrument otherwise provides, interest runs from the date of the bill, and if the bill is undated from the issue thereof.

9. Bill payable on demand.

(1) A bill is payable on demand –

(a) which is expressed to be payable on demand, or at sight, or on presentation; or

(b) in which no time for payment is expressed.

(2) Where a bill is accepted or endorsed when it is overdue, it shall, as regards the acceptor who so accepts, or any endorser who so endorses it, be deemed a bill payable on demand.

10. Bill payable at a future time.

(1) A bill is payable at a determinable future time within the meaning of this Act which is expressed to be payable –

(a) at a fixed period after date or sight;

(b) on or at a fixed period after the occurrence of a specified event which is certain to happen, though the time of happening may be uncertain.

(2) An instrument expressed to be payable on a contingency is not a bill, and the happening of the event does not cure the defect.

11. Omission of date in bill payable after date.

Where a bill expressed to be payable at a fixed period after date is issued undated, or where the acceptance of a bill payable at the fixed period after sight is undated, any holder may insert therein the true date of issue or acceptance, and the bill shall be payable accordingly but –

(a) where the holder in good faith and by mistake inserts a wrong date; and

(b) in every case where a wrong date is inserted, if the bill subsequently comes into the hands of a holder in due course the bill shall not be avoided thereby, but shall operate and be payable as if the date so inserted had been the true date.

12. Ante-dating and post-dating.

(1) Where a bill or an acceptance or any endorsement on a bill is dated, the date shall, unless the contrary be proved, be deemed to be the true date of the drawing, acceptance, or endorsement.

(2) A bill is not invalid by reason only that is in ante-dated or post-dated, or that it bears date on a Sunday.

13. Computation of time of payment.

Where a bill is not payable on demand, the date on which it falls due is determined as follows –

(a) three days, called "days of grace", are in every case where the bill itself does not otherwise provide, added to the time of payment as fixed by the bill, and the bill is due and payable on the last day of grace; but –

  (i) when the last day of grace falls on Sunday, Christmas Day or Good Friday, the bill is, except in the case hereinafter provided for, due and payable on the preceding business day;

  (ii) when the last day of grace is a public holiday, other than Christmas Day or Good Friday, or when the last day of grace is a Sunday and the second day of grace is a public holiday, the bill is due and payable on the succeeding business day;

(b) where a bill is payable at a fixed period after date, after sight, or after the happening of a specified event, the time of payment is determined by excluding the day from which the time is to begin to run and by including the day of payment;

(c) where a bill is payable at a fixed period after sight, the time begins to run from the date of the acceptance if the bill be accepted, and from the date of noting or protest if the bill be noted or protested for non-acceptance, or for non-delivery;

(d) the term "month" in a bill means a calender month.

14. Case of need.

The drawer of bill and any endorser may insert therein the name of a person to whom the holder may resort in case of need, that is to say, in case the bill is dishonoured by non-acceptance or non-payment. Such person is called the "referee in case of need". It is in the option of the holder to resort to the referee in case of need or not as he or she may think fit.

15. Optional stipulations by drawer or endorser.

The drawer of a bill and any endorser may insert therein an express stipulation–
(a) negativing or limiting his or her own liability to the holder;
(b) waiving as regards himself or herself some or all of the holder's duties.

16. Definition and requisites of acceptance.

(1) The acceptance of a bill is the signification by the drawee of his or her assent to the order of the drawer.
(2) An acceptance is invalid unless it complies with the following conditions, namely –
  (a) it must be written on the bill and be signed by the drawee. The mere signature of the drawee without additional words is sufficient;
  (b) it must not express that the drawee will perform his or her promise by any other means than the payment of money.

17. Time for acceptable.

(1) A bill may be accepted –
  (a) before it has been signed by the drawer, or while otherwise incomplete;
  (b) when it is overdue, or after it has been dishonoured by a previous refusal to accept, or by non-payment.
(2) When a bill payable after sight is dishonoured by non-acceptance, and the drawee subsequently accepts it, the holder, in the absence of any different agreement, is entitled to have the bill accepted as of the date of first presentment to the drawee for acceptance.

18. General and qualified acceptances.

(1) An acceptance is either –
  (a) general; or
  (b) qualified.
(2) A general acceptance assents without qualification to the order of the drawer
(3) A qualified acceptance in express terms varies the effect of the bill as drawn and in particular an acceptance is qualified which is –
  (a) conditional, that is to say, which makes payment by the acceptor dependent on the fulfillment of a condition in it; stated;
  (b) partial, that is to say, an acceptance to pay part only of the amount for which the bill is drawn;
  (c) local, that is to say, an acceptance to pay only at a particular specified place; but an acceptance to pay at the particular place is a general

acceptance unless it expressly states that the bill is to be paid there only and not else where;

(d) qualified as to time;

(e) the acceptance of some one or more of the drawees, but not of all.

19. Inchoate instruments.

(1) Where a simple signature on a blank stamped paper is delivered by the signer in order that it maybe converted into a bill, it operates as a prima facie authority to fill it up as a complete bill for any amount the stamp will cover, using the signature for that of the drawer, or the acceptor, or an endorser; and, in like manner, when a bill is wanting in any material particular, the person in possession of it has a prima facie authority to fill up the omission in any way he or she thinks fit.

(2) In order that any such instrument when completed may be enforceable against any person who became a party thereto prior to its completion, it must be filled up within a reasonable time, and strictly in accordance with the authority given. Reasonable time for this purpose is a question of fact; but if any such instrument after completion is negotiated to a holder in due course it shall be valid and effectual for all purposes in his or her hands, and he or she may enforce it as if it had been filled up within a reasonable time and strictly in accordance with the authority given.

20. Delivery.

(1) Every contract on a bill, whether it be the drawer's, the acceptor's, or an endorser's, is incomplete and revocable, until delivery of the instrument in order to give effect to it; except that where an acceptance is written on a bill, and the drawee gives notice to or according to the directions of the persons entitled to the bill that he or she has accepted it, the acceptance then becomes complete and irrevocable.

(2) As between immediate parties, and as regards a remote party other than a holder in due course, the delivery –

(a) in order to be effectual must be made either by or under the authority of the party drawing, accepting, or endorsing, as the case may be;

(b) may be shown to have been conditional or for a special purpose only, and not for the purpose of transferring the property in the bill, but if the bill be in the hands of a holder in due course, a valid delivery of the bill by all parties prior to him so as to make them liable to him or her is conclusively presumed.

(3) Where a bill is no longer in the possession of a party who has signed it as drawer, acceptor, or endorser, a valid and unconditional delivery by him or her is presumed until the contrary is proved.

Capacity and authority of parties

21. Capacity of parties.

(1) Capacity to incur liability as a party to a bill is co-extensive with capacity to contract; but nothing in this section shall enable a corporation to make itself liable as drawer, acceptor, or endorser of a bill unless it is competent to it so to do under the law for the time being in force relating to corporations.

(2) Where a bill is drawn or endorsed by an infant, minor, or corporation having no capacity or power to incur liability on a bill, the drawing or endorsement entitles the holder to receive payment of the bill, and to enforce it against any other party thereto.

22. Signature essential to liability.

No person is liable as drawer, endorser, or acceptor of a bill who has not signed it as such; except that –

(a) where a person signs a bill in a trade or assumed name, he or she is liable thereon as if he or she had signed it in this own name;

(b) the signature of the name of a firm is equivalent to the signature by the person so signing of the names of all persons liable as partners in that firm.

23. Forged or unauthorised signature.

Subject to the provisions of this Act, where a signature on a bill is forged or placed on the bill without the authority of the person whose signature it purports to be, the forged or unauthorised signature is wholly inoperative, and no right to retain the bill or to give a discharge therefore or to enforce payment of it against any party thereto can be required through or under that signature, unless the party against whom it is sought to retain or enforce payment of the bill is precluded from setting up the forgery or want of authority; but nothing in this section shall affect the ratification of an unauthorized signature not amounting to forgery.

24. Procuration signature.

A signature by procuration operates as notice that the agent has but a limited authority to sign, and the principal is only bound by such signature if the agent in so signing was acting within the actual limits of his or her authority.

25. Person signing as agent or in representative capacity.

(1) Where a person signs a bill as drawer, or acceptor and adds words to his or her signature, indicating that he or her signs for or on behalf of a principal, or in a representative character, he or she is not personally liable thereon but the mere addition to his or her signature of words describing him or her as an agent or as filling a representative character, does not exempt him from personal liability.

(2) In determining whether a signature on a bill is that of the principal or that of the agent by whose hand it is written, the construction most favourable to the validity of the instrument shall be adopted.

The Consideration for a bill

26. Value and holder for value.

(1) Valuable consideration for a bill may be constituted by –
   (a) any consideration sufficient to support a simple contract;
   (b) an antecedent debt or ability such a debt or liability is deemed valuable consideration whether the bill is payable on demand or at a future time.

(2) Where value has at any time been given for a bill, the holder is deemed to be a holder for value as regards the acceptor and all parties to the bill who became parties prior to that time.

(3) Where the holder of a bill has a lien on it, arising either from contract or by implication of law; he or she is deemed to be a holder for value to the extent of the sum for which he or she had a lien.

27. Accommodation bill or party.

(1) An accommodation party to a bill is a person who has signed a bill as drawer, acceptor, or endorser, without receiving value therefor, and for the purpose of lending his or her name to some other person.

(2) An accommodation party is liable on the bill to a holder for value; and it is immaterial whether, when such holder took the bill, he or she knew such party to be an accommodation party or not.

28. Holder in due course

(1) A holder in due course is a holder who has taken a bill, complete and regular on the face of it, under the following conditions, namely –
   (a) that he or she became the holder of it before it was overdue, and without notice that it had been previously dishonoured, if that was the fact;
   (b) that he or she took the bill in good faith and for value and that at the time the bill was negotiated to him he or she had no notice of any defect in the title of the person who negotiated it.

(2) The title of a person who negotiates a bill is defective within the meaning of this Act when he or she obtained the bill, or the acceptance of it, by fraud, duress or force and fear, or other unlawful means, or for an illegal consideration, or when he or she negotiates it in breach of faith, or under such circumstance as amount to a fraud.

(3) A holder (whether for value or not) who derives his or her title to a bill through a holder in due course, and who is not himself or herself a party to any fraud or illegality affecting it, has all the rights of that holder in due course as regards the acceptor and all parties to the bill prior to that holder.

29. Presumption of value and good faith.

(1) Every party whose signature appears on a bill is prima facie deemed to have become a party to it for value.

(2) Every holder of a bill is prima facie deemed to be a holder in due course; but if in an action on a bill it is admitted or proved that the acceptance, issue or

subsequent negotiation of the bill is affected with fraud, duress, or force and fear, or illegality, the burden of proof is shifted, until the holder proves that subsequent to the alleged fraud or illegality, value has in good faith been given for the bill.

Negotiation of bills

30. Negotiation of bill.

(1) A bill is negotiated when it is transferred from one person to another in such a manner as to constitute the transferee the holder of the bill.
(2) A bill payable to bearer is negotiated by delivery.
(3) A bill payable to order is negotiated by the endorsement of the holder completed by delivery.
(4) Where the holder of a bill payable to his or her order transfers it for value without endorsing it, the transfer gives the transferee such title as the transferor had in the bill, and the transferee in addition acquires the right to have the endorsement of the transferor.
(5) Where any person is under obligation to endorse a bill in a representative capacity, he or she may endorse the bill in such terms as to negative personal liability.

31. Requisition of a valid endorsement.

An endorsement in order to operate as a negotiation must comply with the following conditions, namely –

(a) it must be written on the bill itself and be signed by the endorser. The simple signature of the endorser on the bill, without additional words, is sufficient. An endorsement written on an allonge, or on a "copy" of a bill issued or negotiated in a country where "copies" are recognised is deemed to be written on the bill itself;
(b) it must be an endorsement of the entire bill. A partial endorsement, that is to say, an endorsement which purports to transfer to the endorsee a part only of the amount payable, or which purports to transfer the bill to two or more endorsees severally, does not operate as a negotiation of the bill;
(c) where a bill is payable to order of two or more payees or endorsees who are not partners, all must endorse, unless the one endorsing has authority to endorse for the others;
(d) where, in a bill payable to order, the payee or endorsee is wrongly designated, or his or her name is mis-spelt, he or she may endorse the bill as therein described, adding, if he or she thinks fit, his proper signature;
(e) where there are two or more endorsements on a bill, each endorsement is deemed to have been made in the order in which it appears on the bill, until the contrary is proved;
(f) an endorsement may be made in blank or special; it may also contain terms making it restrictive.

32. Conditional endorsement.

Where a bill purports to be endorsed conditionally, the condition may be disregarded by the payer, and payment to the endorsee is valid whether the condition has been fulfilled or not.

33. Endorsement in blank and special endorsement.

(1) An endorsement in blank specifies no endorsee, and a bill so endorsed becomes payable to bearer.

(2) A special endorsement specifies the person to whom, or to whose order, the bill is to be payable.

(3) The provisions of this Act relating to a payee apply with the necessary modifications to an endorsee under a special endorsement.

(4) When a bill has been endorsed in blank, any holder may convert the blank endorsement into a special endorsement by writing above the endorser's signature a direction to pay the bill to or to the order of himself or herself or some other person.

34. Restrictive endorsement.

(1) An endorsement is restrictive which prohibits the further negotiation of the bill or which expresses that it is a mere authority with the bill as thereby directed and not a transfer of the ownership of the bill, as, for example, if a bill be endorsed "Pay D only", or "Pay D for the account of X" or "Pay D or order for collection".

(2) A restrictive endorsement gives the endorsee the right to receive payment of the bill and to sue any party to it that his or her endorser could have sued, but gives him or her no power to transfer his or her rights as endorsee unless it expressly authorises him or her to do so.

(3) Where a restrictive endorsement authorises further transfer, all subsequent endorsees take the bill with the same rights and subject to the same liabilities as the first endorsees under the restrictive endorsement.

35. Negotiation of overdue or dishonoured bill.

(1) Where a bill is negotiable in its origin it continues to be negotiable until it has been –

(a) restrictively endorsed; or

(b) discharged by payment or otherwise.

(2) Where an overdue bill is negotiated, it can only be negotiated subject to any defect of title affecting it at its maturity, and thenceforward no person who takes it can acquire or give a better title than that which the person from whom he or she took it had.

(3) A bill payable on demand is deemed to be overdue within the meaning and for the purposes of this section when it appears on the face of it to have been in circulation for an unreasonable length of time what is an unreasonable length of time for this purpose is a question of fact.

(4) Except where an endorsement bears date after the maturity of the bill, every negotiation is prima facie deemed to have been effected before the bill was overdue.

(5) Where a bill which is not overdue has been dishonoured, any person who takes it with notice of the dishonour takes it subject to any defect of title attaching thereto at the time of dishonour, but nothing in this subsection shall affect the rights of a holder in due course.

36. Negotiation of bill to party already liable thereon

Where a bill is negotiated back to the drawer, or to a prior endorser, or to the acceptor, such party may, subject to the provisions of this Act, re-issue and further negotiate the bill, but he or she is not entitled to enforce payment of the bill against any intervening party to whom he or she was previously liable.

37. Rights of the holder.

The rights and powers of the holder of a bill are as follows –

(a) he or she may sue on the bill in his or her own name;

(b) where he or she is a holder in due course, he or she holds the bill free from any defect of title of prior parties, as well as from mere personal defences available to prior parties among themselves, and may enforce payment against all parties liable on the bill;

(c) where his or her title is defective –

(i) if he or she negotiates the bill to a holder in due course, that holder obtains a good and complete title to the bill; and

(ii) if he obtains payment of the bill, the person who pays him or her in due course gets a valid discharge for the bill.

General duties of the holder

38. When presentment for acceptance is necessary.

(1) Where a bill is payable after sight, presentment for acceptance is necessary in order to fix the maturity of the instrument.

(2) Where a bill expressly stipulates that it shall be presented for acceptance, or where a bill is drawn payable elsewhere than at the residence or place of business of the drawee, it must be presented for acceptance before it can be presented for payment.

(3) In no other case is presentment for acceptance necessary in order to render liable any party to the bill.

(4) Where the holder of a bill, drawn payable elsewhere than at the place of business or residence of the drawee, has not time, with the exercise of reasonable diligence, to present the bill for acceptance before presenting it for payment on the day that it falls due, the delay caused by presenting the bill for acceptance before presenting it for payment is excused, and does not discharge the drawer and endorsers.

39. Time for presenting bill payable after sight.

(1) Subject to the provision of this Act, when a bill payable after sight is negotiated, the holder must either present it for acceptance or negotiate it within a reasonable time.

(2) If he or she does not do so, the drawer and all endorsers prior to that holder are discharged.

(3) In determining what is a reasonable time within the meaning of this section, regard shall be had to the nature of the bill, the usage of trade with respect to similar bills, and the facts of the particular case.

40. Rules as to presentment for acceptance and excuses for non presentment.

(1) A bill is duly presented for acceptance which is presented in accordance with the following rules –

(a) the presentment must be made by or on behalf of the holder to the drawee or to some person authorised to accept or refuse acceptance on his behalf at a reasonable hour on a business day and before the bill is overdue.

(b) where a bill is addressed to two or more drawees, who are not partners, presentment must be made to them all; unless one has authority to accept for all, then presentment may be made to him or her only;

(c) where the drawee is dead, presentment may be made to his or her personal representative;

(d) where the drawee is bankrupt, presentment may be made to him or her or to his trustee;

(e) where authorised by agreement or usage, a presentment through the Post Office is sufficient.

(2) Presentment in accordance with these rules is excused, and a bill may be treated as dishonoured by non-acceptance –

(a) where the drawee is dead or bankrupt, or is a fictitious person or a person not having capacity to contract by bill;

(b) where, after the exercise of reasonable diligence, such presentment cannot be effected;

(c) where, although the presentment has been irregular, acceptance has been refused on some other ground.

(3) The fact that the holder has reason to believe that the bill, on presentment, will be dishonoured, does not excuse presentment.

41. Non-acceptance.

When a bill is duly presented for acceptance, and is not accepted within the customary time, the person presenting it must treat it as dishonoured by non-acceptance. If he or she does not, the holder shall lose his or her right of recourse against the drawer and endorsers.

42. Dishonour by nonacceptance and its consequences.

(1) A bill is dishonoured by non-acceptance –

(a) when it is duly presented for acceptance, and such an acceptance as is prescribed by this Act is refused or cannot be obtained; or

(b) when presentment for acceptance is excused and the bill is not accepted.

(2) Subject to the provisions of this Act, when a bill is dishonoured by non-acceptance, an immediate right of recourse against the drawer and endorsers accrues to the holder, and no presentment for payment is necessary.

43. Duties as to qualified acceptances.

(1) The holder of a bill may refuse to take a qualified acceptance, and if he or she does not obtain an unqualified acceptance, may treat the bill as dishonoured by non-acceptance.

(2) Where a qualified acceptance is taken, and the drawer or an endorser has not expressly or impliedly authorised the holder to take a qualified acceptance, or does not subsequently assent to it, such drawer or endorser is discharged from his or her liability on the bill; but–

(a) the provisions of this subsection shall not apply to a partial acceptance, of which due notice has been given;

(b) where a foreign bill has been accepted as to part, it must be protested as to the balance.

(3) When the drawer or endorser of a bill receives notice of a qualified acceptance, and does not, within a reasonable time, express his or her dissent to the holder, he or she shall be deemed to have assented to it.

44. Rules as to presentment for payment.

(1) Subject to the provisions of this Act, a bill must be duly presented for payment.

(2) If it be not so presented, the drawer and endorsers shall be discharged

(3) A bill is duly presented for payment which is presented in accordance with the following rules –

(a) where the bill is not payable on demand, presentment must be on the day it falls due;

(b) where the bill is payable on demand, then, subject to the provisions of this Act, presentment must be made within a reasonable time after its issue in order to render the drawer liable, and within a reasonable time after its endorsement, in order to render the endorser liable. In determining what is a reasonable time, regard shall be had to the nature of the bill, the usage of trade with regard to similar bills, and the facts of the particular case;

(c) presentment must be made by the holder, or by some person authorised to receive payment on his behalf, at a reasonable hour on a business day at the proper place, as hereinafter defined in paragraph (d) of this subsection either to the person designated by the bill as payer, or to some person authorised to pay or refuse payment on his or her behalf, if with the exercise of reasonable diligence such person can there be found;

(d) a bill is presented at the proper place –
  (i) where a place of payment is specified in the bill and the bill is there presented;
  (ii) where no place of payment is specified, but the address of the drawee or acceptor is given in the bill, and the bill is there presented;
  (iii) where no place of payment is specified, and no address given, and the bill is presented at the drawee's or acceptor's place of business, if known, and if not, at his ordinary residence if known;
  (iv) in any other case, if presented to the drawee or acceptor wherever he can be found, or if presented at his last-known place of business or residence;

(e) where a bill is presented at the proper place, and after the exercise of reasonable diligence, no person authorised to pay or refuse payment can be found there, no further presentment to the drawee or acceptor is required;

(f) where a bill is drawn upon, or accepted by two or more persons who are not partners, and no place of payment is specified, presentment must be made to them all;

(g) where the drawee or acceptor of a bill is dead, and no place of payment is specified, presentment must be made to a personal representative, if such there be, and with the exercise of reasonable diligence he or she can be found;

(h) where authorised by agreement or usage, a presentment through the Post Office is sufficient.

45. Excuses for delay or non-presentment for payment.

(1) Delay in making presentment for payment is excused when the delay is caused by circumstances beyond the control of the holder, and not imputable to his or her default, misconduct or negligence. When the cause of delay ceases to operate, presentment must be made with reasonable diligence.

(2) Presentment for payment is dispensed with –
  (a) where, after the exercise of reasonable diligence, presentment, as required by this Act, cannot be effected. The fact that the holder has reason to believe that the bill will, on presentment, be dishonoured, does not dispense with the necessity for presentment;
  (b) where the drawee is a fictitious person;
  (c) as regards the drawer, where the drawee or acceptor is not bound, as between himself or herself and the drawer, to acceptor or pay the bill, and the drawer has no reason to believe that the bill would be paid if presented;
  (d) as regards an endorser, where the bill was accepted or made for the accommodation of that endorser, and he or she has no reason to expect that the bill would be paid if presented;
  (e) by waiver of presentment, expressed or implied.

46. Dishonour by non-payment

(1) A bill is dishonoured by non-payment –
   (a) when it is duly presented for payment and payment is refused or cannot be obtained; or
   (b) when presentment is excused and the bill is overdue and unpaid.

(2) Subject to the provisions of this Act, when a bill is dishonoured by non-payment, an immediate right of recourse against the drawer and endorsers accrues to the holder.

47. Notice of dishonour and effect of non-notice.

Subject to the provisions of the Act, when a bill has been dishonoured by non-acceptance or by non-payment, notice of dishonour must be given to the drawer and each endorser, and any drawer or endorser to whom such notice is not given is discharged; except that –

(a) where a bill is dishonoured by non-acceptance, and notice of dishonour is not given, the rights of a holder in due course subsequent to the omission;

(b) where a bill is dishonoured by non-acceptance, and due notice of dishonour is not given, it shall be necessary to give notice of a subsequent dishonour by non-payment unless the bill shall in the meantime have been accepted.

48. Rules as to notice of dishounour.

Notice of dishonour in order to be valid and effectual must be given in accordance with the following rules –

(a) the notice must be given by or on behalf of the holder, or by or on behalf of an endorser who, at the time of giving it, is himself or herself liable on the bill;

(b) notice of dishonour may be given by an agent either in his or her own name, or in the name of any party entitled to give notice, whether that party is his or her principal or not;

(c) where the notice is given by or on behalf of the holder, it ensures for the benefit of all subsequent holders and all prior endorsers who have a right of recourse against the party to whom it is given;

(d) where notice is given by or on behalf of an endorser entitled to give notice as hereinbefore provided, it enures for the benefit of the holder and all endorsers subsequent to the party to whom notice is given.

(e) the notice may be given in writing or by personal communication, and may be given in any terms which sufficiently identify the bill, and intimate that the bill has been dishonoured by non-acceptance or non-payment;

(f) the return of a dishonoured bill to the drawer or an endorser is, in point of form, deemed a sufficient notice of dishonour;

(g) a written notice need not be signed, and an insufficient written notice may be supplemented and validated by verbal communication. A mis-description of the bill shall not vitiate the notice unless the party by whom the notice is given is in fact misled thereby;

(h) where notice of dishonour is required to be given to any person, it may be given either to the party himself or to his or her agent for that purpose;

(i) where the drawer or endorser is dead, and the party giving notice knows it, the notice must be given to a personal representative, if such there be, and with the exercise of reasonable diligence he or she can be found;

(j) where the drawer or endorser is bankrupt, notice may be given either to the party himself or herself or to the trustee;

(k) where there are two or more drawers or endorsers who are not partners, notice must be given to each of them, unless one of them has authority to receive such notice for the others;

(l) the notice may be given as soon as the bill is dishonoured, and must be given within a reasonable time thereafter. In the absence of special circumstances, notice is not deemed to have been given within a reasonable time unless –

- (i) where the person giving and the person to receive notice reside in the same place, notice is given or sent off in time to reach the latter on the day after the dishonour of the bill;
- (ii) where the person giving and the person to receive notice reside in different places, the notice is sent off on the day after the dishonour of the bill, if there be a post at the convenient hour on that day, and if there be no such post on that day, then by the next post thereafter;

(m) where a bill when dishonoured is in the hands of an agent, he or she may either himself or herself give notice to the parties liable on the bill or he or she may give notice to his or her principal. If he or she gives notice to his principal, he must do so within the same time as if he were the holder, and the principal upon receipt of such notice has himself or herself the same time for giving notice as if the agent had been an independent holder;

(n) where a party to a bill receives due notice of dishonour he or she has, after the receipt of such notice, the same period of time for giving notice to antecedent parties that the holder has after the dishonour;

(o) where a notice of dishonour is duly addressed and posted, the sender is deemed to have given due notice of dishonour, notwithstanding any miscarriage by the Post Office.

49. Excecuse for non-notice and delay.

(1) Delay in giving notice of dishonour is excused where the delay is caused by circumstances beyond the control of the party giving notice, and not imputable to his or her default, misconduct or negligence. When the cause of delay ceases to operate, the notice must be given with reasonable diligence.

(2) Notice of dishonour is dispensed with –

- (a) when, after the exercise of reasonable diligence, notice as required by this Act cannot be given to or does not reach the drawer or endorser sought to be charged;
- (b) by waiver express or implied. Notice of dishonour may be waived before the time of giving notice has arrived or after the omission to give due notice;
- (c) as regards the drawer in the following cases, namely –
  - (i) where the drawer and drawee are the same person;

(ii) where the drawee is a fictitious person or a person not having capacity to contract;

(iii) where the drawer is the person to whom the bill is presented for payment;

(iv) where the drawee or acceptor is, as between himself or herself and the drawer, under no obligation to accept or pay the bill;

(v) where the drawer has countermanded payment,

(d) as regards the endorser in the following cases, namely –

(i) where the drawee is a fictitious person or a person not having capacity to contract and the endorser was aware of the fact at the time he or she endorsed the bill;

(ii) where the endorser is the person to whom the bill is presented for payment;

(iii) where the bill was accepted or made for his or her accommodation.

50. Noting or protest of bill.

(1) Where an inland bill has been dishonoured, it may, if the holder thinks fit, be noted for non-acceptance or non-payment; but it shall not be necessary to note or protest any such bill in order to preserve the recourse against the drawer or endorser.

(2) Where a foreign bill, appearing on the face of it to be such, has been dishonoured by non-acceptance, it must be duly protested for non-acceptance, and where such a bill, which has not been previously dishonoured by non-acceptance, is dishonoured by non-payment, it must be duly protested for non-payment. If it be not so protested the drawer and endorsers are discharged. Where a bill does not appear on the face of it to be a foreign bill, protest of the bill in case of dishonour is unnecessary.

(3) A bill which has been protested for non-acceptance may be subsequently protested for non-payment.

(4) Subject to the provisions of this Act, when a bill is noted or protested, it may be noted on the day of its dishonour and must be noted not later than the next succeeding business day. When a bill has been duly noted, the protest may be subsequently extended as of the date of the noting.

(5) Where the acceptor of a bill becomes bankrupt or insolvent or suspends payment before it matures, the holder may cause the bill to be protested for better security against the drawers and endorsers.

(6) A bill must be protested at the place where it is dishonoured; except that –

(a) when a bill is presented through the Post Office, and returned by post dishonoured, it may be protested at the place to which it is returned and on the day of its return if received during business hours, and if not received during business hours, then not later than the next business day;

(b) when a bill drawn payable at the place of business or residence of some person other than the drawee has been dishonoured by non-acceptance, it must be protested for non-payment at the place where it is expressed to be payable, and no further presentment for payment to, or demand on, the drawee is necessary.

(7) A protest must contain a copy of the bill, and must be signed by the notary making it, and must specify –
   (a) the person at whose request the bill is protested;
   (b) the place and date of protest, the cause or reason for protesting the bill, the demand made, and the answer given, if any, or the fact that the drawee or acceptor could not be found.

(8) Where a bill is lost or destroyed, or is wrongly detained from the person entitled to hold it, protest may be made on a copy or written particulars thereof.

(9) Protest is dispensed with by any circumstances which would dispense with notice of dishonour. Delay in noting or protesting is excused when the delay is caused by circumstances beyond the control of the holder, and not imputable to his or her default, misconduct or negligence. When the cause of delay ceases to operate, the bill must be noted or protested with reasonable diligence.

51. Duties of older as regards drawee or acceptor.

(1) When a bill is accepted generally, presentment for payment is not necessary in order to render the acceptor liable.

(2) When by the terms of a qualified acceptance presentment for payment is required, the acceptor, in the absence of an express stipulation to that effect, is not discharged by the omission to present the bill for payment on the day that it matures.

(3) In order to render the acceptor of a bill liable it is not necessary to protest it, or that notice of dishonour should be given to him or her.

(4) Where the holder of a bill presents it for payment, he or she shall exhibit the bill to the person from whom he or she demands payment, and when a bill is paid the holder shall forthwith deliver it up to the party paying it.

Liabilities of parties

52. Bill not assignment of funds in hands of drawee.

A bill of itself does not operate as an assignment of funds in the hands of the drawee available for the payment of it, and the drawee of a bill who does not accept as required by this Act is not liable on the instrument.

53. Liability of acceptor.

The acceptor of a bill, by accepting it –

(a) engages that he or she will pay it according to the tenor of his or her acceptance;

(b) is precluded from denying to a holder in due course –
   (i) the existence of the drawer, the genuineness of his or her signature, and his or her capacity and authority to draw the bill;
   (ii) in the case of a bill payable to drawer's order, the then capacity of the drawer to endorse, but not the genuineness or validity of his or herendorsement;
   (iii) in the case of a bill payable to the order of a third person, the existence of the payee and his or her then capacity to endorse, but not the genuineness or validity of his or her endorsement.

54. Liability of drawer or endorser.

(1) The drawer of a bill by drawing it –

(a) engages that on due presentment it shall be accepted and paid according to its tenor, and that if it be dishonoured he or she will compensate the holder or any endorser who is compelled to pay it, provided that the requisite proceedings on dishonour be duly taken;

(b) is precluded from denying to a holder in due course, the existence of the payee and his or her then capacity to endorse.

(2) The endorser of a bill by endorsing it –

(a) engages that on due presentment it shall be accepted and paid according to its tenor and that if it is dishonoured he or she will compensate the holder or subsequent endorser who is compelled to pay it provided that the requisite proceedings on dishonour are duly taken;

(b) is precluded from denying to a holder in due course the genuineness and regularity in all respects of the drawer's signature and all previous endorsements;

(c) is precluded from denying to his or her immediate or subsequent endorsee that the bill was at the time of his or her endorsement a valid and subsisting bill, and that he or she had then a good title to it.

55. Stranger signing bill liable as endorser.

Where a person signs a bill otherwise than as drawer or acceptor, he thereby incurs the liabilities of an endorser to a holder in due course.

56. Measure of damages against parties to dishonoured bill.

Where a bill is dishonoured, the measure of damages, which shall be deemed to be liquidated damages, shall be as follows –

(a) the holder may recover from any party liable on the bill, and the drawer who has been compelled to pay the bill may recover from the acceptor, and an endorser who has been compelled to pay the bill may recover from the acceptor or from the drawer or from a prior endorser –

(i) the amount of the bill;

(ii) interest thereon from the time of presentment for payment if the bill is payable on demand, and from the maturity of the bill in any other case;

(iii) the expenses of noting, or when protest is necessary, and the protest has been extended, the expenses of protest;

(b) in the case of a bill which has been dishonoured abroad, in lieu of the above damages, the holder may recover from the drawer or an endorser, and the drawer or an endorser who has been compelled to pay the bill may recover from any party liable to him or her, the amount of the exchange with interest thereon until the time of payment;

(c) where by this Act interest may be recovered as damages, such interest may, if justice require it, be withheld wholly or in part, and where a bill is expressed to be payable with interest at a given rate, interest as damages may or may not be given at the same rate as interest proper.

57. Transferor by delivery and transferee.

(1) Where the holder of a bill payable to bearer negotiates it by delivery without endorsing it, he or she is called a "transferor by delivery".
(2) A transferor by delivery is not liable on the instrument.
(3) A transferor by delivery who negotiates a bill thereby warrants to his or her immediate transferee, being a holder for value, that the bill is what it purports to be, that he or she has a right to transfer it, and that at the time of transfer he or she is not aware of any fact which renders it valueless.

Discharge of bill

58. Payment in due course.

(1) A bill is discharged by payment in due course by or on behalf of the drawee or acceptor.
(2) "Payment in due course" means payment made at or after the maturity of the bill to the holder of it in good faith and without notice that his or her title to the bill is defective.
(3) Subject to the provisions hereinafter contained, when a bill is paid by the drawer or endorser, it is not discharged, but –
    (a) where a bill payable to, or to the order of, a third party is paid by the drawer the drawer may enforce payment of it against the acceptor, but may not re-issue the bill;
    (b) where a bill is paid by an endorser, or where a bill payable to drawer's order is paid by the drawer, the party paying it is remitted to his or her former rights as regards the acceptor or antecedent parties, and he or she may, if he or she thinks fit, strike out his or her own and subsequent endorsements, and again negotiate the bill.
(4) Where an accommodation bill is paid in due course by the party accommodated, the bill is discharged.

59. Banker paying demand draft on which endorsement is forged.

(1) When a bill payable to order on demand is drawn on a banker, and the banker on whom it is drawn pays the bill in good faith and in the ordinary course of business, it is not incumbent on the banker to show that the endorsement of the payee or any subsequent endorsement was made by or under the authority of the person whose endorsement it purports to be, and the banker is deemed to have paid the bill in due course, although such endorsement has been forged or made without authority.
(2) Any draft or order (other than a bill or a cheque) drawn upon a banker for a sum of money payable to order or demand which shall, when presented for payment, purport to be endorsed by the person to whom the same shall be drawn payable, shall be a sufficient authority to such banker to pay the amount of such draft or order to the bearer of it; and it shall not be incumbent on such banker to prove that such endorsement, or any subsequent endorsement, was made by or under

the direction or authority of the person to whom the said draft or order was or is made payable either by the drawer or endorser of the draft or order.

60. Acceptor the holder at maturity.

When the acceptor of a bill is or becomes the holder of it at or after its maturity, in his or her own right, the bill is discharged.

61. Express waiver.

(1) Where the holder of a bill at or after its maturity absolutely and unconditionally renounces his or her rights against the acceptor the bill is discharged. The renunciation must be in writing, unless the bill is delivered up to the acceptor.

(2) The liabilities of any party to a bill may in like manner be renounced by the holder before, at, or after its maturity, but nothing in this section shall affect the rights of a holder in due course without notice of the renunciation.

62. Cancellation.

(1) Where a bill is intentionally cancelled by the holder or his or her agent, and the cancellation is apparent thereon, the bill is discharged.

(2) In like manner any party liable on a bill may be discharged by the intentional cancellation of his or her signature by the holder or his or her agent. In such case any endorser who would have had a right of recourse against the party whose signature is cancelled is also discharged.

(3) A cancellation made unintentionally, or under a mistake, or without the authority of the holder, is inoperative, but where a bill or any signature thereon appears to have been cancelled the burden of proof lies on the party who alleges that the cancellation was made unintentionally, or under a mistake, or without authority.

63. Alteration of bill.

(1) Where a bill or acceptance is materially altered without the assent of all parties liable on the bill, the bill is avoided, except as against a party who has himself or herself made, authorised, or assented to the alteration, and subsequent endorser; except that where a bill has been materially altered, but the alteration is not apparent, and the bill is in the hands of a holder in due course, the holder may avail himself or herself of the bill as if it had not been altered, and may enforce payment of it according to its original tenor.

(2) In particular the following alterations are material, namely, any alteration of the date, the sum payable, the time of payment, the place of payment, and, where a bill has been accepted generally, the addition of a place of payment without the acceptor's consent.

Acceptance and payment for honour

64. Acceptance for honour supra protest.

(1) Where a bill of exchange has been protested for dishonour by non-acceptance, or protested for better security, and is not overdue, any person, not being a party

already liable on it, may with the consent of the holder, intervene and accept the bill supra protest, for the honour of any party liable on it, or for the honour of the person for whose account the bill is drawn.

(2) A bill may be accepted for honour for part only of the sum for which it is drawn.

(3) An acceptance for honour supra protest in order to be valid must –

(a) be written on the bill, and indicate that is it an acceptance for the honour;

(b) be signed by the acceptor for honour.

(4) Where an acceptance for honour does not expressly state for whose honour it is made, it is deemed to be an acceptance for the honour of the drawer.

(5) Where a bill payable after sight is accepted for honour, its maturity is calculated from the date of the noting for non-acceptance, and not from the date of the acceptance for honour.

65. Liability of acceptor for honour.

(1) The acceptor for honour of a bill by accepting it engages that he or she will, on due presentment, pay the bill according to the tenor of his or her acceptance, if it is not paid by the drawee, provided it has been duly presented for payment, and protested for non-payment and that he or she receives notice of these facts.

(2) The acceptor for honour is liable to the holder and to all parties to the bill subsequent to the party for whose honour he or she has accepted.

66. Presentment to acceptor for honour.

(1) Where a dishonoured bill has been accepted for honour supra protest, or contains a reference in case of need, it must be protested for non-payment before it is presented for payment to the acceptor for honour or referee in case of need.

(2) Where the address of the acceptor for honour is in the same place where the bill is protested for non-payment, the bill must be presented to him or her not later than the day following its maturity; and where the address of the acceptor for honour is in some place other than the place where it was protested for non-payment, the bill must be forwarded not later than the day following its maturity for presentment to him or her.

(3) Delay in presentment or non-presentment is excused by any circumstance which would excuse delay in presentment for payment or non-presentment for payment.

(4) When a bill of exchange is dishonoured by the acceptor for honour it must be protested for non-payment by him or her.

67. Payment for honour supra protest

(1) Where a bill has been protested for non-payment any person may intervene and pay it supra protest for the honour of any party liable on it, or for the honour of the person for whose account the bill is drawn.

(2) Where two or more persons offer to pay a bill for the honour of different parties, the person whose payment will discharge most parties to the bill shall have the preference.

(3) Payment for honour supra protest, in order to operate as such and not as a mere voluntary payment, must be attested by a notarial act of honour which may be appended to the protest or form an extension of it.

(4) The notarial act of honour must be founded on a declaration made by the payer for honour, or his or her agent in that behalf, declaring his or her intention to pay the bill for honour, and for whose honour he or she pays.

(5) Where a bill has been paid for honour, all parties subsequent to the party for whose honour it is paid are discharged, but the payer for honour is subrogated for, and succeeds to both the rights and duties of, the holder as regards the party for whose honour he or she pays, and all parties liable to that party.

(6) The payer for honour on paying to the holder the amount of the bill and the notarial expenses incidental to its dishonour is entitled to receive both the bill itself and the protest. If the holder does not on demand deliver them up he or she shall be liable to the payer for honour in damages.

(7) Where the holder of a bill refuses to receive payment supra protest he or she shall lose his or her right of recourse against any party who would have been discharged by such payment.

Lost instruments

68. Holder's right to duplicate of lost bill.

(1) Where a bill has been lost before it is overdue, the person who was the holder of it may apply to the drawer to give him or her another bill of the same tenor, giving security to the drawer, if required, to indemnify him or her against all persons whatever in case the bill alleged to have been lost shall be found again.

(2) If the drawer on request as aforesaid refuses to give such duplicate bill he or she may be compelled to do so.

69. Action on lost bill.

In any action of proceeding upon a bill, the court or a judge may order that the loss of the instrument shall not be set up, provided an indemnity be given to the satisfaction of the court or judge against the claims of any other person upon the instrument in question.

Bill in a set

70. Rules as to sets.

(1) Where a bill is drawn in a set, each part of the set being numbered, and contain a reference to the other parts, the whole of the parts constitute one bill.

(2) Where the holder of a set endorses two or more parts to different persons, he or she is liable on every such part, and every endorser subsequent to him or her is liable on the part he or she has himself or herself endorsed as if the said parts were separate bills.

(3) Where two or more parts of a set are negotiated to different holders in due course, the holder whose title first accrues is as between such holders deemed the true owner of the bill, but nothing in this subsection shall affect the rights of a person who in due course accepts or pays the parts first presented to him or her.

(4) The acceptance may be written on any part, and it must be written on one part only. If the drawee accepts more than one part, and such accepted parts get

into the hands of different holders in due course, he or she is liable on every such part as if it were a separate bill.

(5) When the acceptor of a bill drawn in a set pays it without requiring the part bearing his or her acceptance to the delivered up to him, or her and that part at maturity is outstanding in the hands of a holder in due course, he or she is liable to the holder of it.

(6) Subject to the preceding rules, where any one part of a bill drawn in a set is discharged by payment or otherwise, the whole bill is discharged.

Conflict of laws

71. Rules where laws conflict.

Where a bill drawn in one country is negotiated, accepted, or payable in another, the rights, duties, and liabilities of the parties thereto are determined as follows –

(a) the validity of a bill as regards requisites in form is determined by the law of the place of issue, and the validity as regards requisites in form of the supervening contracts, such as acceptance, or endorsement or acceptance supra protest, is determined by the law of the place where the contract was made; except that –

(i) where a bill is issued out of Uganda it is not invalid by reason only that it is not stamped in accordance with the law of the place of issue;

(ii) where a bill issued out of Uganda conforms, as regards requisites in form, to the law of Uganda, it may, for the purpose of enforcing payment thereof, be treated as valid as between all persons who negotiate, hold, or become parties to it in Uganda;

(b) subject to the provisions of this Act, the interpretation of the drawing, endorsement, acceptance, or acceptance supra protest of a bill, is determined by the law of the place where such contract is made; except that where an inland bill is endorsed in a foreign country the endorsement shall, as regards the payer, be interpreted according to the law of Uganda;

(c) the duties of the holder with respect to presentment for acceptance or payment, and the necessity for or sufficiency of a protest or notice of dishonour, or otherwise, are determined by the law of the place where the act is done or the bill is dishonoured;

(d) where a bill is drawn out of but payable in Uganda and the sum payable is not expressed in the currency of Uganda, the amount shall, in the absence of some express stipulation, be calculated according to the rate of exchange for sight drafts at the place of payment on the day the bill is payable.

(e) where a bill is drawn in one country and is payable in another, the due date thereof is determined according to the law of the place where it is payable.

PART III – CHEQUES ON A BANKER.

72. Cheque defined.

(1) A cheque is a bill of exchange drawn on a banker payable on demand.
(2) Except as otherwise provided in this Part of this Act, the provisions of this Act applicable to a bill of exchange payable on demand apply to a cheque.

73. Presentment of cheque for payment.

Subject to the provisions of this Act –
(a) where a cheque is not presented for payment within a reasonable time of its issue, and the drawer or the person on whose account it is drawn had the right at the time of such presentment as between him or her and the banker to have the cheque paid and suffers actual damage through the delay, he or she is discharged to the extent of such damage, that is to say, to the extent to which such drawer or person is a creditor of the banker to a larger amount than he or she would have been had the cheque been paid;
(b) in determining what is a reasonable time regard shall be had to the nature of this instrument, the usage of trade and of bankers, and the facts of the particular case;
(c) the holder of such cheque as to which such drawer or person is discharged shall be a creditor, in lieu of such drawer or person, of the banker to the extent of such discharge, and entitled to recover the amount from him or her.

74. Revocation of banker's authority.

The duty and authority of a banker to pay a cheque drawn on him by his customer are determined by –
(a) countermand of payment;
(b) notice of the customer's death.

Crossed cheques

75. General and special crossings defined.

(1) Where a cheque bears across its face an addition of –
    (a) the words "and company" or any abbreviation of it between two parallel transverse lines, either with or without the words "not negotiable"; or
    (b) two parallel transverse lines simply, either with or without the words "not negotiable", that addition constitutes a crossing, and the cheque is crossed generally.
(2) When a cheque bears across its face an addition of the name of a banker, either with or without the words "not negotiable", that addition constitutes a crossing, and the cheque is crossed specially and to that banker.

76. Crossing by drawer or after issue.

(1) A cheque may be crossed generally or specially by the drawer.
(2) Where a cheque is uncrossed, the holder may cross it generally or specially.
(3) Where a cheque is crossed generally, the holder may cross it specially.
(4) Where a cheque is crossed generally or specially the holder may add the words "not negotiable".
(5) Where a cheque is crossed specially, the banker to whom it is crossed may again cross it specially to another banker for collection.
(6) Where an uncrossed cheque, or a cheque crossed generally, is sent to a banker for collection, he or she may cross it specially to himself or herself.

77. Crossing a material part of cheque.

A crossing authorised by this Act is a material part of the cheque; it shall not be lawful for any person to obliterate or, except as authorised by this Act, to add to or alter the crossing.

78. Duties of banker as to crossed cheques.

(1) Where a cheque is crossed specially to more than one banker, except when crossed to an agent for collection being a banker, the banker on whom it is drawn shall refuse payment thereof.
(2) When the banker on whom a cheque is drawn which is so crossed nevertheless pays it, or pays a cheque crossed generally otherwise than to a banker, or if crossed specially otherwise than to the banker to whom it is crossed, or his or her agent for collection being a banker, he or she is liable to the true owner of the cheque for any loss he or she may sustain owing to the cheque having been so paid; where a cheque is presented for payment which does not at the time of presentment appear to be crossed, or to have had a crossing which has been obliterated, or to have been added to or altered otherwise than as authorised by this Act, the banker paying the cheque in good faith and without negligence shall not be responsible or incur any liability, nor shall the payment be questioned by reason of the cheque having been crossed, or of the crossing having been obliterated or having been added to or altered otherwise than as authorised by this Act, and of payment having been made otherwise than to a banker or to the banker to whom the cheque is or was crossed, or to his agent for collection being a banker, as the case may be.

79. Protection to banker and drawer where cheque is crossed.

Where the banker, on whom a crossed cheque is drawn in good faith and without negligence pays it, if crossed generally, to a banker, and if crossed specially, to the banker to whom it is crossed, or his or her agent for collection being a banker, the banker paying the cheque, and, if the cheque has come into the hands of the payee, the drawer, shall respectively be entitled to the same rights and be placed in the same position as if payment of the cheque had been made to the true owner of the cheque.

80. Effect of words "not negotiable".

Where a person takes a crossed cheque which bears on it the words "not negotiable", he or she shall not have, and shall not be capable of giving, a better title to the cheque than that which the person from whom he or she took it had.

81. Protection to collecting banker.

(1) Where a banker in good faith and without negligence receives payment for a customer of a cheque crossed generally or specially to himself or herself and the customer has no title or a defective title thereto, the banker shall not incur any liability to the true owner of the cheque by reason only of having received that payment.

(2) A banker receives payment of a crossed cheque for a customer within the meaning of this section notwithstanding that he or she credits his or her customer's account with the amount of the cheque before receiving payment thereof.

(3) Sections 75 to 81 of this Act shall apply to a banker's draft as if the draft were a cheque. For the purposes of this subsection, "banker's draft" means a draft payable on demand drawn by or on behalf of a bank upon itself, whether payable at the head office or some other office of the bank.

PART IV – PROMISSORY NOTES.

82. Promissory note defined.

(1) A promissory note is an unconditional promise in writing made by one person to another signed by the maker, engaging to pay, on demand or at a fixed or determinable future time, a sum certain in money, to, or to the order of, a specified person or to bearer.

(2) An instrument in the form of a note payable to maker's order is not a note within the meaning of this section unless and until it is endorsed by the maker.

(3) A note is not invalid by reason only that it contains also a pledge of collateral security with authority to sell or dispose of it.

(4) A note which is, or on the face of it purports to be, both made and payable within Uganda is an inland note. Any other note is a foreign note.

83. Delivery necessary.

A promissory note is inchoate and incomplete until delivery thereof to the payee or bearer.

84. Joint and several notes.

(1) A promissory note may be made by two or more makers and they may be liable on it jointly, or jointly and severally according to its tenor.

(2) Where a note runs "I promise to pay", and is signed by two or more persons, it is deemed to be their joint and several note.

85. Note payable on demand.

(1) Where a note payable on demand has been endorsed, it must be presented for payment within a reasonable time of the endorsement. If it be not so presented the endorser is discharged.

(2) In determining what is a reasonable time, regard shall be had to the nature of the instrument, the usage of trade, and the facts of the particular case.

(3) Where a note payable on demand is negotiated, it is not deemed to be overdue, for the purpose of affecting the holder with defects of title of which he or she had no notice, by reason that it appears that a reasonable time for presenting it for payment has elapsed since its issue.

86. Presentment of note for payment.

(1) Where a promissory note is in the body of it made payable at a particular place, it must be presented for payment at that place in order to render the maker liable. In any other case, presentment for payment is not necessary in order to render the maker liable.

(2) Presentment for payment is necessary in order to render the endorser of a note liable.

(3) Where a note is in the body of it made payable at a particular place, presentment at that place is necessary in order to render an endorser liable; but when a place of payment is indicated by way of memorandum only presentment at the place is sufficient to render the endorser liable, but a presentment to that maker elsewhere, if sufficient in other respects, shall also suffice.

87. Liability of maker.

The maker of a promissory note by making it –

(a) engages that he or she will pay it according to its tenor;

(b) is precluded from denying to a holder in due course the existence of the payee and his or her then capacity to endorse.

88. Application of Part II to notes.

(1) Subject to the provisions in this Part and, except as by this section provided, the provisions of this Act relating to bills of exchange apply, with the necessary modifications, to promissory notes.

(2) In applying those provisions the maker of a note shall be deemed to correspond with the acceptor of a bill, and the first endorser of a note shall be deemed to correspond with the drawer of an accepted bill payable to drawer's order.

(3) The following provisions as to bills do not apply to notes, namely, provisions relating to –

- (a) presentment for acceptance;
- (b) acceptance;
- (c) acceptance supra protest;
- (d) bills in a set.

(4) Where a foreign note is dishonoured, protest thereof is unnecessary.

Part V – Supplementary.

89. Good faith.

A thing is deemed to be done in good faith within the meaning of this Act where it is in fact done honestly, whether it is done negligently or not.

90. Signature.

(1) Where, by this Act, any instrument or writing is required to be signed by any person, it is not necessary that he or she should sign it with his or her own hand but it is sufficient if his or her signature is written thereon by some other person by or under his or her authority.

(2) In the case of a corporation, where by this Act any instrument or writing is required to be signed, it is sufficient if the instrument or writing be sealed with the corporate seal.

(3) Nothing in this section shall be construed as requiring the bill or note of a corporation to be under seal.

91. Computation of time.

(1) Where, by this Act, the time limited for doing any act or thing is less than three days, in reckoning time, non-business days are excluded.

(2) "Non-business days" for the purposes of this Act means Sundays and public holidays, and any other day is a business day.

92. When noting equivalent to protest.

For the purposes of this Act, where a bill or note is required to be protested within a specified time, or before some further proceeding is taken, it is sufficient that the bill has been noted for protest before the expiration of the specified time or the taking of the proceeding; and the formal protest may be extended at any time thereafter as of the date of the noting.

93. Protest when notary not accessible.

(1) Where a dishonoured bill or note is authorised or required to be protested, and the services of a notary cannot be obtained at the place where the bill is dishonoured, any householder or substantial resident of the place may, in the presence of two witnesses, give a certificate, signed by them, attesting the dishonour of the bill, and the certificate shall in all respects operate as if it were a formal protest of the bill.

(2) The form given in the Schedule to this Act may be used with necessary modifications, and if used shall be sufficient.

94. Dividend warrants may be crossed.

The provisions of this Act as to crossed cheques shall apply to warrant for payment of dividend.

95. Savings.

(1) The rules in bankruptcy relating to bills of exchange, promissory notes and cheques, shall continue to apply thereto notwithstanding anything in this Act contained.

(2) The rules of common law including the law merchant, save in so far as they are inconsistent with the express provisions of this Act, shall continue to apply to bills of exchange, promissory notes and cheques.

(3) Nothing in this Act shall affect –

(a) the provisions of the Stamps Act or any law or enactment for the time being in force relating to the revenue;

(b) the provisions of the Companies Act or any Act relating to joint stock banks or companies;

(c) the validity of any usage relating to dividend warrants, or the endorsements thereof.

Schedule.

Form of protest which may be used when the services of a notary cannot be obtained.

Know all men that I, ... (*householder*), of.........................., at the request of ....., there being no notary public available, did on the .... day of ...., 20... at .... demand payment (or acceptance) of the bill of exchange hereunder written, from ...., to which demand he or she made answer (*state answer, if any*), wherefore I now, in the presence of....... and ...., do protest the said bill of exchange.

(Signed) ....

Householder

....

Witness

....

Witness

N.B: The bill itself should be annexed, or a copy of the bill, and all that is written thereon should be underwritten.

CHAPTER 7

THE EVIDENCE (BANKERS' BOOKS) ACT

Arrangement of Sections

Section

THE EVIDENCE (BANKERS' BOOKS) ACT.

Commencement: 7 October, 1930.

An Act relating to the law of evidence with respect to banker's books

1. Interpretation.

In this Act, unless the context otherwise requires –

(a) "bank" or "banker" means any person carrying on the business of banking in Uganda (including the Post Bank Uganda Limited established under the provisions of the Uganda Communications Act, and any branch of that bank), and, for the purpose of sections 2, 3 and 4 of this Act, includes any person carrying on the business of banking in Kenya and Tanzania; the fact that any such bank is a Post Bank Uganda Limited may be proved by a certificate purporting to be under the hand of the managing director or an assistant managing director;

(b) "bankers' books" includes ledgers, day books, cash books, account books, and all other books used by the ordinary business of the bank;

(c) "legal proceeding" means any civil or criminal proceeding or inquiry (including an arbitration) in which evidence is or may be given, in Uganda, and, for the purposes of section 6, of this Act includes any proceeding or inquiry in Kenya or Tanzania.

2. Mode of proof of entries in bankers' books.

Subject to the provisions of this Act, a copy of an entry in the bankers' book shall in all legal proceedings be received as prima facie evidence of such entry, and of matters, transactions, and accounts in it recorded.

3. Proof that a book is a banker's book.

(1) A copy of an entry in a banker's book shall not be received in evidence under this Act unless it be first proved that the book was at the time of the making of the entry one of the ordinary books of the bank, and that the entry was made in the usual and ordinary course of business, and that the book is in the custody or control of the bank.

(2) Such proof may be given by a partner or officer of the bank, and may be given orally or by an affidavit sworn before any commissioner or person authorised to take affidavits.

4. Verification of copy.

(1) A copy of an entry in a banker's book shall not be received in evidence under this Act unless it is further proved that the copy has been examined with the original entry and is correct.

(2) Such proof shall be given by some person who has examined the copy with the original entry, and may be given either orally or by an affidavit sworn before any commissioner or person authorised to take affidavits.

5. Case in which banker, etc not compellable to produce book, etc.

A banker or officer of a bank shall not, in any legal proceeding to which the banker is not party, be compellable to produce any banker's book the contents of which can be proved under this Act, or to appear as a witness to prove the matters, transactions, and accounts recorded in a banker's book, unless by order of a court made for special cause.

6. Court or judge may order inspection etc.

(1) On the application of any party to a legal proceeding a court may order that such party be at liberty to inspect and take copies of any entries in a banker's book for any of the purposes of such proceedings.

(2) An order under this section may be made either with or without summoning the bank or any other party, and shall be served on the bank three clear days before the same is to be obeyed, unless the court otherwise directs.

7. Costs.

(1) The costs of any application to a court under or for the purposes of this Act, and the costs of anything done or to be done under an order of a court made under or for the purposes of this Act, shall be in the discretion of the court, which may order the same or any part thereof to be paid to any party by the bank, where the costs have been occasioned by any default or delay on the part of the bank.

(2) Any such order against a bank may be enforced as if the bank was a party to the proceeding.

8. Computation of time.

Sunday and any day declared to be a public holiday under the Public Holidays Act shall be excluded from the computation of time under this Act.

CHAPTER 67

THE BANKRUPTCY ACT

Arrangement of Section

Section

PART I – INTERPRETATION.

PART II – PROCEEDING FROM ACT OF BANKRUPTCY TO DISCHARGE.

Acts of bankruptcy

Receiving order

Proceedings consequent on order

Public examination of the debtor

Composition or scheme of arrangement

Adjudication of bankruptcy

Control over person and property of debtor

PART III – ADMINISTRATION OF PROPERTY

Proof of debts

Property available for payment of debts

Effect of bankruptcy on antecedent and other transactions

Realisation of property

Distribution of property

PART IV – OFFICIAL RECEIVER AND STAFF.

PART V – TRUSTEE IN BANKRUPTCY.

Official name

Appointment

Control over trustee

PART VII – SUPPLEMENTARY PROVISIONS.

Application of act

General rules

Fees and salaries, etc.

Evidence

Miscellaneous

Unclaimed funds or dividends

Part VIII – Bankruptcy Offences.

Part IX – Provisions for Reciprocity with other Territories.

Part X – General.

Schedules

CHAPTER 67

THE BANKRUPTCY ACT

An act relating to bankruptcy

Commencement : 1st January, 1931.

PART I – INTERPRETATION.

1. Interpretation.

In this Act unless the context otherwise requires –

(a) "affidavit" includes a statutory declaration and an affirmation;

(b) "available act of bankruptcy" means any act of bankruptcy available for a bankruptcy petition at the date of the presentation of the petition on which the receiving order is made;

(c) "bailiff" means any person charged with the execution of any process;

(d) "court" means the court having jurisdiction in bankruptcy under this Act;

(e) "debt provable in bankruptcy" or "provable debt" includes any debt or liability by this Act made provable in bankruptcy;

(f) "gazetted" means published in the Gazette;

(g) "general rules" includes forms;

(h) "goods" includes all chattels personal;

(i) "local bank" means any bank in Uganda;

(j) "ordinary resolution" means a resolution decided by a majority in value of the creditors present, personally or by proxy, at a meeting of creditors and voting on the resolution;

(k) "prescribed" means prescribed by general rules within the meaning of this Act;

(l) "property" includes money, goods, things in action, land, and every description of property whether movable or immovable and whether situate in Uganda or elsewhere; also obligations, easements, and every description of estate, interest, and profit, present or future, vested or contingent, arising out of or incident to property as above defined;

(m) "reciprocating court" means a court having jurisdiction in bankruptcy or insolvency in a reciprocating territory;

(n) "reciprocating territory" means any territory declared a reciprocating territory under section 148 of this Act;

(o) "relative by consanguinity or affinity" means a husband, wife, grandparent, parent, son, daughter, brother, sister, uncle, aunt, nephew, niece, cousin, or adopted child;

(p) "resolution" means ordinary resolution;

(q) "secured creditor" means a person holding a mortgage, charge or lien on the property of the debtor, or any part thereof, as a security for a debt due to him or her from the debtor;

(r) "special resolution" means a resolution decided by a majority in number and three-fourths in value of the creditors present, personally or by proxy, at a meeting of creditors and voting on the resolution;

(s) "trustee" means the trustee in bankruptcy of a debtor's estate.

PART II – PROCEEDINGS FROM ACT OF BANKRUPTCY TO DISCHARGE.

Acts of bankruptcy

2. Acts of bankrupty.

(1) A debtor commits an act of bankruptcy in each of the following cases–

(a) if in Uganda or elsewhere he or she makes a conveyance or assignment of his or her property to a trustee or trustees for the benefit of his or her creditors generally;

(b) if in Uganda or elsewhere he or she makes a fraudulent conveyance, gift, delivery, or transfer of his or her property, or of any part thereof;

(c) if in Uganda or elsewhere he or she makes any conveyance or transfer of his or her property, or any part thereof, or creates any charge thereon, which would under this or any other Act be void as a fraudulent preference if he or she were adjudged bankrupt;

(d) if with intent to defeat or delay his or her creditors he or she does any of the following things, namely, departs out of Uganda, or being out of Uganda remains out of Uganda, or departs from his or her dwelling-house, or otherwise absents himself, or herself or begins to keep house;

(e) if execution against him or her has been levied by seizure of his or her goods in any civil proceeding in any court, and the goods have been either sold or held by the bailiff for twenty-one days; except that, where an interpleader summons has been taken out in regard to the goods seized, the time elapsing between the date at which such summons is taken out and the date at which the proceedings on which such summons are finally disposed of, settled, or abandoned, shall not be taken into account in calculating such period of twenty-one days;

(f) if he or she files in the court a declaration of his or her inability to pay his or her debts or presents a bankruptcy petition against himself or herself;

(g) if a creditor has obtained a final decree or final order against him or her for any amount, and, execution thereon not having been stayed, has served on him or her in Uganda, or, by leave of the court, elsewhere, a bankruptcy notice under this Act, and he or she does not within seven days after service of the notice, in case the service is effected in Uganda, and in case the service is effected elsewhere, then within the time limited in that behalf by the order giving leave to effect the service, either comply with the requirements of the notice or satisfy the court that he or she has a counterclaim, set-off or cross-demand counterclaim, set-off or cross-demand which equals or exceeds the amount of the decree or sum ordered to be paid, and which he or she could not set up in the action in which the decree was obtained, or the proceedings in which the order was obtained. For the purposes of this paragraph and section 3 of this Act, any person who is, for the time being, entitled to enforce a final decree or final order shall be deemed to be a creditor who has obtained a final decree or final order;

(h) if the debtor gives notice to any of his or her creditors that he or she has suspended, or that he or she is about to suspend, payment of his or her debts.

(2) In this Act unless the context otherwise requires "debtor" includes any person, whether domiciled in Uganda or not, who at the time when any act of bankruptcy was done or suffered by him or her –

(a) was personally present in Uganda; or

(b) was ordinarily resident or had a place of residence in Uganda; or

(c) was carrying on business in Uganda, personally, or by means of an agent or manager;

(d) was a member of a firm or partnership which carried on business in Uganda and for the purposes of Part IX of this Act includes a person against whom bankruptcy proceedings have been instituted in a reciprocating territory and who has property in Uganda.

3. Bankruptcy notices.

(1) A bankruptcy notice under this Act shall be in the prescribed form, and shall require the debtor to pay the amount in the decree or sum ordered to be paid in accordance with the terms of the decree or order, or to secure or compound for it to the satisfaction of the creditor or the court, and shall state the consequences of non-compliance with the notice, and shall be served in the prescribed manner:

(2) A bankruptcy notice –

(a) may specify an agent to act on behalf of the creditor in respect of any payment or other thing required by the notice to be made to, or done to the satisfaction of, the creditor:

(b) shall not be invalidated by reason only that the sum specified in the notice as the amount due exceeds the amount actually due, unless the debtor within the time allowed for payment gives notice to the creditor that he or she disputes the validity of the notice on the ground of such misstatement; but, if the debtor does not give such notice, he or she shall be deemed to have complied with the bankruptcy notice if within the time allowed he or she takes such steps as would have constituted a compliance with the notice had the actual amount due been correctly specified therein.

Receiving order

4. Jurisdication to make a receiving order.

Subject to the conditions hereinafter specified if a debtor commits an act of bankruptcy the account may, on a bankruptcy petition being presented either by a creditor or by the debtor, make an order, in this Act called a receiving order, for the protection of the estate.

5. Conditions on which a creditor may petition

(1) A creditor shall not be entitled to present a bankruptcy petition against a debtor unless –

(a) the debt owing by the debtor to the petitioning creditor, or, if two or more creditors join in the petition, the aggregate amount of debts owing to the several petitioning creditors, amounts to one thousand shillings;

(b) the debt is a liquidated sum, payable either immediately or at some certain future time;

(c) the act of bankruptcy on which the petition is grounded has occurred within three months before the presentation of the petition;

(d) the debtor is domiciled in Uganda, or within a year before the date of the presentation of the petition has ordinarily resided, or had a dwelling-house or place of business or has carried on business in Uganda business or has carried on business in Uganda personally or by means of an agent or manager, or is or within the said period has been a member of a firm or partnership of persons which has carried on business in Uganda by means of a partner or partners, or an agent or manager, nor, where a deed of arrangement has been executed, shall a creditor be entitled to present a bankruptcy petition founded on the execution of the deed, or on any other act committed by the debtor in the course or for the purpose of the proceedings preliminary to execution of the deed, in cases where he or she is prohibited from so doing by any law for the time being in force relating to deeds of arrangement.

(2) If the petitioning creditor is a secured creditor, he or she must in his or her petition either state that he or she is willing to give up his or her security for the benefit of the creditors in the event of the debtor being adjudged bankrupt, or give an estimate of the value of his or her security.

(3) In the latter case, he or she may be admitted as a petitioning creditor to the extent of the balance of the debt due to him or her, after deducting the value so estimated, in the same manner as if he or she were an unsecured creditor.

6. Proceedings and order on creditor's petition.

(1) A creditor's petition shall be verified by affidavit of the creditor, or of some person on his or her behalf having knowledge of the facts, and served in the prescribed manner.

(2) At the hearing the court shall require proof of the debt of the petitioning creditor, of the service of the petition, and of the act of bankruptcy, or, if more than one act of bankruptcy is alleged in the petition, of some one of the alleged acts of bankruptcy and, if satisfied with the proof, may make a receiving order in pursuance of the petition.

(3) If the court is not satisfied with the proof of the petitioning creditor's debt, or of the act of bankruptcy, or of the service of the petition, or is satisfied by the debtor that he or she is able to pay his or her debts, or that for other sufficient cause no order ought to be made, the court may dismiss the petition.

(4) When the act of bankruptcy relied on is non-compliance with a bankruptcy notice to pay, secure, or compound for a judgment debt, or sum ordered to be

paid, the court may, if it thinks fit, stay or dismiss the petition on the ground that an appeal is pending from the judgment or order.

(5) Where the debtor appears on the petition, and denies that he or she is indebted to the petitioner, or that he or she is indebted to such an amount as would justify the petitioner in presenting a petition against him or her, the court, on such security, if any, being given as the court may require for payment to the petitioner of any debt which may be established against him or her in due course of law, and of the costs of establishing the debt, may, instead of dismissing the petition, stay all proceedings on the petition for such time as may be required for trial of the question relating to the debt.

(6) Where proceedings are stayed, the court may, if by reason of the delay caused by the stay of proceedings or for any other cause it thinks just, make a receiving order on the petition of some other creditor, and shall thereupon dismiss, on such terms as it thinks just, the petition in which proceedings have been stayed under subsection (5).

(7) A creditor's petition shall not, after presentment, be withdrawn without the leave of the court.

7. Debtor's petition and order on the petition.

(1) A debtor's petition shall allege that the debtor is unable to pay his or her debts, and the presentation thereof shall be deemed an act of bankruptcy without the previous filing by the debtor of any declaration of inability to pay his or her debts, and the court shall thereupon make a receiving order; except that such order shall be refused unless and until the debtor shall have filed with the official receiver a statement of and in relation to his or her affairs prepared in accordance with the provisions of section 15 of this Act.

(2) A debtor's petition shall not, after presentation be withdrawn without the leave of court.

8. Effect of a receiving order.

(1) On the making of a receiving order the official receiver shall be thereby constituted receiver of the property of the debtor, and thereafter, except as directed by this Act, no creditor to whom the debtor is indebted in respect of any debt provable in bankruptcy shall have any remedy against the property or person of the debt or in respect of the debt, or shall commence any action or other legal proceedings, unless with the leave of the court and on such terms as the court and on such terms as the court may impose.

(2) This section shall not affect the power of any secured creditor to realise or otherwise deal with his or her security in the same manner as he or she would have been entitled to realise or deal with it if this section had not been passed.

9. Power to appoint an interim receiver.

The court may, if it is shown to be necessary for the protection of the estate, at any time after the presentation of a bankruptcy petition, and before a receiving order is made, appoint the official receiver to be interim receiver of the property of the debtor, or of any part thereof, and direct him to take immediate possession thereof, or of any part thereof.

10. Power to stay pending proceedings.

(1) The court may, at any time after the presentation of a bankruptcy petition, stay any action, execution or other legal process against the property or person of the debtor, and any court in which proceedings are pending against a debtor may, on proof that a bankruptcy petition has been presented by or against the debtor, either stay the proceedings or allow them to continue on such terms as it may think just.

(2) Where the court makes an order staying any action or proceeding, or staying proceedings generally, the order may be served by sending a copy thereof, under the seal of the court, by post to the address for service of the plaintiff or other party prosecuting such proceedings.

11. Power to appoint a special manager.

(1) The official receiver of a debtor's estate may, on the application of any creditor or creditors, and if satisfied that the nature of the debtor's estate or business or the interests of the creditors generally require the appointment of a special manager of the estate or business other than the official receiver, appoint a manager thereof accordingly to act until a trustee is appointed, and with such powers (including any of the powers of a receiver) as may be entrusted to him or her by the official receiver.

(2) The special manager shall give security and account in such manner as the official receiver may direct.

(3) The special manager shall receive such remuneration as the creditors may, by resolution at an ordinary meeting, determine, or, in default of any such resolution, as may be prescribed.

12. Advertisement of a receiving order.

Notice of every receiving order, stating the name, residential and business addresses and description of the debtor, the date of the order, the court by which the order is made, and the date of the petition, shall be gazetted in the prescribed manner .

Proceedings consequent on a receiving order

13. First meeting of creditors.

As soon as may be after the making of a receiving order against a debtor a general meeting of his or her creditors (in this Act referred to as the first meeting of creditors) shall be held for the purpose of considering whether a proposal for a composition or scheme of arrangement shall be accepted, or whether it is expedient that the debtor shall be adjudged bankrupt, and generally as to the mode of dealing with the debtor's property.

14. Meetings to be governed by rules.

With respect to the summoning of the proceedings at the first and other meetings of creditors, the rules in the first Schedule to this Act shall be observed.

15. Debtor's statement of affairs.

(1) The debtor shall make out and submit to the official receiver a statement of and in relation to his or her affairs in the prescribed form, verified by affidavit, and showing the particulars of the debtor's assets, debts and liabilities, the names, residences and occupations of his or her creditors, the securities held by them respectively, the dates when the securities were respectively given, and such further or other information as may be prescribed or as the official receiver may require.

(2) The statement shall be so submitted –

(a) prior to, but not more than three days before, the date of the presentation of the debtor's petition;

(b) within fourteen days of the date of the receiving order made on the petition of a creditor, but the court may, for special reasons, extend the time.

(3) In the case of a creditor's petition, if the debtor fails without reasonable excuse to comply with the requirements of this section, he or she shall be guilty of an offence against the Act, and the court may, on the application of the official receiver, or of any creditor, adjudge the debtor bankrupt, and the debtor shall, in addition to any other punishment to which he or she may be liable, commits of a contempt of court and may be punished accordingly.

(4) Any person stating himself or herself in writing to be a creditor of the bankrupt may, personally or by agent, inspect the statement at all reasonable times, and take any copy thereof or extract therefrom, but any person untruthfully so stating himself or herself to be a creditor commits a contempt of court and shall be punishable accordingly on the application of the trustee or official receiver.

Public examination of the debtor

16. Public examination of debtor.

(1) Where the court makes a receiving order, it shall, save as in this Act provided, hold a public sitting, on a day to be appointed by the court, for the examination of the debt, and the debtor shall attend thereat, and shall be examined as to his or her conduct, dealings, and property.

(2) The examination shall be held as soon as conveniently may be after the expiration of the time for the submission of the debtor's statement of affairs.

(3) The court may adjourn the examination from time to time.

(4) Any creditor who has tendered a proof, or his or her representative authorised in writing, may question the debtor concerning his or her affairs and the causes of his or her failure.

(5) The official receiver shall take part in the examination of the debtor, and for the purpose may employ an advocate if he or she so desires.

(6) If a trustee is appointed before the conclusion of the examination, he or she may take part therein.

(7) The court may put such questions to the debtor as it may think expedient.

(8) The debtor shall be examined upon oath, and it shall be his or her duty to answer all such questions as the court may put or allow to be put to him or her.

(9) Such notes of the examination as the court thinks proper shall be taken down in writing, and shall be read over either to or by the debtor and signed by him and may thereafter, save as in this Act provided, be used in evidence against him; they shall also be open to the inspection of any creditor at all reasonable times.

(10) When the court is of opinion that the affairs of the debtor have been sufficiently investigated, it shall by order declare that his or her examination is concluded, but such order shall not be made until after the day appointed for the first meeting of creditors.

(11) Where the debtor is a lunatic or suffers from any such mental or physical affliction or disability as in the opinion of the court makes him or her unfit to attend his or her public examination, the court may make an order dispensing with such examination or directing that the debtor be examined on such terms, in such manner and at such place as to the court seems expedient.

Composition or scheme of arrangement

17. Compositions and schemes of arrangement.

(1) Where a debtor intends to make a proposal for a composition in satisfaction of his or her debts or a proposal for a scheme of arrangement of his or her affairs, he or she shall, within four days of submitting his statement of affairs, or within such time thereafter as the official receiver may fix, lodge with the official receiver a proposal in writing, signed by him or her, embodying the terms of the composition or scheme which he or she is desirous of submitting for the consideration of his or her creditors, and setting out particulars of any sureties proposed.

(2) In such case the official receiver shall hold a meeting of creditors, before the public examination of the debtor is concluded, and send to each creditor, before the meeting, a copy of the debtor's proposal, with a report thereon; and if at that meeting a majority in number and three-fourths in value of all the creditors who have proved, resolved to accept the proposal, it shall be deemed to be duly accepted by the creditors, and when approved by the court shall be binding on all the creditors.

(3) The debtor may at the meeting amend the terms of his or her proposal, if the amendment is, in the opinion of the official receiver calculated to benefit the general body of creditors.

(4) Any creditor who has proved his or her debt may assent to or dissent from the proposal by a letter, in the prescribed form, addressed to the official receiver, so as to be received by him or her not later than the day preceding the meeting and any such assent or dissent shall have effect as if the creditor had been present and had voted at the meeting.

(5) The debtor or the official receiver may, after the proposal is accepted by the creditors, apply to the court to approve it, and notice of the time appointed for hearing the application shall be given to each creditor who has proved.

(6) The application shall not be heard until after the conclusion of the public examination of the debtor.

(7) Any creditor who has proved may be heard by the court in opposition to the application, notwithstanding that he or she may at a meeting of creditors have voted for the acceptance of the proposal.

(8) For the purpose of approving a composition or scheme by joint debtors, the court may, if it thinks fit, and on the report of the official receiver that it is expedient so to do; dispense with the public examination of one of the joint debtors if he or she is unavoidably prevented from attending the examination by illness or absence from Uganda.

(9) The court shall, before approving the proposal, hear a report of the official receiver as to the terms thereof, and as to the conduct of the debtor, and any objections which may be made by or on behalf of any creditor.

(10) If the court is of opinion that the terms of the proposal are not reasonable, or are not calculated to benefit the general body of creditors, the court shall refuse to approve the proposal.

(11) If any facts are proved on proof of which the court would be required either to refuse, suspend or attach conditions to the debtor's discharge, were he or she adjudged bankrupt, the court shall refuse to approve the proposal, unless it provides reasonable security for the payment of not less than five shillings in the pound on all the unsecured debts provable against the debtor's estate.

(12) In any other case the court may either approve or refuse to approve the proposal.

(13) If the court approves the proposal, the approval may be testified by the seal of the court being attached to the instrument containing the terms of the proposed composition or scheme, or by the terms being embodied in an order of the court.

(14) A composition or scheme accepted and approved in pursuance of this section shall be binding on all the creditors so far as relates to any debts due to them from the debtor and provable in bankruptcy, but shall not release the debtor from any liability under a judgment against him or her in an action for seduction or affiliation, or under a judgment against him or her as a co-respondent in a matrimonial cause, except to such an extent and under such conditions as the court expressly orders in respect of such liability.

(15) A certificate of the official receiver that a composition or scheme has been duly accepted and approved shall, in the absence of fraud, be conclusive as to its validity.

(16) The provisions of a composition or scheme under this section may be enforced by the court on application by any person interested, and any disobedience of an order of the court made on the application shall be deemed a contempt of court.

(17) If default is made in payment of any installment due in pursuance of the composition or scheme, or if it appears to the court, on satisfactory evidence, that the composition or scheme cannot, in consequence of legal difficulties, or for any sufficient cause, proceed without injustice or undue delay to the creditors or to the debtor, or that the approval of the court was obtained by fraud, the court may, if it thinks fit, on application by the official receiver or the trustee or by any creditor, adjudge the debtor bankrupt, and annul the composition or scheme, but without prejudice to the validity of any sale, disposition or payment duly made or thing duly done, under or in pursuance of the composition or scheme.

(18) Where a debtor is adjudged bankrupt under subsection (17) any debt provable in other respects, which has been contracted before the adjudication, shall be provable in the bankruptcy.

(19) If under or in pursuance of a composition or scheme a trustee is appointed to administer the debtor's property or manage his or her business, or to distribute the composition, section 27 and Part V of this Act shall apply as if the trustee were a trustee in a bankruptcy, and as if the terms "bankruptcy", "bankrupt", and "order of adjudication" include respectively a composition or scheme of arrangement, a compounding or arranging debtor, and an order approving the composition or scheme.

(20) Part III of this Act shall, so far as the nature of the case and the terms of the composition or scheme admit, apply thereto, the same interpretation being given to the terms "trustee", "bankruptcy", "bankrupt" and "order of adjudication" as in subsection (19)

(21) No composition or scheme shall be approved by the court which does not provide for the payment in priority to other debts of all debts directed to be so paid in the distribution of the property of a bankrupt.

(22) The acceptance by a creditor of a composition or scheme shall not release any person who under this Act would not be released by an order of discharge if the debtor had been adjudged bankrupt.

18. Effect of a composition or scheme.

Notwithstanding the acceptance and approval of a composition or scheme, the composition or scheme shall not be binding on any creditor so far as regards a debt or liability from which, under the provisions of this Act, the debtor would not be released by an order of discharge in bankruptcy, unless the creditor assents to the composition or scheme.

Adjudication of bankruptcy

19. Adjudication of bankruptcy where a composition is not accepted or approved.

(1) Where a receiving order is made against a debtor, then, if the creditors at the first meeting, or any adjournment thereof by ordinary resolution, resolve that the debtor be adjudged bankrupt, or pass no resolution, or if the creditors do not meet, or if a composition or scheme is not approved in pursuance of this Act within fourteen days after the conclusion of the examination of the debtor, or such further time as the court may allow, the court shall adjudge the debtor bankrupt, and there upon the property of the bankrupt shall become divisible among his or her creditors, and shall vest in a trustee, and the court shall at the same time specify on such order of adjudication the period within which the debtor shall apply for his or her discharge.

(2) Notice of every order adjudging a debtor bankrupt, stating the name, residential and business addresses and description of the bankrupt, and the date of the adjudication shall be gazetted in the prescribed manner, and the date of the order shall, for the purposes of this Act, be the date of the adjudication.

20. Appointment of a trustee.

(1) Where a debtor is adjudged bankrupt, or the creditors have resolved that he or she be adjudged bankrupt, the creditors may by ordinary resolution appoint some fit person, whether a creditor or not, to fill the office of trustee of the property of the bankrupt; or they may resolve to leave his or her appointment to the committee of inspection hereinafter mentioned.

(2) A person shall be deemed not fit to act as trustee of the property of the bankrupt where he or she has been previously removed from the office of trustee of a bankrupt's property for misconduct or neglect of duty.

(3) Any person, other than the official receiver, so appointed shall give security in a manner prescribed to the satisfaction of the court, and the court, if satisfied with the security, shall certify that his or her appointment has been duly made, unless the court objects to the appointment on the ground that it has not been made in good faith by a majority in value of the creditors voting, or that the person appointed is not fit to act as trustee, or that his or her connection with or relation to the bankrupt, or his or her estate or any particular creditor makes it difficult for him or her to act with impartiality in the interests of the creditors generally.

(4) The appointment of a trustee shall take effect as from the date of the certificate.

(5) The official receiver may be appointed the trustee by the creditors, and, should he or she so desire, in such case, there shall be no committee of inspection, and the official receiver may do all things which may be done by a trustee with the permission of the committee of inspection.

(6) If a trustee is not appointed by the creditors within four weeks from the date of the adjudication, or in the event of there being negotiations for a composition or scheme pending at the expiration of those four weeks, then within seven days from the close of those negotiations by the refusal of the creditors to accept, or of the court to approve, the composition or scheme, the official receiver shall report the matter to the court, and thereupon the court shall appoint some fit person to be trustee of the bankrupt's property, and shall certify the appointment; but that the creditors or the committee of inspection (if so authorised by resolution of the creditors) may, at any subsequent time, if they think fit, appoint a trustee, and, on the appointment being made and certified, the person appointed shall become trustee in the place of the person appointed by the court.

(7) When a debtor is adjudged bankrupt after the first meeting of creditors has been held, and a trustee has been not been appointed prior to the adjudication, the official receiver shall forthwith summon a meeting of creditors for the purpose of appointing a trustee.

21. Committee of inspection.

(1) The creditors qualified to vote may, at their first or any subsequent meeting by resolution, appoint a committee of inspection for the purpose of superintending the administration of the bankrupt's property by the trustee.

(2) The committee of inspection shall consist of not more than five nor less than three persons, possessing one or other of the following qualifications–

(a) that of being a creditor or the holder of a general power of attorney from a creditor, but no creditor and no holder of a general proxy or general proxy or general power of attorney from a creditor shall be qualified to act as a member of the committee of inspection until the creditor has proved his debt and the proof has been admitted; or

(b) that of being a person to whom a creditor intends to give a general proxy or general power of attorney; but no such person shall be qualified to act as a member of the committee of inspection until he holds such a proxy or power of attorney, and until the creditor has proved his or her debt and the proof has been admitted.

(3) The committee of inspection shall meet at such times as they shall from time to time appoint, and, failing such appointment, at least once a month; and the trustee or any member of the committee may also call a meeting of the committee as and when he or she thinks necessary.

(4) The committee may act by a majority of their members present at a meeting, but shall not act unless a majority of the committee are present at the meeting.

(5) Any member of the committee may resign his or her office by notice in writing signed by him or her, and delivered to the trustee.

(6) If a member of the committee becomes bankrupt or compounds or arranges with his or her creditors, or is absent from five consecutive meetings of the committee, his or her office shall thereupon become vacant.

(7) Any member of the committee may be removed by an ordinary resolution at any meeting of creditors of which seven days' notice has been given stating the object of the meeting.

(8) On a vacancy occurring in the office of a member of the committee, the trustee shall forthwith summon a meeting of creditors for the purpose of filling the vacancy, and the meeting may by resolution appoint another creditor, or other person eligible as above, to fill the vacancy.

(9) The continuing members of the committee, provided there be not less than two such continuing members, may act notwithstanding any vacancy in their body; and, where the number of members of the committee of inspection is for the time being less than five, the creditors may increase that number so that it does not exceed five.

(10) If there be no committee of inspection, any act or things or any direction or permission by this Act authorised or required to be done or given by the committee may be done or given by the court or the official receiver on the application of the trustee.

22. Power to accept a composition or scheme after a bankruptcy adjudication.

(1) Where a debtor is adjudged bankrupt the creditors may, if they think fit, at anytime after the adjudication, by a majority in number and three-fourths in value of all the creditors who have proved, resolve to accept a proposal for a composition in satisfaction of debts due to them under the bankruptcy, or for a scheme of arrangement of the bankrupt's affairs; and thereupon the same proceedings shall be taken and the same consequences shall ensue as in the case of a composition or scheme accepted before adjudication.

(2) If the court approves the composition or scheme, it may make an order annulling the bankruptcy and vesting the property of the bankrupt in him or her or in such other person as the court may appoint, on such terms, and subject to such conditions, if any, as the court may declare.

(3) If default is made in payment of any installment due in pursuance of the composition or scheme or if it appears to the court that the composition or scheme cannot proceed without injustice or undue delay, or that the approval of the court was obtained by fraud, the court may, if it thinks fit, on application by any person interested, adjudge the debtor bankrupt, and annul the composition or scheme, but without prejudice to the validity of any sale, disposition or payment duly made, or thing duly done, under or in pursuance of the composition or scheme.

(4) Where a debtor is adjudged bankrupt under this subsection all debts, provable in other respects, which have been contracted before the date of such adjudication, shall be provable in the bankruptcy.

Control over the person and property of the debtor

23. Duties of the debtor as to discovery and realisation of property.

(1) Every debtor against whom a receiving order is made shall, unless prevented by sickness or other sufficient cause, attend the first meeting of his or her creditors, and shall submit to such examination and give such information as the meeting may require.

(2) Every debtor shall give such inventory of his or her property, such list of his or her creditors and debtors, and of the debts due to and from them respectively, submit to such examination in respect of his or her property or his or her creditors, attend such other meeting of his or her creditors, wait at such times on the official receiver, special manager, or trustee, execute such powers of attorney, conveyances, deeds, and instruments and generally do all such acts and things in relation to his property and the distribution of the proceeds amongst his creditors, as may be reasonably required by the official receiver, special manager or trustee or as may be prescribed by general rules, or be directed by the court by any special order or orders made in reference to any particular case, or made on the occasion of any special application by the official receiver, special manager, trustee or any creditors or person interested.

(3) Every debtor shall, if adjudged bankrupt, aid, to the utmost of his or her power, in the realisation of his or her property and the distribution of the proceeds among his or her creditors.

(4) If a debtor wilfully fails to perform the duties imposed on him or her by this section, or to deliver up possession of any part of his or her property which is divisible amongst his or her creditors under this Act, and which is for the time being in his possession or under his or her control, to the official receiver or to the trustee, or to any person authorised by the court to take possession of it, he or she shall, in addition to any other punishment to which he or she may be subject, commits a contempt of court, and may be punished accordingly.

24. Address and particulars of employment to be furnished.

(1) Every debtor residing in Uganda against whom an order of adjudication is made in Uganda on or after the 30th April, 1948, shall, so long as such order remains in force, keep the official receiver or the trustee, as the case may be, informed of his or her residential and postal addresses and shall submit every three months from the date of the said order a return, verified by affidavit, giving full particulars as to his or her employment, salary, earnings and other income during the preceding three months.

(2) The provisions of this section shall apply in like manner to every debtor resident in Uganda against whom an order of adjudication has been made on or before the 30th April, 1948.

(3) Any person who fails to comply with the provisions of this section commits an offence.

25. Arrest of a debtor under certain circumstances.

(1) The court may, by warrant addressed to any police officer of prescribed officer of the court, cause a debtor to be arrested, and any books, papers, money and goods in his or her possession to be seized, and him or her and them to be safely kept as prescribed until such time as the court may order in any of the following circumstances –

(a) if, after a bankruptcy notice has been issued under this Act, or after presentation of a bankruptcy petition by or against him or her, it appears to the court that there is probable reason for believing that he or her has absconded or is about to abscond, with a view of avoiding payment of the debt in respect of which the bankruptcy notice was issued, or of avoiding service of a bankruptcy petition, or of avoiding appearance to any such petition, or of avoiding examination in respect of his or her affairs, or of otherwise avoiding, delaying or embarrassing proceedings in bankruptcy against him or her;

(b) if, after presentation of a bankruptcy petition by or against him or her, it appears to the court that there is probable cause for believing that he or she is about to remove his or her goods with a view of preventing or delaying possession being taken of them by the official receiver or trustee, or that there is probable ground for believing that he or she has concealed or is about to conceal or destroy any of his or her goods, or any books, documents or writings which might be of use to his or her creditors in the course of his or her bankruptcy;

(c) if, after service of a bankruptcy petition on him or her, or after a receiving order is made against him or her, he or she removes any goods in his or her possession above the value of one hundred shillings, without the leave of the official receiver or trustee;

(d) if, without good cause shown, he or she fails to attend any examination ordered by the court:

(2) No arrest upon a bankruptcy notice shall be valid and protected, unless the debtor before or at the time of his or her arrest is served with such bankruptcy notice.

(3) No payment or composition made or security given after arrest made under this section shall be exempt from the provisions of this Act relating to fraudulent preferences.

26. Re-direction of a debtor's letters, etc.

Where a receiving order is made against a debtor, the court, on the application of the official receiver or trustee, may from time to time order that for such time not exceeding six months, as the court thinks fit, letters, telegrams, cablegrams, and other postal articles, addressed to the debtor at any place or places mentioned in the order for re-direction, shall be re-directed, sent or delivered by the managing director of the Uganda Post Limited, or the officers acting under him or her, or by any other person in charge of the transmission and receipt of telegrams and cablegrams, to the official receiver, or the trustee, or otherwise as the court directs, and the same shall be done accordingly.

27. Inquiry as to debtor's conduct, dealings and property.

(1) The court may on the application of the official receiver or trustee, at any time after a receiving order has been made against a debtor, summon before it the debtor or his or her wife, or any person known or suspected to have in his or her possession any of the estate or effects belonging to the debtor, or supposed to be indebted to the debtor, or any person whom the court may deem capable of giving information respecting the debtor, his or her dealings or property, and the court may require any such person to produce any documents in his or her custody or power relating to the debtor, his or her dealings or property.

(2) If any person so summoned, after having been tendered a reasonable sum, refuses to come before the court at the time appointed, or refuses to produce any such documents, having no lawful impediment made known to the court at the time of its sitting and allowed by it, the court may, by warrant, cause him or her to be apprehended and brought up for examination.

(3) The court may examine on oath, either by word of mouth or by written interrogatories, any person so brought before it concerning the debtor, his or her dealings, or property.

(4) If any person on examination before the court admits that he or she is indebted to the debtor, the court may, on the application of the official receiver or trustee, order him or her to pay to the official receiver or trustee, at such time and in such manner as to the court seems expedient, the amount admitted, or any part thereof, either in full discharge of the whole amount in question or not, as the court thinks fit with or without costs of the examination.

(5) If any person on examination before the court admits that he or she has in his or her possession any property belonging to the debtor, the court may, on the application of the official receiver or trustee, order him or her to deliver to the official receiver or trustee such property or any part thereof, at such time, and in such manner, and on such terms, as to the court may seem just.

(6) The court may, if it thinks fit, order that any person who if in Uganda would be liable to be brought before it under this section shall be examined in any other place out of Uganda.

28. Bankrupt to apply for a discharge.

(1) Where, on or after the 30th April, 1948, any order of adjudication is made, then the bankrupt shall, within a period specified by the court, apply to the court for an order of discharge, and the court shall appoint a day for hearing the application, but the application shall not be heard until the public examination of the bankrupt is concluded.

(2) An application for an order of discharge shall, except when the court in accordance with rules made under this Act otherwise directs, be heard in open court:

(3) On the hearing of the application the court shall take into consideration a report of the official receiver of Uganda or any reciprocating territory as to the bankrupt's conduct and affairs (including a report as to the bankrupt's conduct during the proceedings under his or her bankruptcy), and may either grant or refuse an absolute order of discharge, or suspend the operation of the order for a specified time, or grant an order of discharge subject to any conditions with respect to any earnings or income which may afterwards become due to the bankrupt, or with respect to his or her after-acquired property; except that –

(a) where the bankrupt has committed any offence under this Act or any other offence connected with his or her bankruptcy whether in Uganda or any reciprocating territory, or where in any case any of the facts hereinafter mentioned are proved to have occurred either in Uganda or any reciprocating territory the court shall –

(i) refuse the discharge; or

(ii) suspend the discharge for such period as the court thinks proper; or

(iii) suspend the discharge until the debtor has paid to his or her creditors such dividend as the court in its absolute discretion may determine; or

(iv) require the bankrupt as a condition of his discharge to consent to a decree being entered against him or her by the official receiver or trustee for any balance or part of any balance of the debts provable under the bankruptcy which is not satisfied at the date of the discharge, such balance or part of any balance of the debts to be paid out of the future earnings or after-acquired property of the bankrupt in such manner and subject to such conditions as the court may direct; but execution shall not be issued on the decree without leave of the court, which leave may be given on proof that the bankrupt has since his or her discharge acquired property or income available towards payment of his or her debts;

(b) if at any time after the expiration of two years from the date of any order made under this section the bankrupt satisfies the court that there is no reasonable probability of his or her being in a position to comply with the terms of such order, or of any substituted order, in such manner and upon such conditions as it may think fit.

(4) The facts referred to in subsection (3) (a)–

(a) that the bankrupt's assets are not of a value equal to ten shillings in the pound on the amount of his or her unsecured liabilities, unless he or she satisfies the court that the fact that the assets are not of a value equal to ten shillings in the pound on the amount of his or her unsecured liabilities has arisen from circumstances for which he or she cannot justly be held responsible;

(b) that the bankrupt has omitted to keep such books of account as are usual and proper in the business carried on by him or her and as sufficiently disclose his or her business transactions and financial position within the three years immediately preceding his or her bankruptcy;

(c) that the bankrupt has continued to trade after knowing himself or herself to be insolvent;

(d) that the bankrupt has contracted any debt provable in the bankruptcy without having at the time of contracting it any reasonable or probable ground of expectation (proof whereof shall lie on him or her) of being able to pay it;

(e) that the bankrupt has failed to account satisfactorily for any loss of assets or for any deficiency of assets to meet his or her liabilities.

(f) that the bankrupt has brought on, or contributed to, his or her bankruptcy by rash and hazardous speculations, or by unjustifiable extravagance in living, or by gambling, or by culpable neglect of his or her business affairs;

(g) that the bankrupt has put any of his or her creditors to unnecessary expense by a frivolous or vexatious defence to any action properly brought against him or her;

(h) that the bankrupt has brought on or contributed to his or her bankruptcy by incurring unjustifiable expense in bringing any frivolous or vexatious action;

(i) that the bankrupt has, within three months preceding the date of the receiving order, when unable to pay his or her debts as they become due, given an undue preference to any of his or her creditors;

(j) that the bankrupt has, within three months preceding the date of the receiving order, incurred liabilities with a view of making his or her assets equal to ten shillings in the pound on the amount of his or her unsecured liabilities;

(k) that the bankrupt has, on any previous occasion, been adjudged bankrupt, or made a composition or arrangement with his or her creditors;

(l) that the bankrupt has been guilty of any fraud or fraudulent breach of trust;

(m) that the bankrupt has made default in payment of any sum ordered by the court under the provisions of section 53 of this Act.

(5) With a view to removing any legal disqualification on account of bankruptcy which is removed if the bankrupt obtains from the court his or her discharge with a certificate to the effect that the bankruptcy was caused by misfortune

without any misconduct on his or her part, the court may, if it thinks fit, grant such a certificate, and a refusal to grant such a certificate shall be subject to appeal.

(6) For the purposes of this section, a bankrupt's assets shall be deemed of a value equal to ten shillings in the pound on the amount of his or her unsecured liabilities when the court is satisfied that the property of the bankrupt has realised, or is likely to realise, or with due care in realisation might have realised, an amount equal to ten shillings in the pound on his or her unsecured liabilities, and a report by the official receiver or the trustee shall be *prima facie* evidence of the amount of such liabilities.

(7) For the purposes of this section, the report of the official receiver shall be *prima facie* evidence of the statements therein contained.

(8) Notice of the appointment by the court of the day for hearing the application for discharge shall be published in the prescribed manner, and sent fourteen days at least before the day so appointed to each creditor who has proved, and the court may hear the official receiver and the trustee, and may also hear any creditor.

(9) At the hearing the court may put such questions to the debtor and receive such evidence as it may think fit.

(10) The powers of suspending and of attaching conditions to a bankrupt's discharge may be exercised concurrently.

(11) A discharged bankrupt shall, notwithstanding his or her order discharge, give such assistance as the trustee may require in the realisation and distribution of such of his or her property as is vested in the trustee, and, if he or she fails to do so, he or she or she commits a contempt of court; and the court may also, if it thinks fit, revoke his or her discharge, but without prejudice to the validity of any sale, disposition or payment duly made or thing duly done subsequent to the discharge but before its revocation.

29. Failure to apply for a discharge.

If the bankrupt does not appear on the day fixed for hearing his application for discharge or on such subsequent day as the court may direct, or if the bankrupt does not apply for an order of discharge within the period specified under the provisions of subsection (1) of section 28 of this Act, he or she commits an offence against this Act.

30. Fraudulent settlements.

In either of the following cases, that is to say –

(a) in the case of a settlement made before and in consideration of marriage where the settlor is not at the time of making the settlement able to pay all his or her debts without the aid of the property comprised in the settlement; or

(b) in the case of any covenant or contract made in consideration of marriage for the future settlement on or for the settlor's wife or children of any money or property wherein he had not at the date of his marriage any estate or interest (not being money or property of or in right of his wife),

if the settlor is adjudged bankrupt or compounds or arranges with his creditors, and it appears to the court that such settlement, covenant, or contract was made in order to defeat or delay creditors, or was unjustifiable having regard to the state of the settlor's affairs at the time when it was made, the court may refuse or suspend an order of discharge, or grant an order subject to conditions, or refuse to approve a composition or arrangement, as the case may be, in like manner as in cases where the debtor has been guilty of fraud.

31. Effect of an order of discharge.

(1) An order of discharge shall not release the bankrupt –

(a) from any debt on a recognizance nor from any debt with which the bankrupt may be chargeable at the suit of the Government or of any person for any offence against any law relating to any branch of the general revenue of Uganda, or at the suit of the bailiff or other public officer on a bail bond entered into for the appearance of any person prosecuted for any such offence; and he or she shall not be discharged from such excepted debts unless the Secretary to the Treasury certifies in writing his or her consent to the bankrupt being discharged therefrom;

(b) from any debt or liability incurred by means of any fraud or fraudulent breach of trust to which he or she was a party, nor from any debt or liability whereof he or her has obtained forbearance by any fraud to which he or she was a party; or

(c) from any liability under a judgment against him or her in an action for seduction or affiliation, or under a judgment against him or her as a co-respondent in a matrimonial cause, except to such an extent and under such conditions as the court expressly orders in respect of such liability.

(2) An order of discharge shall release the bankrupt from all other debts provable in bankruptcy.

(3) An order of discharge shall be conclusive evidence of the bankruptcy, and to the validity of the proceedings therein, and in any proceedings that may be instituted against a bankrupt who has obtained an order of discharge in respect of any debt from which he or she is released by the order, the bankrupt may plead that the cause of action occurred before his or her discharge.

(4) An order of discharge shall not release any person who at the date of the receiving order was a partner or co-trustee with the bankrupt, or was jointly bound or had made any joint contract with him or her, or any person who was surety or in the nature of a surety for him or her.

32. Power for count to annul adjudication in certain cases.

(1) Where in the opinion of the court a debtor ought not to have been adjudged bankrupt, or where it is proved to the satisfaction of the court that the debts of the bankrupt are paid in full, the court may, on the application of any person interested, by order annul the adjudication.

(2) Where adjudication is annulled under this section, all sales and dispositions of property and payments duly made, and all acts theretofore done, by the official receiver, trustee, or other persons acting under their authority, or by the court, shall be valid, but the property of the debtor who was adjudged bankrupt shall vest in such person as the court may appoint, or, in default of any such appointment, revert to the debtors. For all his or her estate or interest therein on

such terms and subject to such conditions, if any, as the court may declare by order.

(3) Notice of the order annulling an adjudication shall be forthwith gazetted.

(4) For the purposes of this section, any debt disputed by a debtor shall be considered as paid in full if the debtor enters into a bond, in such sum and with such sureties as the court approves, to pay the amount to be recovered in any proceeding for the recovery of or concerning the debt, with costs, and any debt due to a creditor who cannot be found or cannot be identified shall be considered as paid in full if paid into court.

PART III – ADMINISTRATION OF PROPERTY.

Proof of debts

33. Description of debts provable in bankrupcy.

(1) Demands in the nature of unliquidated damages arising otherwise than by reason of a contract, promise, or breach of trust shall not be provable in bankruptcy.

(2) A person having notice of any act of bankruptcy available against the debtor shall not prove in bankruptcy any debt or liability contracted by the debtor subsequently to the date of his so having notice.

(3) Save as aforesaid, all debts and liabilities, present of future, certain or contingent, to which the debtor is subject at the date of the receiving order, or to which he or she may become subject before his or her discharge by reason of any obligation incurred before the date of the receiving order, shall be deemed to be debts provable in bankruptcy.

(4) An estimate shall be made by the trustee of the value of any debt or liability provable as aforesaid, which by reason of its being subject to any contingency or contingencies, or for any other reason, does not bear a certain value.

(5) Any person aggrieved by any estimate made by the trustee as under subsection may appeal to the court.

(6) If, in the opinion of the court, the value of the debt or liability is incapable of being fairly estimated, the court may make an order to that effect, and thereupon the debt or the liability shall, for the purposes of this Act, be deemed to be a debt not provable in bankruptcy.

(7) If, in the opinion of the court, the value of the debt or liability is capable of being fairly estimated, the court may assess the value, and the amount of the value when assessed shall be deemed to be a debt provable in bankruptcy.

(8) "Liability" shall, for the purposes of this Act, include –

(a) any compensation for work or labour done;

(b) any obligation or possibility of an obligation to pay money or money's worth on the breach of any express or implied covenant, contract, agreement, or undertaking, whether the breach does or does not occur, or is or is not likely to occur or capable of occurring, before the discharge of the debtor;

(c) generally, any express or implied engagement, agreement, or undertaking, to pay, or capable of resulting in the payment of money or money's worth; whether the payment is, as respects amount, fixed or unliquidated; as respects time, present or future, certain or dependent on any one contingency or on two or more contingencies; as to mode of valuation, capable of being ascertained by fixed rules or as matter of opinion.

34. Mutual credit and set-off.

Where there have been mutual credits, mutual debts or other mutual dealings, between a debtor against whom a receiving order is made under this Act and any other person proving or claiming to prove a debt under the receiving order, an account shall be taken of what is due from the one party to the other in respect of such mutual dealings, and the sum due from the one party shall be set off against any sum due from the other party, and the balance of the account, and no more, shall be claimed or paid on either side respectively; but a person shall not be entitled under this section to claim the benefit of any set-off against the property of a debtor in any case where he or she had, at the time of giving credit to the debtor, notice of an act of bankruptcy committed by the debtor and available against him or her.

35. Rules as to proof of debts.

With respect to the mode of proving debts, the right of proof by secured and other creditors, the admission and rejection of proofs, and other matters referred to in the Second Schedule to this Act, the rules in the Schedule shall be observed.

36. Priority of debts.

(1) In the distribution of the property of a bankrupt there shall be paid in priority to all other debts –

(a) all taxes and local rates due from the bankrupt at the date of the receiving order, and having become due and payable within twelve months next before that date not exceeding in the whole one year's assessment; Uganda Land Commission or a district land board

(b) all rents payable to a controlling authority as defined in the Public Lands Act which are not more than five years in arrear;

(c) all wages or salary, whether or not earned wholly or in part by way of commission, of any clerk or servant in respect of service rendered to the bankrupt during four months before the date of the receiving order, not exceeding two thousand shillings;

(d) all wages of any labourer or workman not exceeding two thousand shillings whether payable for time or for piecework in respect of services rendered to the bankrupt during four months before the date of the receiving order, or, in the case of an African labourer or workman, during twelve months before such date;

(e) all sums of money deposited by Africans with the bankrupt for safe custody, whether the bankrupt held himself or herself out as a banker or not;

(f) all amounts due in respect of compensation under the Workers Compensation Act the liability wherefor accrued before the date of the receiving order, unless the bankrupt had at the said date, under such a contract with insurers as is mentioned in section 20 of the said Act, rights capable of being transferred to or vested in the worker. Where any such compensation is a weekly payment, the amount due in respect thereof shall be taken to be the amount of the lump sum for which the weekly payment could be redeemed if the employer made an application for that purpose under section 20 of the said Act.

(g) All amounts due in respect of contributions payable during the period of 12 months immediately preceding the date of the receiving order by the bankrupt as the employer of any person under the National Social Security Act.

(2) The foregoing debts shall rank equally between themselves, and shall be paid in full, unless the property of the bankrupt is insufficient to meet them, in which case they shall abate in equal proportions between themselves.

(3) Subject to the retention of such sums as may be necessary for the costs of administration or otherwise, the foregoing debts shall be discharged forthwith so far as the property of the debtor is sufficient to meet them.

(4) In the event of a landlord or other person distraining or having distrained on any goods or effects of a bankrupt within three months next before the date of the receiving order the debts to which priority is given by this section shall be a first charge on the goods or effects so distrained, on or the proceeds of the sale thereof; except that in respect of any money paid under any such charge the landlord or other person shall have the same rights of priority as the person to whom such payment is made.

(5) If a debtor by or against whom a bankruptcy petition has been presented dies, this section shall apply as if he or she were bankrupt, and as if the date of his or her death were substituted for the date of the receiving order.

(6)

(a) In the case of partners the joint estate shall be applicable in the first instance in payment of their joint debts, and the separate estate of each partner shall be applicable in the first instance in payment of his or her separate debts.

(b) If there is a surplus of the separate estates, it shall be dealt with as part of the joint estate.

(c) If there is a surplus of the joint estate, it shall be dealt with as part of the respective separate estates in proportion of the right and interest of each partner in the joint estate.

(7) Subject to the provisions of this Act, all debts proved in the bankruptcy shall be paid pari passu.

(8) If there is any surplus after payment of the foregoing debts, it shall be applied in payment of interest from the date of the receiving order at the rate of 6 percent on all debts proved in the bankruptcy.

(9) Nothing in this section shall prejudice the provisions of any enactment relating to deeds of arrangement respecting the payment of expenses incurred by the trustee under a deed of arrangement which has been avoided by the bankruptcy of the debtor.

37. Preferential claim in case of apprenticeship.

(1) Where at the time of the presentation of the bankruptcy petition any person is apprenticed or is an articled clerk to the bankrupt, the adjudication of bankruptcy shall, if either the bankrupt or apprentice or clerk gives notice in writing to the trustee to that effect, be a complete discharge of the indenture of apprenticeship or articles of agreement; and, if any money has been paid by or on behalf of the apprentice or clerk to the bankrupt as a fee, the trustee may, on the application of the apprentice or clerk, or of some person on his or her behalf, pay such sum as the trustee, subject to an appeal to the court, thinks reasonable, out of the bankrupt's property, to or for the use of the apprentice or clerk, regard being had to the amount paid by him or on his or her behalf, and to the time during which he or she served with the bankrupt under the indenture or articles before the commencement of the bankruptcy, and to the other circumstances of the case.

(2) Where it appears expedient to a trustee, he or she may on the application of any apprentice or articled clerk to the bankrupt, or any person acting on behalf of such apprentice or articled clerk, instead of acting under subsection (1), transfer the indenture of apprenticeship or articles of agreement to some other person.

38. Landlord's power of distress in case of bankrupcty.

The landlord or other person to whom any rent is due from the bankrupt may at any time, either before or after the commencement of the bankruptcy, distrain upon the goods or effects of the bankrupt for the rent due to him or her from the bankrupt, with this limitation, that if such distress for rent be levied after the commencement of the bankruptcy, it shall be available only for six months' rent accrued due prior to the date of the order of adjudication and shall not be available for rent payable in respect of any period subsequent to the date when the distress was levied but the landlord or other person to whom the rent may be due from the bankrupt may prove under the bankruptcy for the surplus due for which the distress may not have been available.

39. Postponement of claims of relatives.

Where a receiving order has been made against a debtor, any relative by consanguinity or affinity of such debtor who has a claim against the debtor for salary or wages due or in respect of any money or other estate lent or entrusted to the debtor such relative shall not be entitled to claim as a creditor in respect thereof until all claims of other creditors for valuable consideration or money's worth have been satisfied.

Property available for payment of debts

40. Relation back of trustee's title.

(1) The bankruptcy of a debtor, whether it takes place on the debtor's own petition or upon that of a creditor or creditors, shall be deemed to have relation back to, and to commence at, the time of the act of bankruptcy being committed on which a receiving order is made against him or her, or, if the bankrupt is proved to have committed more acts of bankruptcy than one, to have relation back to

and commence at the time of the first of the acts of bankruptcy proved to have been committed by the bankrupt within three months immediately before the the date of the presentation of the bankruptcy petition; but no bankruptcy petition, receiving order or adjudication shall be rendered invalid by reason of any act of bankruptcy anterior to the debt of the petitioning creditor.

(2) Where a receiving order is made against a judgment debtor in pursuance of section 100 of this Act the bankruptcy of the debtor shall be deemed to have relation back to, and to commence at, the time of the order, or if the bankrupt is proved to have committed any previous act of bankruptcy, then to have relation back to, and to commence at, the time of the first of the acts of bankruptcy proved to have been committed by the debtor within three months next preceding the date of the order.

41. Description of bankrupt's property divisible amongst creditors.

(1) The property of the bankrupt divisible amongst his creditors, and in this Act referred to as the property of the bankrupt, shall not comprise the following particulars –

(a) property held by the bankrupt on trust for any other person;

(b) the tools, if any, of his or her trade and the necessary wearing apparel and bedding of himself or herself, his or her wife and children, to a value, inclusive of tools and apparel and bedding, not exceeding three hundred shillings in the whole, except that in any case the court, having regard to the bankrupt's station in life, may in its discretion order that this allowance be increased to any value not exceeding eight hundred shillings in the whole.

(2) The property of the bankrupt shall comprise the following particulars –

(a) all such property as may belong to or be vested in the bankrupt at the commencement of the bankruptcy, or may be acquired by or devolve on him or her before his or her discharge;

(b) the capacity to exercise and to take proceedings for exercising all such powers in or over or in respect of property as might have been exercised by the bankrupt for his or her own benefit at the commencement of his or her bankruptcy or before his or her discharge; and

(c) all goods, being at the commencement of the bankruptcy in the possession, order or disposition of the bankrupt, in his or her trade or business, by the consent and permission of the true owner, under such circumstances that he or she is the reputed owner thereof; but things in action other than debts due or growing due to the bankrupt in the course of his or her trade or business shall not be deemed goods within the meaning of this paragraph.

42. Provisions as to a second bankruptcy.

(1) Where a second or subsequent receiving order is made against a bankrupt, or where an order is made for the administration in bankruptcy of the estate of a deceased bankrupt, then for the purposes of any proceedings consequent upon any such order, the trustee in the last preceding bankruptcy shall be deemed to

be a creditor in respect of any unsatisfied balance of the debts provable against the property of the bankrupt in that bankruptcy

(2) In the event of a second or subsequent receiving order made against a bankrupt being followed by an order adjudging him or her bankrupt, or in the event of an order being made for the administration in bankruptcy of the estate of a deceased bankrupt, any property acquired by him or her since he or she was last adjudged bankrupt, which at the date when the subsequent petition was presented had not been distributed amongst the creditors in such last preceding bankruptcy, shall (subject to any disposition thereof made by the official receiver or trustee in that bankruptcy, without knowledge of the presentation of the subsequent petition, and subject to the provisions of section 50 of this Act) vest in the trustee in the subsequent bankruptcy or administration in bankruptcy.

(3) Where the trustee in any bankruptcy receives notice of a subsequent petition in bankruptcy against the bankrupt, or after his or her decease of a petition for the administration of his estate in bankruptcy, the trustee shall hold any property then in his or her possession which has been acquired by the bankrupt since he or she was adjudged bankrupt until the subsequent petition has been disposed of, and, if on the subsequent petition an order of adjudication or an order of the administration of the estate in bankruptcy is made, he or she shall transfer all such property or the proceeds thereof (after deducting his or her costs and expenses) to the trustee in the subsequent bankruptcy or administration in bankruptcy, as the case may be.

Effect of bankruptcy on Antecedent and other transactions

43. Restrictions of rights of a creditor under execution of attachment.

(1) Where a creditor has issued execution against the goods or lands of a debtor, or has attached any debt due to him or her, he or she shall not be entitled to retain the benefit of the execution or attachment against the trustee in bankruptcy of the debtor, unless he or she has completed the execution or attachment before the date of the receiving order, and before notice of the presentation of any bankruptcy petition by or against the debtor or of the commission of any available act of bankruptcy by the debtor.

(2) For the purpose of this Act, an execution against goods is completed by seizure and sale; an attachment of a debt is completed by receipt of the debt; and an execution against land is completed by seizure, or, in the case of an equitable interest, by the appointment of a receiver.

(3) An execution levied by seizure and sale on the goods of a debtor is not invalid by reason only of its being an act of bankruptcy, and a person who purchases the goods in good faith under a sale by the bailiff shall, in all cases, acquire a good title to them against the trustee in bankruptcy.

44. Duties of a bailif as to goods taken in execution.

(1) Where any goods of a debtor are taken in execution, and before the sale thereof, or the completion of the execution by the receipt or recovery of the full amount

of the levy, notice is served on the bailiff that a receiving order has been made against the debtor, the bailiff shall, on request, deliver the goods and any money seized or received in part satisfaction of the execution to the official receiver, but the costs of the execution shall be a first charge on the goods or money so delivered, and the official receiver or trustee may sell the goods, or an adequate part thereof, for the purpose of satisfying the charge.

(2) Where, under an execution in respect of a decree for a sum exceeding four hundred shillings, the goods of a debtor are sold or money is paid in order to avoid sale, the bailiff shall deduct his or her costs of the execution from the proceeds of sale or the money paid, and retain the balance for fourteen days, and, if within that time notice is served on him or her of a bankruptcy petition having been presented by or against the debtor thereon and a receiving order is made against the debtor on the bankruptcy petition or on any other petition of which the bailiff has notice, the bailiff shall pay the balance to the official receiver, or, as the case may be, to the trustee, who shall be entitled to retain it as against the execution creditor.

(3) Where any goods in the possession of an execution debtor at the time of seizure by a bailiff are sold by such bailiff without any claim having been made to the same, the purchaser of the goods so sold shall acquire a good title to such goods, and no person shall be entitled to recover against such bailiff or any other person lawfully acting under his or her authority, for any sale of such goods or for paying over the proceeds thereof prior to the receipt of a claim to such goods, unless it is proved that the person from whom recovery is sought had notice, or might by making reasonable inquiry have ascertained that such goods were not the property of the execution debtor.

(4) Nothing in this subsection shall affect the right of any claimant, who may prove that at the time of sale he had a title to such goods, to any remedy to which he may be entitled against any person other than such bailiff.

45. Avoidance of certain settlements.

(1) Any settlement of property, not being a settlement made before and in consideration of marriage, or made in favour of a purchaser or incumbrancer in good faith and or for valuable consideration, or a settlement made on or for the wife or children of the settlor of property which has accrued to the settlor after marriage in right of his or her wife, shall, if the settlor becomes bankrupt within two years after the date of the settlement, be void against the trustee in the bankruptcy, and shall, if the settlor becomes bankrupt, at any subsequent time within ten years after the date of the settlement be void against the trustee in bankruptcy unless the parties claiming under the settlement can prove that the settlor was, at the time of making the settlement, able to pay all his or her debts without the aid of the property comprised in the settlement, and that the interest of the settlor in such property passed to the trustee of such settlement on the execution thereof.

(2) Any covenant or contract made by any person (hereinafter called the settlor) in consideration of his or her marriage, either for the future payment of money for the benefit of the settlors wife or husband, or for the future settlement on or for

the settlor's wife or husband or children, or property, wherein the settlor had not at the date of the marriage any estate or interest, whether vested or contingent, in possession or remainder, and not being money or property in right of the settlor's wife or husband, shall, if the settlor is adjudged bankrupt and the covenant or contract has not been executed at the date of the commencement of his or her bankruptcy, be void against the trustee in the bankruptcy, except so far as it enables the persons entitled under the covenant or contract to claim for dividend in the settlors bankruptcy, under or in respect of the covenant or contract, but any such claim to dividend shall be postponed until all claims of the other creditors for valuable consideration in money or money's worth have been satisfied.

(3) Any payment of money (not being payment of premiums on a policy of life assurance) or any transfer of property made by the settlor in pursuance of such a covenant or contract as aforesaid shall be void against the trustee in the settlor's bankruptcy unless the persons to whom the payment or transfer was made prove either –

(a) that the payment or transfer was made more than two years before the date of the commencement of the bankruptcy; or

(b) that at the date of the payment or transfer the settlor was able to pay all his or her debts without the aid of the money so paid or the property so transferred; or

(c) that the payment or transfer was made in pursuance of a covenant or contract to pay or transfer money or property expected to come to the settlor from or on the death of a particular person named in the covenant or contract, and was made within three months after the money or property came into the possession or under the control of the settlor, but, if in the event of any such payment or transfer being declared void, the persons to whom it was made shall be entitled to claim for dividend under or in respect of the covenant or contract in like manner as if it had not been executed at the commencement of the bankruptcy.

(4) "Settlement" shall, for the purposes of this section include any conveyance or transfer of property.

46. Avoidance of general assignments of book debts unless registered.

(1) Where a person engaged in any trade or business makes an assignment to any other person of his or her existing or future book debts or any class thereof, and is subsequently adjudicated bankrupt, the assignment shall be void against the trustee as regards any book debts which have not been paid at the commencement of the bankruptcy, unless the assignment has been registered as if the assignment were a bill of sale given otherwise than by way of security for the payment of a sum of money, and the provisions of the law with respect to the registration of bills of sale shall apply accordingly:

(2) Nothing in this section shall have effect so as render void any assignment of book debts due at the date of assignment from specified debtors, or of debts growing due under specified contracts, or any assignment of book debts included in a transfer of a business made bona fide and for value, or any assignment of assets for the benefit of creditors generally.

(3) For the purposes of this section "assignment" includes assignment by way of security and other charges on book debts.

47. Avoidance of preference in certain cases.

(1) Every conveyance or transfer of property, or charge thereon made, every payment made, every obligation incurred, and every judicial proceeding taken or suffered by any person unable to pay his debts as they become due from his own money in favour of any creditor or of any person in trust for any creditor, with a view of giving such creditor, or any surety or guarantor for the debt due to such creditor, a preference over the other creditors, shall, if the person making, taking, paying or suffering the same is adjudged bankrupt on a bankruptcy petition presented within six months after the date of making, taking, paying or suffering the same, be deemed fraudulent and void as against the trustee in the bankruptcy.

(2) This section shall not affect the rights of any person making title in good faith and for valuable consideration through or under a creditor of the bankrupt.

(3) Where a receiving order is made against a judgment debtor in pursuance of section 100 of this Act, this section shall apply as if the debtor had been adjudged bankrupt on a bankruptcy petition presented at the date of the receiving order.

48. Protection of bona fide transactions without notice.

Subject to the foregoing provisions of this Act with respect to the effect of bankruptcy on an execution or attachment, and with respect to the avoidance of certain settlements, assignments and preferences, nothing in this Act shall invalidate, in the case of bankruptcy –

(a) any payment by the bankrupt to any of his or her creditors;
(b) any payment or delivery to the bankrupt;
(c) any conveyance or assignment by the bankrupt for valuable consideration;
(d) any contract, dealing or transaction by or with the bankrupt for valuable consideration; if both the following conditions are complied with, namely–
    (i) that the payment, delivery, conveyance, assignment, contract, dealing, or transaction, as the case may be, takes place before the date of the receiving order; and
    (ii) that the person (other than the debtor) to, by, or with whom the payment, delivery, conveyance, assignment, contract, dealing, or transaction, was made, executed, or entered into, has not at the time of the payment, delivery, conveyance, assignment, contract dealing, or transaction, available act of bankruptcy committed by the bankrupt before that time.

49. Validity of certain payments to a bankrupt and an assignee.

A payment of money or delivery of property to a person subsequently adjudged bankrupt, or to a person claiming by assignment from him, shall, notwithstanding anything in this Act be a good discharge to the person paying the money or delivering the property, if the payment or delivery is made before the actual date on which the receiving order is made and without notice of the presentation of a bankruptcy petition, and is either pursuant to the ordinary course of business or otherwise bona fide.

50. Dealings with an undischarged bankrupt.

(1) All transactions by a bankrupt with any person dealing with him bona fide and for value, in respect of property, whether movable or immovable, acquired by the bankrupt after the adjudication, shall if completed before any intervention by the trustee, be valid against the trustee, and any estate or interest in such property which by virtue of this Act is vested in the trustee shall determine and pass in such manner and to such extent as may be required for giving effect to any such transaction.

(2) For the purposes of subsection (1) the receipt of any money, security or negotiable instrument from, or by the order or direction of, a bankrupt by his or her banker, and any payment and any delivery of any security or negotiable instrument made to or by the order or direction of, a bankrupt by his or her banker, shall be deemed to be a transaction by the bankrupt with such banker dealing with him or her for value.

(3) Where a banker has ascertained that a person having an account with him is an undischarged bankrupt, then, unless the banker is satisfied that the account is on behalf of some other person, it shall be his or her duty forthwith to inform the trustee in the bankruptcy or the official receiver of the existence of the account, and thereafter he or she shall not make any payments out of the account, except under an order of the court or in accordance with instructions from the trustee in the bankruptcy, unless by the expiration of one month from the date of giving the information no instructions have been received from the trustee or the official receiver.

Realisation of property

51. Possession of property by the trustee.

(1) The trustee shall, as soon as may be, take possession of the deeds, books, and documents of the bankrupt, and all other parts of his property capable of manual delivery.

(2) The trustee shall, in relation to and for the purpose of acquiring or retaining possession of the property of the bankrupt, be in the same position position as if he were a receiver of the property appointed by the court, and the court may, on his or her application, enforce such acquisition or retention accordingly.

(3) Where any part of the property of the bankrupt consists of stock, shares in ships, shares, or any other property transferable in the books of any company, office, or person, the trustee may exercise the right to transfer the property to the same extent as the bankrupt might have exercised it if he or she had not become bankrupt.

(4) Where any part of the property of the bankrupt consists of things in action, such things shall be deemed to have been duly assigned to the trustees.

(5) Subject to the provisions of this Act with respect to property acquired by a bankrupt after adjudication, any treasurer or other officer, or any banker, attorney, or agent of a bankrupt, shall pay and deliver to the trustee all money and securities in his or her possession or power, as such officer, banker, attorney, or agent,

which he or she is not by law entitled to retain as against the bankrupt or the trustee. If he or she does not, he or she commits a contempt of court, and may be punished accordingly on the application of the trustee.

52. Seizure of the property of a bankrupt.

Any person acting under warrant of the court may seize any part of the property of a bankrupt, or of a debtor against whom a receiving order has been made, in the custody or possession of the bankrupt or the debtor, or of any other person, and with a view to such seizure may break open any house, building or room of the bankrupt or the debtor, where the bankrupt or the debtor is supposed to be, or any building or receptacle of the bankrupt or the debtor where any of his or her property is supposed to be; and where the court is satisfied that there is reason to believe that property of a bankrupt, or of a debtor against whom a receiving order has been made, is concealed in a house or place not belonging to him or her, the court may, if it thinks fit, grant a search warrant to any police officer or officer of the court, who may execute it according to its tenor.

53. Appropriation of a proportion of pay or salary to creditors.

(1) Where a bankrupt is an officer of the Armed Forces of Uganda, or a public officer, the trustee shall receive for distribution amongst the creditors so much of the bankrupt's pay or salary as the court, on the application of the trustee, with the consent of the head of the Ministry or department under which the pay or salary is enjoyed, may direct.

(2) Before making any order under subsection (1), the court shall communicate with the head of the Ministry or department as to the amount, time, and manner of the payment to the trustee, and shall obtain the written consent of the head of the Ministry to the terms of such payment.

(3) Where a bankrupt is in receipt of a salary or income other than as referred to in subsections (1) and (2), the court, on the application of the trustee, shall from time to time make such order as it thinks just for the payment of the salary or income, or of any part thereof, to the trustee, to be applied by him or her in such manner as the court may direct.

(4) Where a bankrupt is an employee and earning wages irrespective of whether payment of such wages is made by the day or any other period of time, the court, on the application of the trustee, shall from time to time make such order as it thinks just for the payment of any part of such wages to the trustee to be applied by him or her in such manner as the court may direct.

(5) Nothing in this section shall take away or abridge any power conferred by or under any written law to dismiss or terminate the service of any officer to whom the provisions of subsection (1) of this section apply.

54. Appropriation of income of property restrained from anticipation.

Where a married woman who has been adjudged bankrupt has property the income of which is subject to a restraint on anticipation, the court shall have power, on the application of the trustee, to order that, during such time as the court may order, the whole or some part of such income be paid to the trustee for distribution amongst the creditor, and in the exercise of such power the court shall have regard to the means of subsistence available for the woman and her children.

55. Vesting and transfer of property.

(1) Until a trustee is appointed, the official receiver shall be the trustee for the purposes of this Act, and, immediately on a debtor being adjudged bankrupt, the property of the bankrupt shall vest in the trustee.

(2) On the appointment of a trustee, the property shall forthwith pass to and vest in the trustee appointed.

(3) The property of the bankrupt shall pass from trustee to trustee, including under that term the official receiver when he or she fills the office of trustee, and shall vest in the trustee for the time being during his or her continuance in office, any conveyance, assignment, or transfer whatever.

(4) The certificate of appointment of a trustee shall, for all purposes of any law in force in any part of Uganda requiring registration or recording of conveyances or assignments of property, be deemed to be a conveyance or assignment of property, and may be registered and recorded accordingly.

56. Disclaimer of onerous property.

(1) Where any part of the property of the bankrupt consists of land of any tenure burdened with onerous covenants, of shares or stock in companies, of unprofitable contracts, or of any other property that is unsaleable, or not readily saleable, by reason of its binding the possessor thereof to the performance of any onerous act, or to the payment of any sum of money, the trustee, notwithstanding that he or she has endeavoured to sell or has taken possession of the property, or exercised any act of ownership in relation thereto, but subject to the provisions of this section, may, by writing signed by him or her, at any time twelve months after the first appointment of a trustee or such extended period as may be allowed by the court, disclaim the property; except that, where any such property has not come to the knowledge of the trustee within one month after such appointment, he or she may disclaim such property at any time within twelve months after he or she has become aware thereof or such extended period as may be allowed by the court.

(2) The disclaimer shall operate to determine, as from the date of disclaimer, the rights, interests, and liabilities of the bankrupt and his or her property in or in respect of the property disclaimed, and shall also discharge the trustee from all personal liability in respect of the property disclaimed as from the date when property vested in him or her, but shall not, except as far as is necessary for the purpose of releasing the bankrupt and his or her property and the trustee from liability, affect the rights or liabilities of any other person.

(3) A trustee shall not be entitled to disclaim a lease without the leave of the court, except in any cases which may be prescribed by general rules, and the court may, before or on granting such leave, require such notices to be given to persons interested, and impose such terms as a condition of granting leave, and make such orders with respect to fixtures, tenant's improvements, and other matters arising out of the tenancy, as the court thinks just.

(4) The trustee shall not be entitled to disclaim any property in pursuance of this section in any case where an application in writing has been made to the trustee by any person interested in the property requiring him or her to decide whether he or she will disclaim or not, and the trustee has for a period of twenty-eight days after the receipt of the application, or such extended period as may be allowed by the court, declined or neglected to give notice whether he or she disclaims the property or not; and, in the case of a contract, if the trustee, after such application as aforesaid, does not within the said period or extended period disclaim the contract, he or she shall be deemed to have adopted it.

(5) The court may, on the application of any person who is, as against the trustee, entitled to the benefit or subject to the burden of a contract made with the bankrupt, make an order rescinding the contract on such terms as to payment by or to either party of damages for the non-performance of the contract, or otherwise as to the court may seem equitable, and any damages payable under the order to any such person may be proved by him or her as a debt under the bankruptcy.

(6) The court may, on application by any person either claiming any interest in any disclaimed property or under any liability not discharged by the Act in respect of any disclaimed property, and on hearing such persons as it thinks fit, make an order for the vesting of the property in or delivery thereof to any person entitled thereto, or to whom it may seem just that the same should be delivered by way of compensation for such liability as aforesaid, or a trustee for him or her, and on such terms as the court thinks just; and on any such vesting order being made, the property comprised therein shall vest accordingly in the person therein named in that behalf without any conveyance or assignment for the purpose; but where the property disclaimed is of a leasehold nature, the court shall not make a vesting order in favour of any person claiming under the bankrupt, whether as under-lessee or as a mortgagee by demise, except upon the terms of making that person –

(a) subject to the same liabilities and obligations as the bankrupt was subject to under the lease in respect of the property at the date when the bankruptcy petition was filed; or

(b) if the court thinks fit, subject only to the same liabilities and obligations as if the lease had been assigned to that person at that date, and in either event (if the case so requires) as if the lease had comprised only the property comprised in the vesting order; and any mortgagee or under-lessee declining to accept a vesting order upon such terms shall be excluded from all interest in and security upon the property, and, if there is no person claiming under the bankrupt who is willing to accept an order upon such terms, the court shall have power to vest the bankrupt's estate and interest in the property in any person liable either personally or in a representative character, and either alone or jointly with the bankrupt to perform the lessee's covenants in the lease, freed and discharged from all estates, incumbrances, interests created therein by the bankrupt.

(7) Where, on the release, removal, resignation, or death of a trustee in bankruptcy, an official receiver is acting as trustee, he or she may disclaim any property which might be disclaimed by a trustee under the foregoing provisions,

notwithstanding that the time prescribed by this section for such disclaimer has expired, but such power of disclaimer shall be exercisable only within twelve months after the official receiver has become trustee in the circumstances aforesaid, or, has become aware of the existence of such property, whichever period may last expire.

(8) Any person injured by the operation of a disclaimer under this section shall be deemed to be a creditor of the bankrupt to the extent of the injury, and may accordingly prove the same as a debt under the bankruptcy.

57. Power of the trustee to deal with property.

Subject to the provisions of this Act, the trustee may do all or any of the following things–

(a) sell all or any part of the property of the bankrupt (including the goodwill of the business, if any, and the book debts due or growing due to the bankrupt), by public auction or private contract, with power to transfer the whole thereof to any person or company, or to sell the same in parcels;

(b) give receipts for any money received by him or her, which receipts shall effectually discharge the person paying the money from all responsibility in respect of the application thereof;

(c) prove, rank, claim, and draw a dividend in respect of any debt due to the bankrupt;

(d) exercise any powers, the capacity to exercise which is vested in the trustee under this Act, and execute any powers of attorney, deeds and other instruments, for the purpose of carrying into effect the provisions of this Act;

(e) deal with any property to which the bankrupt is beneficially entitled as tenant in tail in the same manner as the bankrupt might have dealt with it.

58. Powers exercisable by the trustee with permission of the committee of inspection.

(1) The trustee may, with the permission of the committee of inspection, do all or any of the following things –

(a) carry on the business of the bankrupt, so far as may be necessary, for the beneficial winding-up of the same;

(b) bring, institute, or defend any action or other legal proceedings relating to the property of the bankrupt;

(c) employ an advocate or other agent to take any proceedings or do any business which may be sanctioned by the committee of inspection;

(d) accept as the consideration for the sale of any property of the bankrupt a sum of money payable at a future time subject to such stipulations as to security and otherwise as the committee think fit;

(e) mortgage or pledge any part of the property of the bankrupt for the purpose of raising money for the payment of his or her debts;

(f) refer any dispute to arbitration, compromise any debts, claims, and liabilities, whether present or future, certain or contingent, liquidated or un-liquidated, subsisting or supposed to subsist between the bankrupt and any person who may have incurred any liability to the bankrupt, on the receipt of such sums, payable at such times, and generally on such terms as may be agreed on;

(g) make such compromise or other arrangement as may be thought expedient with creditors, or persons claming to be creditors, in respect of any debts provable under the bankruptcy;

(h) make such compromise or other arrangement as may be thought expedient with respect to any claim arising out of or incidental to the property of the bankrupt, made or capable of being made on the trustee by any person or by the trustee on any person;

(i) divide in its existing form amongst the creditors, according to its estimated value, any property which from its peculiar nature or other special circumstances cannot be readily or advantageously sold.

(2) The permission given for the purposes of this section shall not be a general permission to do all or any of the above-mentioned things, but shall only be a permission to do the particular thing or things for which permission is sought in the specified case or cases.

59. Power to allow the bankrupt to manage property.

The trustee, with the permission of the committee of inspection, may appoint the bankrupt himself or herself to superintend the management of the property of the bankrupt or of any part thereof, or to carry on the trade, if any, of the bankrupt for the benefit of his or her creditors, and in any other respect to aid in administering the property, in such manner and on such terms as the trustee may direct.

60. Allowance to the bankrupt for maintenance or service.

The trustee may from time to time, with the permission of the committee of inspection, make such allowance as he may think just to the bankrupt out of his or her property for the support of the bankrupt and his or her family, or in consideration of his or her services if he or she is engaged in winding up his or she estate, but any such allowance may be reduced by the court.

61. Right of the trustee to inspect goods pawned, etc.

Where any goods of a debtor against whom a receiving order has been made are held by any person by way of pledge, pawn or other security, it shall be lawful for the official receiver or trustee, after giving notice in writing of his or her intention to do so, to inspect the goods, and where such notice has been given, such person as aforesaid shall not be entitled to realise his or her security until he or she has given the trustee a reasonable opportunity of inspecting the goods and of exercising his or her right of redemption if he or she thinks fit to do so.

62. Limitation of the trustee's powers in relation to copyright.

Where the property of a bankrupt comprises the copyright in any work or any interest in such copyright, and he or she is liable to pay to the author of the work royalties or a share of the profits in respect thereof, the trustee shall not be entitled to sell, or authorise the sale of, any copies of the work, or to perform or authorise the performance of the work, except on the terms of paying to the author such sums by way of royalty or share of the profits as would have been payable by the bankrupt, nor shall he or she, without the consent of the author or of the court, be entitled to assign the right or transfer the interest or to grant any interest in the right by licence, except upon terms which will secure to the author payments by way of royalty or share of the profits at a rate not less than that which the bankrupt was liable to pay.

63. Protection of the official receiver and trustee from personal liability in certain cases.

Where the official receiver or trustee has seized or disposed of any goods, chattels, property, or other effects in the possession or on the premises of a debtor against whom a receiving order has been made, without notice of any claim by any person in respect of the same, and it is thereafter made to appear that the said goods, chattels, property, or other effects were not, at the date of the receiving order, the property of the debtor, the official receiver or trustee shall not be personally liable for any loss or damage arising from such seizure or disposal sustained by any person claiming such property, nor for the costs of any proceedings taken to establish a claim thereto, unless the court is of opinion that the official receiver or trustee has been guilty of negligence in respect of the same.

Distribution of property

64. Declaration and distribution of dividends.

(1) Subject to the retention of such sums as may be necessary for the costs of administration, or otherwise, the trustee shall, with all convenient speed, declare and distribute dividends amongst the creditors who have proved their debts.

(2) The first dividend, if any, shall be declared and distributed within four months after the conclusion of the first meeting of creditors, unless the trustee satisfies the committee of inspection that there is sufficient reason for postponing the declaration to a later date.

(3) Subsequent dividends shall, in the absence of sufficient reason to the contrary, be declared and distributed at intervals of not more than six months.

(4) Before declaring a dividend, the trustee shall cause notice of his or her intention to do so to be gazetted in the prescribed manner, and shall also send reasonable notice thereof to each creditor mentioned in the bankrupt's statement who has not proved his or her debt.

(5) When the trustee has declared a dividend, he or she shall send to each creditor who has proved a notice showing the amount of the dividend and when and how it is payable and a statement in the prescribed form as to the particulars of the estate.

65. Joint and separate dividends.

(1) Where one partner of a firm is adjudged bankrupt, a creditor to whom the bankrupt is indebted jointly with the other partners of the firm, or any of them, shall not receive any dividend out of the separate property of the bankrupt until all the

separate creditors have received the full amount of their respective debts.

(2) Where joint and separate properties are being administered, dividends of the joint and separate properties shall, unless otherwise directed by the court on the application of any person interested, be declared together, and the expenses of and incidental to such dividends shall be fairly apportioned by the trustee between the joint and separate properties, regard being had to the work done for and the benefit received by each property.

66. Provisions for creditors residing at a distance, etc.

(1) In the calculation and distribution of a dividend the trustee shall make provision for debts provable in bankruptcy appearing from the bankrupt's statements, or otherwise, to be due to persons resident in places so distant from the place where the trustee is acting that in the ordinary course of communication they have not had sufficient time to tender their proofs, or to establish them, if disputed, and also for debts provable in bankruptcy the subject of claims not yet determined.

(2) The trustee shall also make provision for any disputed proofs or claims, and for the expenses necessary for the administration of the estate or otherwise.

(3) Subject to the foregoing provisions, the trustee shall distribute as dividends all money in hand.

67. Right of a creditor who has not proved debt before declaration of a dividend.

Any creditor who has not proved his debt before the declaration of any dividend or dividends shall be entitled to be paid out of any money for the time being in the hands of the trustee any dividend or dividends he or she may have failed to receive before that money is applied to the payment of any future dividend or dividends, but he or she shall not be entitled to disturb the distribution of any dividend declared before his or her debt was proved by reason that he or she has not participated therein.

68. Interest on debts.

(1) Where a debt has been proved, and the debt includes interest, or any pecuniary consideration in lieu of interest, such interest or consideration shall, for the purposes of dividend, be calculated at a rate not exceeding eight per centum per annum, without prejudice to the right of a creditor to receive out of the estate any higher rate of interest to which he or she may be entitled after all the debts proved in the estate have been paid in full.

(2) In dealing with the proof of the debt, the following rules shall be observed–

(a) any account settled between the debtor and the creditor within three years preceding the date of the receiving order may be examined, and if it appears that the settlement of the account forms substantially one transaction with any debt alleged to be due out of the debtor's estate (whether in the form of renewal of a loan or capitalisation of interest or ascertainment of loans or otherwise), the account may be reopened and the whole transaction treated as one;

(b) any payment made by the debtor to the creditor before the receiving order, whether by way of bonus or otherwise, and any sums received by the creditor before the receiving order from the realisation of any security for the debt, shall, notwithstanding any agreement to the contrary, be appropriated to principal and interest in the proportion that the principal bears to the sum payable as interest at the agreed rate;

(c) where the debt due is secured and the security is realised after the receiving order, or the value thereof is assessed in the proof, the amount realised or assessed shall be appropriate to the satisfaction of principal and interest in the proportion that the principal bears to the sum payable as interest at the agreed rate.

69. Final dividend.

(1) When the trustee has realised all the property of the bankrupt, or so much thereof as can, in the joint opinion of himself or herself and of the committee of inspection, be realised without needlessly protracting the trusteeship, the trustee shall declare a dividend but before so doing he or she shall give notice in manner prescribed to the persons whose claim to be creditors have been notified to him or her, but not established to his or her satisfaction, that if they do not establish their claims to the satisfaction of the court within a time limited by the notice, he or she will proceed to make a final dividend, without regard to their claims.

(2) After the expiration of the time so limited, or, if the court on application by any such claimant grants him or her further time for establishing his or her claim, then on the expiration of such further time the property of the bankrupt shall be divided among the creditors who have proved their debts, without regard to the claims of any other persons.

70. No action for dividend.

No action for dividend shall lie against the trustee, but, if the trustee refuses to pay any dividend, the court may, if it thinks fit, order him or her to pay it, and also to pay out of his or her own money interest thereon for the time that it is withheld, and the costs of the application.

71. Right of bankrupt to surplus.

The bankrupt shall be entitled to any surplus remaining after payment in full of his or her creditors, with interest, as by the Act provided, and of the costs, charges, and expenses of the proceedings under the bankruptcy petition.

PART IV – OFFICIAL RECEIVER AND STAFF.

72. Appointment of an official receiver and deputy official receivers.

(1) There shall be an official receiver of debtors' estates for Uganda and as many deputy official receivers as may be required from time to time who shall have jurisdiction in such areas as may be specified.

(2) Subject to the provisions of any written law relating to the appointment of persons to the public service the official receiver and the deputy official receiver shall be appointed, be removable by and be under the general authority and directions of the Minister and they shall also be officers of the court.

(3) A deputy official receiver shall have the same powers, rights and duties within the area for which he or she is appointed as an official receiver under this Act.

73. Status of the official receiver.

(1) The duties of the official receiver shall have relation both to the conduct of the debtor and to the administration of his or her estate.

(2) The official receiver may, for the purposes of affidavits verifying proofs, petitions, or other proceedings under this Act, administer oaths.

(3) All provisions in this or any other Act referring to the trustee in a bankruptcy shall, unless the context otherwise requires, or the Act otherwise provides, include the official receiver when acting as trustee.

(4) The trustee shall supply the official receiver with such information, and give him or her such access to and facilities for inspecting the bankrupt's books and documents, and generally shall give him or her such aid as may be requisite for enabling the official receiver to perform his or her duties under this Act.

74. Duties of the official receiver as regards the debtor's conduct.

As regards the debtor, it shall be the duty of the official receiver –

(a) to investigate the conduct of the debtor and to report to the court, stating whether there is reason to believe that the debtor has committed any act which constitutes an offence under this Act, or any enactment repealed by this Act, or which would justify the court in refusing, suspending or qualifying an order for his or her discharge;

(b) to make such other reports concerning the conduct of the debtor as the court may direct;

(c) to take such part as he may deem fit in the public examination of the debtor;

(d) to take such part and give such assistance in relation to the prosecution of any fraudulent debtor as the Director of Public Prosecutions may direct.

75. Duties of the official receiver as to the debtor's estate.

(1) As regards the estate of a debtor, it shall be the duty of the official receiver–

  (a) pending the appointment of a trustee, to act as interim receiver of the debtor's estate, and, where a special manager is not appointed, as manager thereof;

  (b) to authorise the special manager to raise money or make advances for the purposes of the estate in any case where, in the interest of the creditors, it appears necessary so to do;

  (c) to summon and preside at the first meeting of creditors;

  (d) to issue forms of proxy for use at the meetings of creditors;

  (e) to report to the creditors as to any proposal which the debtor may have made with respect to the mode of liquidating his or her affairs;

  (f) to advertise the receiving order, the date of the creditors' first meeting, and of the debtor's public examination, and such other matters as it may be necessary to advertise;

  (g) to act as trustee during any vacancy in the office of trustee.

(2) For the purpose of his or her duties as interim receiver or manager, the official receiver shall have the same powers as if he or she were a receiver and manager appointed by the court, but shall, as far as practicable, consult the wishes of the creditors with respect to the management of the debtor's property, and may for that purpose if he or she thinks it advisable, summon meetings of the persons claiming to be creditors, and shall not, unless the court otherwise orders, incur any expense beyond such as is requisite for the protection of the debtor's property or the disposing of perishable goods; except that, when the debtor cannot prepare a proper statement of affairs, the official receiver may, subject to any prescribed conditions, and at the expense of the estate, employ some person or persons to assist in the preparation of the statement of affairs.

PART V – TRUSTEES IN BANKRUPTCY.

Official name

76. Official name of the trustee.

The official name of a trustee in bankruptcy shall be "the trustee of the property of.......................... a bankrupt" (inserting the name of the bankrupt), and by that name the trustee may, in any part of Uganda or elsewhere, hold property of every description, make contracts, sue and be sued, enter into any engagements binding on himself or herself , and his or her successors in office, and do all other acts necessary or expedient to be done in the execution of his or her office.

Appointment

77. Power to appoint joint or successive trustees.

(1) The creditors may, if they think fit, appoint more persons than one to the office of trustee, and when more persons than one are appointed they shall declare whether any act required or authorised to be done by the trustee is to be done by all or any one or more of such persons, but all such persons are in this Act included under the term "trustee" and shall be joint tenants of the property of the bankrupt.

(2) The creditors may also appoint persons to act as trustees in succession in the event of one or more of the persons first named declining to accept the office of trustee, or failing to give security, or of the appointment of any such person not being certified by the court.

78. Proceedings in case of vacancy in the office of trustee.

(1) If a vacancy occurs in the office of a trustee, the creditors in general meeting may appoint a person to fill the vacancy, and thereupon the same proceedings shall be taken as in the case of a first appointment.

(2) The official receiver shall, on the requisition of any creditor, summon a meeting for the purpose of filling any such vacancy.

(3) If the creditors do not, within three weeks after the occurrence of a vacancy, appoint a person to fill the vacancy, the official receiver shall report the matter to the court, and the court may appoint a trustee; but in such case the creditors or committee of inspection shall have the same power of appointing a trustee in the place of the person so appointed by the court as in the case of a first appointment.

(4) During any vacancy in the office of trustee the official receiver shall act as trustee.

Control over the trustee

79. Discretionary powers of trustee and control thereof.

(1) Subject to the provisions of this Act, the trustee shall, in the administration of the property of the bankrupt and in the distribution thereof amongst his or her creditors, have regard to any directions that may be given by resolution of the creditors at any general meeting, or by the committee of inspection, and any directions so given by the creditors at any general meeting shall, in case of conflict, be deemed to override any directions given by the committee of inspection.

(2) The trustee may from time to time summon general meetings of the creditors for the purpose of ascertaining their wishes, and it shall be his duty to summon meetings at such times as the creditors, by resolution either at the meeting appointing the trustee or otherwise, may direct, and it shall be lawful for any creditor, with the concurrence of one-sixth in value of the creditors (including himself or herself), at any time to request the trustee or official receiver to call a meeting of the creditors, and the trustee or official receiver shall call such meeting accordingly within fourteen days; but the person at whose instance the meeting is summoned shall deposit with the trustee or the official receiver, as the case may be, a sum sufficient to pay the costs of summoning the meeting, such sum to be repaid to him or her out of the estate if the creditors or the court so direct.

(3) The trustee may apply to the court in manner prescribed for directions in relation to any particular matter arising under the bankruptcy.

(4) Subject to the provisions of this Act, the trustee shall use his or her own discretion in the management of the estate and its distribution among the creditors.

80. Appeal to the court against the trustee.

If the bankrupt or any of the creditors, or any other person, is aggrieved by any act or decision of the trustee, he or she may apply to the court, and the court may confirm, reverse, or modify the act or decision complained of, and make such order in the premises as it thinks just.

81. Control of the official receiver over trustees.

(1) The official receiver shall take cognisance of the conduct of the trustees, and, in the event of any trustee not faithfully performing his or her duties, and duly observing all the requirements imposed on him or her by law with respect to the

performance of his or her duties, or in the event of any complaint being made to the official receiver by any creditor in regard there to the official receiver by any creditor in regard there to the official receiver shall inquire into the matter and take such action thereon as may be deemed expedient.

(2) The official receiver may at any time require any trustee to answer any inquiry made by him or her in relation to any bankruptcy in which the trustee is engaged, and, if the official receiver thinks fit, he or she may apply to the court to examine on oath the trustee or any other person concerning the bankruptcy.

(3) The official receiver may also direct a local investigation to be made of the books and vouchers of the trustee.

Remuneration and costs

82. Remuneration of trustee.

(1) Where the creditors appoint any person to be trustee of a debtor's estate, his or her remuneration, if any, shall be fixed by an ordinary resolution of the creditors, or, if the creditors so resolve, by the committee of inspection, and shall be in the nature of a commission or percentage, of which one part shall be payable on the amount realised by the trustee, after deducting any sums paid to secured creditors out of the proceeds of their securities, and the other part of the amount distributed in dividend.

(2) If one-fourth in number or value of the creditors dissent from the resolution, or the bankrupt satisfies the court that the remuneration is unnecessarily large, the court shall fix the amount of the remuneration.

(3) The resolution shall express what expenses the remuneration is to cover, and no liability shall attach to the bankrupt's estate, or to the creditors, in respect of any expenses which the remuneration is expressed to cover.

(4) Where a trustee acts without remuneration, he or she shall be allowed out of the bankrupt's estate such proper expenses incurred by him or her in or about the proceedings of the bankruptcy as the creditors may, with the sanction of the court, approve.

(5) A trustee shall not, under any circumstances whatever, make any arrangement for or accept from the bankrupt, or any advocate, auctioneer, or any other person that may be employed about a bankruptcy, any gift, remuneration, or pecuniary or other consideration or benefit whatever beyond the remuneration fixed by the creditors and payable out of the estate, nor shall he or she make any arrangement for giving up, or give up, any part of his or her remuneration, either as receiver, manager, or trustee, to the bankrupt or any advocate, or other person that may be employed about a bankruptcy.

83. Allowance and taxation of costs.

(1) Where a trustee or manager receives remuneration for his or her services as such, no payment shall be allowed in his or her accounts in respect of the performance by any other person of the ordinary duties which are required by this Act or rules thereunder to be performed by the trustee or manager.

(2) Where the trustee is an advocate, he may contract that the remuneration for his or her services as trustee shall include all professional services.

(3) All bills and charges of advocates, managers, accountants, auctioneers, brokers, and other persons, not being trustees, shall be taxed by the prescribed officer, and no payments in respect thereof shall be allowed in the trustee's accounts without proof of such taxation having been made.

(4) The taxing officer shall satisfy himself or herself before passing such bills and charges that the employment of such advocates and other persons, in respect of the particular matters out of which such charges arise, has been duly sanctioned.

(5) The sanction must be obtained before the employment, except in case of urgency, and in such cases it must be shown that no undue delay took place in obtaining the sanction.

(6) Every such person shall, on request by the trustee (which request the trustee shall make a sufficient time before declaring a dividend), deliver his or her bill of costs or charges to the proper officer for taxation, and, if he fails to do so within seven days after the receipt of the request, or such further time as the court, on application, may grant, the trustee shall declare and distribute the dividend without regard to any claim by him or her, and thereupon any such claim shall be forfeited as well against the trustee personally as against the estate.

Receipts, payments, accounts, audit

84. Trustee to furnish a list of creditors.

The trustee or official receiver shall, whenever required by any creditor so to do, furnish and transmit to him or her by post a list of the creditors showing the amount of the debt due to each creditor, and shall be entitled to charge for such list the sum of fifty cents per each folio of one hundred words, together with the cost of the postage thereof.

85. Trustee to furnish a statement of accounts.

(1) Any creditor, with the concurrence of one-sixth of the creditors (including himself or herself), at any time to call upon the trustee or official receiver to furnish and transmit to the creditors a statement of the accounts up to the date of such notice, and the trustee shall, upon the receipt of such notice, furnish and transmit such statement of the accounts:

(2) The person at whose instance the accounts are furnished shall deposit with the trustee or official receiver, as the case may be, a sum sufficient to pay the costs of furnishing and transmitting the accounts, which sum shall be repaid to him or her out of the estate if the creditors or the court so direct.

86. Booked to be kept by the trustee.

The trustee shall keep, in manner prescribed, proper books in which he shall from time to time cause to be made entries or minutes of proceedings at meetings, and of such other matters as may be prescribed, and any creditor of the bankrupt may, subject to the control of the court, personally or by his or her agent, inspect any such books.

87. Annual statement of proceedings.

(1) Every trustee in a bankruptcy shall from time to time, as may be prescribed, and not less than once in every year during the continuance of the bankruptcy, transmit to the official receiver a statement showing the proceedings in the bankruptcy up to the date of the statement, containing the prescribed particulars, and made out in the prescribed form.

(2) The official receiver shall cause the statements so transmitted to be examined, and shall call the trustee to account for any misfeasance, neglect, or omission, which may appear on the said statements or in his accounts or otherwise, and may require the trustee to make good any loss which the estate of the bankrupt may have sustained by the misfeasance, neglect, or omission.

88. Trustee not to pay into the trustee's private account.

No trustee in a bankruptcy or under any composition or scheme of arrangement shall pay any sums received by him or her as trustee into his or her private banking account.

89. Payment of money into the prescribed bank.

(1) A Bankruptcy Estates Account shall be kept by the official receiver with the prescribed bank, and all moneys received by him or her in respect of proceedings under this Act shall be paid to that account.

(2) Every trustee in bankruptcy shall in such manner and at such times as the official receiver shall direct pay the money received by him or her to the Bankruptcy Estates Account at the prescribed bank, and the official receiver shall furnish him or her with a certificate of receipt of the money so paid; except that–

(a) if it appears to the committee of inspection that, for the purpose of carrying on the debtor's business or of obtaining advances, or because of the probable amount of the cash balance, or if the committee shall satisfy the court that for any other reason it is for the advantage of the creditors that the trustee should have an account with the local bank, the court shall, on the application of the committee of inspection, authorise the trustee to make his or her payments into and out of such local bank as the committee may select;

(b) in any bankruptcy composition or scheme of arrangement in which the official receiver is acting as trustee, or in which a trustee is acting without a committee of inspection, the court may, if for special reasons it thinks fit to do so, upon the application of the official receiver or other trustee, authorise the trustee to make his or her payment into and out of such local bank as the court may direct;

(3) Where the trustee opens an account in a local bank, he or she shall open and keep it in the name of the debtor's estate, and any interest receivable in respect of the account shall be part of the assets of the estate, and the trustee shall make his or her payments into and out of the local bank in the prescribed manner.

(4) Subject to any general rules relating to small bankruptcies under section 117 of this Act, where the debtor at the date of the receiving order has an account at a bank, such account shall not be withdrawn until the expiration of seven days

from the day appointed for the first meeting of creditors, unless the court, for the safety of the account, or other sufficient cause, orders the withdrawal of the account.

(5) If a trustee at any time retains for more than ten days a sum exceeding one thousand shillings, or such other amount as the court in any particular case authorises him or her to retain, then, unless he or she explains the retention to the satisfaction of the court, he or she shall pay interest on the amount so retained in excess at the rate of twenty per centum per annum, and shall have no claim to remuneration, and may be removed from his or her office by the court, and shall be liable to pay any expenses occasioned by reason of his or her default.

90. Investment of surplus funds.

(1) Whenever the cash balance standing to the credit of the Bankruptcy Estates Account is in excess of the amount which in the opinion of the official receiver is required for the time being to answer demands in respect of bankrupts estates, the official receiver may place the same or any part thereof on fixed deposit with the prescribed bank.

(2) Whenever any money so placed on deposit is, in the opinion of the official receiver, required to answer any demand in respect of bankrupts estates, the official receiver shall thereupon withdraw such money from fixed deposit and repay the same to the credit of the cash balance of the Bankruptcy Estates Account.

(3) All interest accruing from any money so placed on deposit shall be paid by the official receiver to the credit of a separate account entitled the Bankruptcy Contingency Fund at the prescribed bank.

(4) Where it appears that it is in the public interest to do so and that other funds are not available or properly chargeable the court may on the application of the official receiver authorise him or her to employ money in the Bankruptcy Contingency Fund to defray the cost in whole or in part of any of the following–

(a) the prosecution of any debtor for any bankruptcy offences alleged to have been committed by him or her;

(b) the institution of proceedings and the payment of expenses of witnesses, if any, for the discovery or recovery of property belonging to any debtor;

(c) the institution of proceedings to set aside an alleged fraudulent preference;

(d) the employment of counsel in matters connected with an estate which by reason of their difficulty or other good cause cannot be dealt with by the official receiver himself or herself;

(e) the employment of interpreters in cases where the court is unable to provide an interpreter;

(f) the payment of expenses involved in arresting a debtor and bringing him or her before the court;

(g) any other expenditure which the court may deem fit.

(5) The court may in its discretion order that the Fund be reimbursed in whole or in part in the event of any money being recovered as a result of the expenditure authorised under subsection (4) of this section.

91. Audit of a trustee's accounts.

(1) Every trustee shall, at such times as may be prescribed, but not less than twice in each year during his or her tenure of office, send to the official receiver an account of his or her receipts and payments as such trustee.

(2) The account shall be in a prescribed form, shall be made in duplicate, and shall be verified by a statutory declaration in the prescribed form.

(3) The official receiver shall cause the accounts so sent to be audited, and, for the purpose of the audit, the trustee shall furnish the auditor with such vouchers and information as the auditor may require, and the auditor may at any time require the production of and inspect any books or accounts kept by the trustee.

(4) When any such account has been audited one copy thereof shall be filed and kept by the official receiver, and the other copy shall be filed with the court, and each copy shall be open to the inspection of any creditor, or of the bankrupt, or of any person interested.

Vacation of office by trustee

92. Release of a trustee.

(1) When the trustee has realised all the property of the bankrupt, or so much thereof as can, in his or her opinion, be realised without needlessly protracting the trusteeship, and distributed a final dividend, if any, or has ceased to act by reason of a composition having been approved, or has resigned, or has been removed from his or her office, the court shall, on his or her application, cause a report on his or her accounts to be prepared, and, on his or her complying with all the requirements of the court, shall take into consideration the report, and any objection which may be urged by the creditor or person interested against the release of the trustee, and shall either grant or withhold the release accordingly.

(2) Where the release of a trustee is withheld, the court may, on the application of any creditor or person interested, make such order as it thinks just, charging the trustee with the consequences of any act or default he or she may have done or made contrary to his or her duty.

(3) An order of the court releasing the trustee shall discharge him or her from all liability in respect of any act done or default made by him or her in the administration of the affairs of the bankrupt, or otherwise in relation to his or her conduct as trustee, but any such order may be revoked on proof that it was obtained by fraud or by suppression or concealment of any material fact.

(4) Subsection (1), (2) and (3) shall apply to the official receiver when he or she is, or is acting as, trustee, and when the official receiver has been released under this section, he or she shall continue to act as trustee for any subsequent purposes of the administration of the debtor's estate, but no liability shall attach to him or her personally by reason of his or her so continuing in respect of any act done, default made, or liability incurred before his or her release.

(5) Where the trustee has not previously resigned or been removed, his or her release shall operate as a removal of him or her from his or her office and thereupon the official receiver shall be the trustee.

(6) Where, on the release of a trustee, the official receiver is, or is acting as, trustee, no liability shall attach to him or her personally in respect of any act done or default made, or liability incurred, by any prior trustee.

93. Office of trustee vacated by insolvency.

If a receiving order is made against a trustee, he or she shall thereby vacate his or her office of trustee.

94. Removal of a trustee.

(1) The creditors may, by ordinary resolution, at a meeting specially called for that purpose, of which seven days' notice has been given, remove a trustee appointed by them, and may, at the same or any subsequent meeting, appoint another person to fill the vacancy as hereinafter provided in case of a vacancy in the office of trustee.

(2) If the court is of opinion–

(a) that a trustee appointed by the creditors is guilty of misconduct or fails to perform his or her duties under this Act;

(b) that his or her trusteeship is being needlessly protracted without any probable advantage to the creditors;

(c) that he or she is by reason of lunacy, or continued sickness or absence, incapable of performing his or her duties; or

(d) that his or her connection with or relation to the bankrupt or his or her estate, or any particular creditor, might make it difficult for him or her to act with impartiality in the interest of the creditors generally, or where, in any other matter he has been removed from office on the ground of misconduct, the court may remove him or her from his or her office.

PART VI – CONSTITUTION, PROCEDURE AND POWERS OF COURT.

Jurisdiction

95. Jurisdication in bankruptcy.

The court having jurisdiction in bankruptcy shall be the High Court; but the Chief Justice may by statutory order delegate all or any part of the jurisdiction of the High Court in bankruptcy to any magistrate's court or subordinate court, either generally or for the purpose of any particular case or class of cases.

96. Judge may exercise his or her powers in chambers.

Subject to the provisions of this Act, and to general rules, a judge of the court may exercise in chambers the whole or any part of his or her powers.

97. Official receiver to make payments in accordance with directions of court.

Where any monies or funds have been received by the official receiver under this Act and the court makes an order declaring that any person is entitled to such monies or funds, the official receiver shall make payment accordingly to that person.

98. General powers of the court.

(1) Subject to the provisions of this Act, the court shall have full power to decide all questions of priorities, and all other questions whatsoever, whether of law or fact, which may arise in any case of bankruptcy coming within its cognisance, or which the court may deem it expedient or necessary to decide for the purpose of doing complete justice or making a complete distribution of property in any such case.

(2) Where default is made by a trustee, debtor, or other person, in obeying any order or direction given by the official receiver, the court may on the application of the official receiver order such defaulting trustee, debtor, or person to comply with the order or directions so given; and the court may also, if it thinks fit upon any such application, make an immediate order for the committal of such defaulting trustee, debtor or person:

(3) `The power given by subsection (2) shall be deemed to be in addition to and not in substitution for any other right or remedy in respect of such default.

99. Disqualification of the bankrupt.

(1) Where a debtor is adjudged bankrupt, he or she shall be disqualified for –

(a) being appointed or acting as a justice of the peace; or

(b) being elected to, or holding or exercising the office of mayor, alderman or municipal councillor, or a member of a town council, school committee or road board.

(2) If a person is adjudged bankrupt whilst holding the office of justice of the peace, mayor, alderman or municipal councillor, or a member of a town council or board, school committee or road board his or her office shall thereupon become vacant.

(3) The disqualifications to which a bankrupt is subject under this section shall be removed and cease if and when–

(a) the adjudication of bankruptcy against him or her is annulled;

(b) period of five years has elapsed from the date of his or her discharge; or

(c) he or her obtains from the court his discharge with a certificate to the effect that his or her bankruptcy was caused by misfortune without any misconduct on his or her part.

(4) The court may grant or withhold such certificate as it thinks fit, but any refusal of such certificate shall be subject to appeal.

Judgement debtors

100. Power to make a receiving order in lieu of a committal order.

(1) Where application is made by a decree holder to the court for committal of a judgment debtor, the court, may, if it thinks fit, decline to commit, and in lieu thereof, with the consent of the decree holder and on payment by him or her of the prescribed fee, make a receiving order against the debtor.

(2) In such case the judgment debtor shall be deemed to have committed an act of bankruptcy at the time the order is made, and the provisions of this Act shall

apply as if for references to the presentation of a petition by or against a person there were substituted references to the making of such a receiving order.

Appeals

101. Appeals in bankruptcy.

(1) The court may review, rescind or vary any order made by it.

(2) Orders of the court in bankruptcy matters shall, at the instance of the person aggrieved, be subject to appeal, but no appeal shall be entertained except in conformity with such general rules as may for the time being be in force in relation to the appeal.

(3) Whereby this Act an appeal to the court is given against any decision of the official receiver, the appeal shall be brought within twenty-one days from the time when the decision appealed against is pronounced or made.

Procedure

102. Discretionary power of the court.

(1) Subject to the provisions of this Act and to general rules, the costs of and incidental to any proceeding in court under this Act shall be in the discretion of the court.

(2) The court may at any time adjourn any proceedings before it upon such terms, if any, as it may think fit to impose.

(3) The court may at any time amend any written process or proceeding under this Act upon such terms, if any, as it may think fit to impose.

(4) Where by this Act, or by general rules, the time for doing any act is limited, the court may extend the time either before or after the expiration thereof upon such terms, if any, as it may think fit to impose.

(5) Subject to general rules, the court may in any matter take the whole or any part of the evidence either *viva voce*, or by interrogatories, or upon affidavit, or, out of Uganda, by commission.

103. Consolidation of petitions.

Where two or more bankruptcy petitions are presented against the same debtor or against joint debtors, the court may consolidate the proceedings, or any of them, on such terms as the court thinks fit.

104. Substitute petitioner.

Where the petitioner does not proceed with due diligence on his petition, the court may substitute as petitioner any other creditor to whom the debtor may be indebted in the amount required by this Act in the case of the petitioning creditor.

105. Continuance of proceedings on death of a debtor.

If a debtor by or against whom a bankruptcy petition has been presented dies, the proceedings in the matter shall, unless the court otherwise orders, be continued as if he or she were alive.

106. Power to stay proceedings.

The court may at any time, for sufficient reason, make an order staying the proceedings under a bankruptcy petition, either altogether or for a limited time, on such terms and subject to such conditions as the court may think just.

107. Power to present a petition against one partner.

Any creditor whose debt is sufficient to entitle him to present a bankruptcy petition against all the partners of a firm may present a petition against any one or more partners of the firm without including the others.

108. Power to dismiss a petition against some respondents only.

Where there are more respondents than one to a petition, the court may dismiss the petition as to one or more of them, without prejudice to the effect of the petition as against the other or others of them.

109. Property of partners to be vested in same trustee.

Where a receiving order has been made on a bankruptcy petition by or against a member of the same partnership, any other bankruptcy petition by or against one member of a partnership shall be filed with the first-mentioned petition, and, unless the court otherwise directs, the same trustee or receiver shall be appointed as may have been appointed in respect of the property of the first-mentioned member of the partnership, and the court may give such directions for consolidating the proceedings as it thinks just.

110. Actions of trustee and bankrupt's partners.

Where a member of a partnership is adjudged bankrupt, the court may authorise the trustee to commence and prosecute any action in the names of the trustee and of the bankrupt's partner; and any release by such partner of the debt or demand to which the action relates shall be void; but notice of the application for authority to commence the action shall be given to him or her, and he or she may show cause against it, and on his or her application the court may, if it thinks fit, direct that he shall receive his proper share of the proceeds of the action, and if he or she does not claim any benefit therefrom, he or she shall be indemnified against costs in respect thereof as the court directs.

111. Actions on joint contracts.

Where a bankrupt is a contractor in respect of any contract jointly with any person or persons, such person or persons may sue or be sued in respect of the contract without the joinder of the bankrupt.

112. Proceedings in partnership name.

Any two or more persons, being partners, or any person carrying on business under a partnership name, may take proceedings or be proceeded against under this Act in the name of the firm, but in such case the court may, on application by any person interested, order the name of the persons who are partners in such firm or the name of such person to be disclosed in such manner, and verified on oath or otherwise, as the court may direct.

113. Court to be auxiliary to other Commonwealth courts.

The court and all the officers thereof shall, in all matters of bankruptcy, act in aid of and be auxiliary to every court elsewhere in the Commonwealth having jurisdiction in bankruptcy or insolvency, and an order of the court seeking aid, with a request to the court, shall be deemed sufficient to enable the court to exercise, in regard to the matters directed by the order, such jurisdiction as either the court or the court which made the request could exercise in regard to similar matters within their respective jurisdictions, save that to enable the official receiver of Uganda to act as the agent of an officer of a reciprocating court or to enable an officer of the court to seek the aid of an official receiver of a reciprocating court in the manner provided in Part IX of this Act, it shall not be necessary for the court or any reciprocating court to make any order or send any request under this section

114. Commitment to prison.

Where the court commits any person to prison, the commitment may be to such convenient prison as the court thinks expedient, and, if the galore any prison refuses to receive any prisoner so committed, he or she shall on conviction be liable for every such refusal to a fine not exceeding two thousand shillings.

PART VII – SUPPLEMENTAL PROVISIONS

Application of the Act

115. Married women.

Every married woman shall be subject to the bankruptcy laws as if she were *feme sole.*

116. Exclusion of companies.

A receiving order shall not be made against any corporation or against any association or company registered under the Companies Act and any Act passed in substitution therefor.

117. Application of the Act in case of small estates.

Where a petition is presented by or against a debtor, if the court is satisfied, by affidavit or otherwise, or the official receiver reports to the court, that the property of the debtor is not likely to exceed in value six thousand shillings, the court may make an order that the debtor's estate be administered in a summary manner, and thereupon the provisions of this Act shall be subject to the following modifications–

(a) if the debtor is adjudged bankrupt the official receiver shall be the trustee in the bankruptcy;

(b) there shall be no committee of inspection, but the official receiver may do all things which may be done by the trustee with the permission of the committee of inspection;

(c) such other modifications may be made in the provisions of this Act as may be prescribed by general rules with the view of saving expense and simplifying procedure, but nothing in this section shall permit the modification of the provisions of this Act relating to the examination or discharge of the debtor; except that the creditors may at any time, by special resolution, resolve that some person other than the official receiver be appointed trustee in the bankruptcy, and thereupon the bankruptcy shall proceed as if an order for summary administration had not been made.

118. Administration in bankruptcy of estate of person dying insolvent.

(1) Any creditor of a deceased debtor whose debt would have been sufficient to support a bankruptcy petition against the debtor, had he been alive, may present to the court a petition in the prescribed form praying for an order for the administration of the estate of the deceased debtor, according to the law of bankruptcy.

(2) Upon the prescribed notice being given to the legal personal representative of the deceased debtor, the court may, in the prescribed manner, upon proof of the petitioner's debt, unless the court is satisfied that there is a reasonable probability that the estate will be sufficient for the payment of the debts owing by the deceased, make an order for the administration in bankruptcy of the deceased debtor's estate, or may, upon cause shown, dismiss the petition with or without costs.

(3) Upon an order being made for the administration of a deceased debtor's estate, the property of the debtor shall vest in the official receiver, as trustee thereof, and he or she shall forthwith proceed to realise and distribute it in accordance with the provisions of this Act; except the creditors shall have the same powers as to appointment of trustees and committees of inspection as they have in other cases where the estate of a debtor is being administered or dealt with in bankruptcy, and the provisions of this Act relating to trustees and committees of inspection shall apply to trustees and committees of inspection appointed under the power so conferred.

(4) If a trustee other than the official receiver is appointed and no committee of inspection is appointed, any act or thing or any direction or permission which might have been done or given by a committee of inspection may be done or given by the court.

(5) With the modifications hereinafter mentioned, all the provisions of Part III of this Act (relating to the administration of the property of a bankrupt) and, subject to any modification that may be made therein by general rules under subsection (11) of this section, the following provisions, namely, section 27 of this Act (which relates to inquiries as to the debtor's conduct, dealings and property), section 83 of this Act, (which relates to the costs of the trustees, managers, and other persons) section 117 of this Act (which relates to the summary administration of small estates), and subsection (4) of section 92 of this Act so far as it relates to

the effect of the release of the official receiver shall, so far as the same are applicable, apply to the case of an administration order under this section in like manner as to an order of adjudication under this Act, and section 38 of this Act shall apply as if for the reference to an order of adjudication there were substituted a reference to an administration order under this section.

(6) In the administration of the property of the deceased debtor under an order of administration, the official receiver or trustee shall have regard to any claim by the legal personal representatives of the deceased debtor to payment of the proper funeral and testamentary expenses incurred by him or her in and about the debtor's estate, and such claims shall be deemed a preferential debt under the order, and shall, notwithstanding anything to the contrary in the provisions of this Act relating to the priority of other debts, be payable in full, out of the debtor's estate, in priority to all other debts.

(7) If, on the administration of a deceased debtor's estate, any surplus remains in the hand of the official receiver or trustee, after payment, in full of all the debts due from the debtor, together with the costs of the administration and interest as provided by this Act in case of bankruptcy, such surplus shall be paid over to the legal personal representative of the deceased debtor's estate, or dealt with in such other manner as may be prescribed.

(8) Notice to the legal personal representative of a deceased debtor of the presentation by a creditor of a petition under this section shall, in the event of an order for administration being made thereon, be deemed to be equivalent to notice of an act of bankruptcy, and after such notice no payment or transfer of property made by the legal personal representative shall operate as a discharge to him or her as between himself or herself and the official receiver or trustee; save as aforesaid nothing in this section shall invalidate any payment made or any act or thing done in good faith by the legal personal representative before the date of the order for administration.

(9) A petition for the administration of the estate of a deceased debtor under this section may be presented by the legal personal representative of the debtor, and, where a petition is so presented by such a representative this section shall apply subject to such modifications as may be prescribed by general rules made under subsection (11) of this section.

(10) Unless the context otherwise requires "creditor" means one or more creditors qualified to present a bankruptcy petition as in this Act provided.

(11) General rules for carrying into effect the provisions of this section may be made in the same manner and to the like and extent as in bankruptcy.

General rules

119. Power to make general rules.

The Chief Justice, with the approval of the Minister, may make general rules for carrying into effect the objects of this Act.

Fees and salaries, etc

120. Fees, etc.

The Chief Justice, with the approval of the Minister, may prescribe a scale of fees and percentages to be charged for or in respect of proceedings under this Act.

121. Salaries and remuneration.

The Chief Justice, with the approval of the Minister, shall direct whether any and what remuneration is to be allowed to any person (other than the official receiver or his or her staff) performing any duties under this Act, and may vary, increase, or diminish such remuneration, as he or she may think fit.

Evidence

122. Gazette to be evidence.

(1) A copy of the Gazette containing any notice inserted therein in pursuance of this Act shall be evidence of the facts stated in the notice.

(2) The production of a copy of the Gazette containing any notice of a receiving order, or of an order adjudging a debtor bankrupt, shall be conclusive evidence in all legal proceedings of the order having been duly made, and of its date.

123. Evidence of proceedings at meetings of creditors.

(1) A minute of proceedings at a meeting of creditors under this Act, signed at the same or the next ensuing meeting, by a person describing himself or herself as, or appearing to be, chairperson of the meeting at which the minute is signed, shall be received in evidence without further proof.

(2) Until the contrary is proved, every meeting of creditors in respect of the proceedings whereof a minute has been so signed shall be deemed to have been duly convened and held, and all resolutions passed or proceedings had thereat to have been duly passed or had.

124. Evidence of proceedings in bankruptcy.

Any petition or copy of a petition in bankruptcy, any order or certificate or copy of an order or certificate made by the court, any instrument or copy of an instrument, affidavit or document made or used in the court of any bankruptcy proceedings or other proceedings had under this Act, shall, if it appears to be sealed with the seal of the court, or purports to be signed by any Judge thereof, or is certified as a true copy by any registrar thereof, be receivable in evidence in all legal proceedings whatever.

125. Swearing of affidavits.

Subject to general rules, any affidavit to be used in the court may be sworn before any person authorised to administer oaths in the court, or before a magistrate or a justice of peace, or in the case of a person residing out of Uganda, before any person qualified to administer oaths in the country where he or she resides (he or she being certified to be qualified as aforesaid by a foreign service officer or diplomatic representative of a Commonwealth country, or by a notary public).

126. Death of a debtor or the witness.

In the case of the death of the debtor or his wife, or of a witness whose evidence has been received by the court in any proceeding under this Act, the deposition of the person so deceased, purporting to be sealed with the seal of the court, or a copy thereof purporting to be so sealed, shall be admitted as evidence of the matters therein deposed to.

127. Certificate of appointment of trustee.

A certificate of the court that a person has been appointed trustee under this Act shall be conclusive evidence of his or her appointment.

Miscellaneous

128. Computation of time.

(1) Where by this Act any limited time from or after any date or event is appointed or allowed for the doing of any act or the taking of any proceeding, then in the computation of that limited time the same shall be taken as exclusive of the day of that date or of the happening of that event, and as commencing at the beginning of the next following day; and the act or proceeding shall be done or taken at latest on the last day of that limited time as so computed, unless the last day is a Sunday or a public holiday or a day on which the offices of the court are wholly closed, in which case any act or proceeding shall be considered as done or taken in due time if it is done or taken on the next day afterwards which is not one of the days in this section specified.

(2) Where by this Act the time limited for doing any act or thing is less than six days, a Sunday, public holiday and any other day on which the offices of the court are wholly closed shall be excluded in computing such time.

(3) Where by this Act any act or proceeding is directed to be done or taken on a certain day, then, if that day happens to be done of the days in this section specified, the act or proceeding shall be considered as done or taken in due time if it is done or taken on the next day afterwards which is not one of the days in this section specified.

129. Services of notices.

All notices and other documents for the service of which no special mode is directed may be sent by post to the last known address of the person to be served therewith.

130. Formal defect not to invalidate proceedings.

(1) No proceeding in bankruptcy shall be invalidated by any formal defect or by any irregularity, unless the court before which an objection is made to the proceeding is of opinion that substantial injustice has been caused by the defect or irregularity, and that the injustice cannot be remedied by any order of the court.

(2) No defect or irregularity in the appointment or election of a receiver, trustee, or member of a committee of inspection shall vitiate any act done by him or her in good faith.

131. Exemption of deeds, etc, from stamp duty.

(1) Every deed, conveyance, assignment or other assurance relating solely to freehold or leasehold property, or to any mortgage charge or other incumbrance on, or any estate, right or interest in, any movable or immovable property which is part of the estate of any bankrupt, and which, after the execution of the deed, conveyance, assignment or other assurance, either at law or in equity, is or remains the estate of the bankrupt or of the trustee under the bankruptcy, and every power of attorney, proxy paper, writ, order, certificate, affidavit, bond or other instrument or writing relating solely to the property of any bankrupt, or to any proceeding under any bankruptcy, shall be exempt from stamp duty, except in respect of fees under this Act.

(2) For the purposes of this section "bankruptcy" shall include any proceeding under this Act whether before or after adjudication and "bankrupt" shall include any debtor proceeded against under this Act.

132. Acting of corporations, partners, etc.

For all or any of the purposes of this Act, a corporation may act by any of its officers authorised in that behalf under the seal of the corporation, a firm may act by any of its members, and a person of unsound mind may act by the manager of his or her estate or other persons appointed under the Administration of Estates of Persons of Unsound Mind Act.

133. Certain provisions to bind the Government.

Save as provided in this Act, the provisions of this Act relating to the remedies against the property of a debtor, the priorities of debts, the effect of a composition or scheme of arrangement, and the effect of a discharge, shall bind the Government.

Unclaimed funds or dividends

134. Unclaimed and undistributed dividends or funds under this Act.

(1) Where the trustee, under any bankruptcy, composition or scheme, pursuant to this Act, has under his or her control any unclaimed dividend which has remained unclaimed for more than six months, or where, after making a final dividend, he or she has in his or her hands or under his control any unclaimed or undistributed money arising from the property of the debtor, he or she shall forthwith pay it to the Bankruptcy Estates Account at the prescribed bank.

(2) The official receiver shall furnish him or her with a certificate of receipt of the money so paid, which shall be an effectual discharge to him or her in respect thereof.

(3) Where any unclaimed or undistributed funds or dividends in the hands or under the control of any trustee or other person empowered to collect, receive or

distribute any funds or dividends under the Deeds of Arrangement Act have remained or remain unclaimed or undistributed for six months after they became claimable or distributable, in any other case for two years after the receipt of the funds or dividends by the trustee or other person, the trustee or other person shall immediately pay them to the bankruptcy estates account at the prescribed bank.

(4) The official receiver shall furnish the trustee or other person with a certificate or receipt of the money so paid, which shall be an effectual discharge to him or her in respect of the money.

(5) The official receiver may at any time order any such trustee or other person to submit to him an account verified by affidavit of the sums received and paid by him or her as aforesaid, and may direct and enforce an audit of the account.

(6) The official receiver may from time to time appoint a person to collect and get in all such unclaimed or undistributed funds or dividends, and for the purposes of this section the court shall have and, at the instance of the official receiver, may exercise, all the powers conferred by this Act with respect to the discovery and realisation of the property of a debtor, and the provisions of Part II of this Act with respect thereto shall, with any necessary modifications, apply to proceedings under this section.

(7) The provisions of this section shall not, except as expressly declared herein, deprive any person of any larger or other right or remedy to which he or she may be entitled against such trustee or other person.

(8) Where any unclaimed dividends or undistributed money paid into the Bankruptcy Estates Account in pursuance of this section shall have remained in that account for a period of two years, the official receiver shall transfer such money to the credit of the Bankruptcy Contingency Fund.

(9) Any person claiming to be entitled to any moneys paid into the Bankruptcy Estates Account or the Bankruptcy Contingency Fund pursuant to this section may apply to the official receiver for payment to him or her of the monies, and the official receiver, if satisfied that the person claiming is so entitled, shall make an order for the payment to such person of the sum due.

(10) If the money claimed under subsection (9) has been paid to the credit of the Bankruptcy Contingency Fund and the said Fund is insufficient to meet the sum required to be paid, the deficiency shall be met out of the Consolidated Fund.

(11) Any person dissatisfied with the decision of the official receiver in respect of his or her claim may appeal to the court.

PART VIII – BANKRUPTCY OFFENCES.

135. Fraudulent debtors.

(1) Any person who has been adjudged bankrupt or in respect of whose estate a receiving order has been made an offence in each of the following cases–

(a) if he or she does not to the best of his or her knowledge and belief fully and truly discover to the trustee all his property, movable and immovable, and how and to whom, and for what consideration and when he or she disposed of any part thereof, except such part as has been disposed of in the ordinary way of his or her trade, if any, or laid out in the ordinary expense of his or her family, unless he or she proves that he or she had no intent to defraud;

(b) if he or she does not deliver up to the trustee, or as he o she directs, all such part of his or she movable and immovable property as is in his or her custody or under his or her control, and which he or she is required by law to deliver up, unless he or she proves that he or she had no intent to defraud;

(c) if he or she does not deliver up to the trustee, or as he or she directs, all books, documents, paper, and writings in his or her custody or under his or her control relating to his or her property or affairs, unless he or she proves that he or she had no intent to defraud;

(d) if, after the presentation of a bankruptcy petition by or against him or her, or within two years immediately before such presentation, he or she conceals any part of his or her property to the value of two hundred shillings or upwards, or conceals any debt due to or from him or her, unless he or she proves that he or she had no intent to defraud;

(e) if, after the presentation of a bankruptcy petition by or against him or her, or within two years immediately before such presentation, he or she fraudulently removes any part of his or her property to the value of two hundred shillings or upwards;

(f) if he or she makes any material omission in any statement relating to his affairs, unless he or she proves that he or she had no intent to defraud;

(g) if, knowing or believing that a false debt has been proved by any person under the bankruptcy, he or she fails for the period of a month to inform the trustee thereof;

(h) if, after the presentation of a bankruptcy petition by or against him or her, he prevents the production of any book, document, paper, or writing affecting or relating to his or her property or affairs, unless he or she proves that he or she had no intent to conceal the state of his or her affairs or to defeat the law;

(i) if, after the presentation of a bankruptcy petition by or against him or her, or within two years next before such presentation, he or she conceals, destroys, mutilates, or falsifies, or is privy to the concealment, destruction, mutilation or falsification of any book or document affecting or relating to his or her property or affairs, unless he or she proves that he or she had no intent to conceal the state of his or her affairs or to defeat the law;

(j) if, after the presentation of a bankruptcy petition by or against him or her, or within two years immediately before such presentation, he or she makes or is privy to the making of any false entry in any book or document affecting or relating to his or her property or affairs, unless he or she proves that he or she had no intent to conceal the state of his or her affairs or to defeat the law;

(k) if, after the presentation of a bankruptcy petition by or against him or her, or within two years next before such presentation, he or her fraudulently parts with, alters, or makes any omission in, or is privy to the fraudulently parting with, altering or making any omission in, any document affecting or relating to his or her property or affairs;

(l) if, after the presentation of a bankruptcy petition by or against him or her, or at any meeting of his or her creditors within two years immediately before such presentation, he or she attempts to account for any part of his or her property by fictitious losses or expenses;

(m) if, within two years immediately before the presentation of a bankruptcy petition by or against him or her, or after the presentation of bankruptcy petition and before the making of a receiving order, he or she, by any false representation or other fraud, has obtained any property on credit and has not paid for the same;

(n) if, within two years next before the presentation of a bankruptcy petition by or against him or her, or after the presentation of a bankruptcy petition and before the making of a receiving order, he or she obtains under false pretence of carrying on business, and, if a trader, of dealing in the ordinary way of his or her trade, any property on credit and has not paid for the same, unless he or she proves that he or she had no intent to defraud;

(o) if, within two years next before the presentation of a bankruptcy petition by or against him or her, or after the presentation of a bankruptcy petition and before the making of a receiving order, he or she pawns, pledges, or disposes of any property which he or she has obtained on credit and has not paid for, unless, in the case of a trader, such pawning, pledging, or disposing is in the ordinary way of his or her trade, and unless in any case he or she proves that he or she had no intent to defraud;

(p) if he or she is guilty of any false representation or other fraud for the purpose of obtaining the consent of his or her creditors or any of them to an agreement with reference to his or her affairs or to his or her bankruptcy;

(q) if he or she makes default in payment for the benefit of creditors of any portion of a salary or other income in respect of the payment of which the court is authorised to make an order;

(r) if, within one year preceding the date of the making of the receiving order, he has continued to trade after knowing himself to be insolvent;

(s) if, within six months before the making of a receiving order, he or she sells goods at a price lower than cost, unless he or she proves that he had no intent to defraud his or her creditors;

(t) if he has contracted any debt provable in the bankruptcy without having at the time of contracting it any reasonable or probable ground of expectation (proof whereof shall lie on him) of being able to pay it.

(2) For the purposes of this subsection, the expression "trustee" means the official receiver of the debtor's estate or trustee administering his or her estate for the benefit of his or her creditors.

(3) Any person guilty of an offence in the cases mentioned in subsection (1) of this section is liable on conviction to imprisonment for any term not exceeding three years except in the cases mentioned respectively in paragraphs *(m), (n),* and

(o), thereof when he or she is liable on conviction to imprisonment for any term not exceeding five years.

(4) Where any person pawns, pledges or disposes of any property in circumstances which amount to an offence under paragraph *(o)* of subsection (1) of this section, every person who takes in pawn or pledge or otherwise receives the property knowing it to be pawned, pledged or disposed of in such circumstance as aforesaid commits an offence and on conviction thereof liable to be punished in the same way as if he or she had received the property knowing it to have been obtained in circumstances amounting to an offence punishable under section 314 of the Penal Code Act.

136. Undischarged bankrupt obtaining credit.

Where a person who has been adjudged bankrupt or insolvent in Uganda or any reciprocating territory and has not obtained his or her discharge–

(a) either alone or jointly with any other person obtains credit to the extent of one hundred shillings or upwards from any person without informing that person that he or she is an undischarged bankrupt; or

(b) engages in any trade or business under a name other than that under which he or she was adjudicated bankrupt without disclosing to all persons with whom he or she enters into any business transaction the name under which he or she was adjudicated bankrupt, he or she commits an offence.

137. Frauds by bankrupts, etc.

(1) If any person who has been adjudged bankrupt or in respect of whose estate a receiving order has been made –

(a) in incurring any debt or liability has obtained credit under false pretences or by means of any other fraud; or

(b) with intent to defraud his or her creditors or any of them, had made or caused to be made any gift or transfer of, or charge on, his or her property; or

(c) with intent to defraud his or her creditors, has concealed or removed any part of his or her property since, or within two months before, the date of any unsatisfied judgment or order for payment of money obtained against him or her, he or she commits an offence.

(2) For the purposes of paragraph *(b)* of subsection (1) of this section if any person who has been adjudged bankrupt, or in respect of whose estate a receiving order has been made, has with intent to defraud his or her creditors or any of them caused or connived at the levying of any execution against his or her property he or she shall be deemed to have made a transfer of or charge on his or her property.

138. Bankrupt guilty of gambling, etc.

(1) Any person who has been adjudged bankrupt, or in respect of whose estate a receiving order has been made, commits an offence, if, having been engaged in any trade or business, and having outstanding at the date of the receiving order any debts contracted in the course and for the purposes of such trade or business–

(a) he or she has within two years prior to the presentation of the bankruptcy petition, materially contributed to or increased the extent of his or her insolvency by gambling or by rash and hazardous speculations, and such gambling or speculations are unconnected with his or her trade or business; or

(b) he or she has, between the date of the presentation of the petition and the date of the receiving order, lost any part of his or her estate by such gambling or rash and hazardous speculations as aforesaid in paragraph (a) of this subsection;

(c) on being required by the official receiver at any time, or in the course of his or her public examination by the court, to account for the loss of any substantial part of his or her estate incurred within a period of a year next preceding the date of the presentation of the bankruptcy petition, or between that date and the date of the receiving order, he or she fails to give a satisfactory explanation of the manner in which such loss was incurred:

(2) In determining for the purposes of this section whether any speculations were rash and hazardous, the financial position of the accused person at the time when he or she entered into the speculations shall be taken into consideration.

(3) A prosecution shall not be instituted against any person under this section except by order of the court.

139. Bankrupt failing to keep proper accounts.

(1) Any person who has been adjudged bankrupt or in respect of whose estate a receiving order has been made commits an offence, if, having been engaged in any trade or business during any period in the three years immediately before the date of the presentation of the bankruptcy petition he or she has not kept proper books of account throughout that period and throughout any further period in which he or she was so engaged between the date of the presentation of the petition and the date of the receiving order, or has not preserved all books of account so kept; except that a person who has not kept or has not preserved books of account shall not be convicted of an offence under this section–

(a) if his or her unsecured liabilities at the date of the receiving order did not exceed, in the case of a person who has not on any previous occasion been adjudged bankrupt or insolvent or made a composition or arrangement with his or her creditors in Uganda or any reciprocating territory, five thousand shillings or in any other case one thousand shillings; or

(b) if he or she proves that in the circumstances in which he or she traded or carried on business the omission was honest and excusable.

(2) A prosecution shall not be instituted against any person under this section except by order of the court.

(3) For the purposes of this section, a person shall be deemed not to have kept proper books of account if he or she has not kept such books or accounts as are necessary to exhibit or explain his or her transactions and financial position in his or her trade or business, including a book containing entries from day to day in sufficient detail of all cash received and cash paid, and, where the trade or business has involved dealings in goods statements of annual stock-takings and

(except in the case of goods sold by way of retail trade to the actual consumer) accounts of all goods sold and purchased showing the buyers and sellers thereof in sufficient detail to enable the goods and the buyers and sellers thereof to be identified.

140. Bankrupt absconding with property.

If any person who is adjudged bankrupt, or in respect of whose estate a receiving order has been made, after the presentation of a bankruptcy petition by or against him or her, or within six months before such presentation, quits Uganda and takes with him or her, or attempts or makes preparation to quit Uganda and take with him or her any part of his or her property to the amount of four hundred shillings or upwards, which ought by law to be divided amongst his or her creditors, he or she shall (unless he proves that he or she had no intent to defraud) commits an offence.

141. False claim, etc.

If any creditor, or any person claiming to be a creditor, in any bankruptcy proceedings, makes any false claim, or any proof, declaration or statement of account, which is untrue in any material particular, he or she commits an offence, unless he or she proves that he or she had no intent to defraud.

142. Order by the court for prosecution on report of trustee.

Where an official receiver or trustee in a bankruptcy reports to the court that in his or her opinion a debtor who has been adjudged bankrupt or in respect of whose estate a receiving order has been made has been committed an offence under this Act, or where the court is satisfied upon the representation of any creditor or member of the committee of inspection that there is ground to believe that the debtor has been guilty of any such offence, the court shall, if it appears to the court that there is reasonable probability that the debtor will be convicted, and that the circumstances are such as to render a prosecution desirable, order that the debtor be prosecuted for such offence.

143. Criminal liability after discharge or composition.

Where a debtor has been guilty of any criminal offence, he or she shall not be exempt from being proceeded against or for it by reason that he or she has obtained his or her discharge or that a composition or scheme of arrangement has been accepted or approved.

144. General penalty.

A person guilty of an offence under this Act in respect of which no special penalty is imposed by this Act shall be liable, on conviction, to imprisonment for a period not exceeding two years.

145. Form of charge.

In a charge for an offence under this Act, it shall be sufficient to set forth the substance of the offence charged in the words of this Act specifying the offence, or as near thereto as circumstances admit, without alleging or setting forth any debt, act of bankruptcy, trading, adjudicating, or any proceeding in, or order, warrant, or document of, the court acting under this Act.

146. Director of Public Prosecutions to act in certain cases.

Where the court orders the prosecution of any person for any offence under this Act or for any offence arising out of or connected with any bankruptcy proceedings, it shall be the duty of the Director of Public Prosecutions to institute and carry on the prosecution; except that, where the order of the court is made on the application of the official receiver and based on his report, the official receiver may institute the prosecution and carry on the proceedings, if or so long as those proceedings are conducted before a magistrate's or subordinate court, unless in the course thereof circumstances arise which render it desirable that the remainder of the proceedings should be carried on by the Director of Public Prosecutions.

147. Evidence as to frauds by agents.

A statement or admission made by any person in any compulsory examination or deposition before the court on the hearing of any matter in bankruptcy shall not be admissible as evidence against that person in any proceeding in respect of any offence relating to frauds by agents, bankers or factors.

PART IX – PROVISIONS FOR RECIPROCITY WITH OTHER TERRITORIES.

148. Declaration of reciprocating territories and courts.

Where the Minister is satisfied that the legislature of any territory, the court of which having jurisdiction in bankruptcy is subordinate to the Court of Appeal, has enacted provisions for reciprocity in bankruptcy which in that territory have the like effect as the provisions in this Part of this Act, the Minister may by statutory instrument declare such territory to be a reciprocating territory, and the court thereof having jurisdiction in bankruptcy, a reciprocating court for the purposes of this Act, and as from the date of publication of such instrument in the Gazette the provisions of this Part of this Act shall apply to all bankruptcy proceedings subsequently instituted in the declared territory against a debtor having property in Uganda.

149. Local effect of receiving order, etc. made by reciprocating court against debtor having property in Uganda.

Where a receiving order or order of adjudication or any appointment of a special manager or interim receiver has been made in any reciprocating territory in bankruptcy proceedings against a debtor having property in Uganda, such order or appointment shall, subject to the other provisions of this Part of this Act, have the like effect as if it had been made in bankruptcy proceedings against the debtor in Uganda, and the debtor and his or her creditors shall be deemed to be in the same position and have the same rights and privileges, and be subject to the same disqualifications, restrictions, obligations and liabilities in every respect as if such order or appointment had been made under this Act.

150. Vesting of bankrupt's local property in trustee appointed in recriprocal territory.

Where an order of adjudication is made by a reciprocating court, the property of the bankrupt situated in Uganda shall, by virtue of such order, vest in the person from time to time discharging the office of trustee of the property of the bankrupt in the reciprocating territory, in the same manner as if the order of adjudication and the appointment of the trustee had been made in Uganda, and the superintendence of such trustee shall continue to be exercised by the committee of inspection appointed in the reciprocating territory or, if there be no such committee, by the reciprocating court.

151. Local powers of official receiver, etc., appointed in the reciprocating territory.

The official receiver, interim receiver, special manager or trustee of a reciprocating territory officiating in bankruptcy proceedings against a debtor having property in Uganda shall, subject to the control of the court by which he or she is appointed, be solely responsible for conducting those proceedings, and managing the affairs of the debtor or bankrupt within Uganda, and for such purposes shall, each in his or her respective capacity, have the same powers, rights, duties, obligations and liabilities as if he or she had derived his or her authority under this Act; and in any such proceedings where by this Act a debtor, creditor or other person interested is required to do any act at the direction of an official receiver, interim receiver, special manager or trustee or is permitted by this Act to move in any matter in connection with such proceedings every such debtor, creditor or person interested shall do such act at the direction of, and in all such matters treat and negotiate with or proceed against the official receiver, interim receiver, special manager or trustee as the case may be of the reciprocating territory, except in so far as any such official may have delegated his or her authority to the official receiver of Uganda as his or her agent in the manner hereinafter provided.

152. Local official receiver to act as agent of official receiver, etc., of reciprocating territory.

Every official receiver, interim receiver, special manager or trustee of a reciprocating territory officiating in bankruptcy proceedings against a debtor having property in Uganda may require the official receiver of Uganda to act as his agent either in regard to any specific matter, or generally to take all such steps as may be lawful under this Act for the discovery, seizure, protection, disclaimer or realisation of any property of the bankrupt situated within Uganda, and in such event it shall be the duty of the official receiver of Uganda to act accordingly.

153. Mode of requesting official receiver to act as agent.

(1) Every request to act as agent as aforesaid shall be made in the manner prescribed under this Act, and shall be published as a notice in the Gazette, and upon such publication and without further formality or authority the official receiver, shall, as regards the debtor or bankrupt and his or her property and creditors situated in Uganda and for the purposes for which he or she is authorised, have the same rights, powers and duties as are conferred under the provisions of this Act upon an official receiver, interim receiver, special manager or trustee as the

case may be; but nothing herein contained shall be taken to confer on the official receiver any interest or title in any such property otherwise than as an agent as aforesaid.

(2) On the receipt of the prescribed request the official receiver shall file with the Registrar of the High Court the original or a properly authenticated copy of the request, and upon such filing the court shall take judicial notice of the appointment as agent under the provisions of this Part of this Act.

(3) Notwithstanding the provisions of subsection (1) of this section, the court may, in any case in which it is made to appear to the court that immediate action is desirable, give the official receiver leave to commence discharging his or her duties as agent as aforesaid in any manner applicable to the circumstances, before the publication of the prescribed request, if upon the receipt of telegraphic or other information the court is satisfied that –

(a) bankruptcy proceedings have been instituted in a reciprocating territory against a debtor having property in Uganda; and

(b) the prescribed request for the official receiver to act has been signed and despatched; and further

(c) that the official receiver has been indemnified against all costs, charges and expenses to be incurred by him or her.

(4) Any provisional authority conferred on an official receiver by the court under subsection (3) of this section may be revoked, unless within such time as may in the circumstances seem reasonable the prescribed request is filed in pursuance of subsection (2) of this section.

(5) Unless the contrary intention appears, every request to act as agent sent to the official receiver of Uganda shall be deemed to permit him or her to delegate at his or her discretion the powers and duties vested in him or her as such agent to any deputy official receiver appointed in pursuance of this Act.

154. Duties of official receiver acting as agent.

It shall be the duty of the official receiver of Uganda to remit the proceeds of the realisation of the property of the bankrupt and all other money of the estate coming into his or her hands as such agent as aforesaid to the person for whom he or she is acting, after deducting such expenses as may have been properly incurred by him or her; and the distribution among the creditors of all such money shall be carried out in accordance with the law of the reciprocating territory in which the adjudicating order was made.

155. Transmission of proofs of local debts.

Where a receiving order or an order of adjudication has been made in a reciprocating territory and the official receiver of Uganda is acting as agent in the manner therein before provided, proofs of debts contracted by the debtor in Uganda may be filed with the local official receiver in the form prescribed by the law of such reciprocating territory, and in every such case he or she shall receive, deal with and forward in the manner prescribed by the rules made under this Part of this Act such proofs to the official receiver or trustee, as the case may be, of such reciprocating territory.

156. Power of local court to make orders under sections 10 and 25.

If on the application of the official receiver or any creditor or other person interested, it appears to the court that bankruptcy proceedings have been instituted in a reciprocating court against a debtor having property situated in Uganda, the court may, notwithstanding that no such proceedings have been instituted in Uganda, exercise as regards the person, property and affairs of the debtor all the powers conferred by sections 10 and 25 of this Act as may in the circumstances be applicable.

157. Local enforcement of warrants of reciprocating court.

Any order, warrant or search warrant made or issued by a reciprocating court shall be enforced by the court of Uganda in the same manner in all respects as if such order, warrant or search warrant had been made or issued by itself.

158. Limitation on powers of local court to entertain proceedings.

Subject to the other provisions of this section, a reciprocating court shall have sole jurisdiction in all matters in or arising out of any bankruptcy proceedings taken before such court against a debtor having property in Uganda, and no court in Uganda shall entertain any suit, application or other matter arising in or out of such proceedings except –

(a) upon the institution of any proceedings by or against the local official receiver in respect of any matters within the scope of his authority in the capacity of agent as aforesaid;

(b) in the case of any civil suit or proceedings within the ordinary civil jurisdiction of such court by or against the official receiver, interim receiver, trustee or special manager of or appointed in a reciprocating territory;

(c) upon the institution of any proceedings affecting the property of the debtor or bankrupt situated in Uganda;

(d) upon the receipt of a request to act in aid of or be auxiliary to such reciprocating court;

(e) for the public examination of the debtor in regard only to his or her property situated within Uganda or his or her dealings with any person ordinarily resident or carrying on business in Uganda; except that such public examination shall not be held until the public examination before the reciprocating court shall have been concluded or adjourned sine die;

(f) for the exercise of powers under Part VIII of this Act in relation only to bankruptcy offences alleged to have been committed within Uganda;

(g) upon the institution of any proceedings for or arising out of the enforcement or execution of any order, warrant or search warrant made or issued by a reciprocating court; or

(h) upon an application for the exercise of the powers conferred on the court by sections 10, 25, 26 and 53 of this Act.

159. Concurrent bankruptcies.

(1) For the purposes of this section "concurrent bankruptcy proceedings" means bankruptcy or insolvency proceedings instituted concurrently against the same debtor in any two or more reciprocating territories, one of which may or may not be Uganda; where concurrent bankruptcy proceedings have been instituted affecting property in Uganda, all such property shall vest in the trustee appointed in the territory where the order of adjudication first is made; but if two or more such orders bear the same date or if for any reason no such adjudication order is made then such property shall vest in or be administered by the trustee or receiver or the territory where the receiving order first is made.

(2) In any case where concurrent bankruptcy proceedings have been instituted in Uganda and in pursuance of subsections (1) and (4) of this section the property of the debtor or bankrupt situated in Uganda vests in or is administered by a trustee or receiver in a reciprocating territory, the court shall rescind its receiving order and annul its order of adjudication, if made, or dismiss the petition upon such terms, if any, as the court may think fit.

(3) The rescission of a receiving order or an annulment of adjudication under subsection (2) shall not invalidate any acts lawfully done by the receiver or trustee of Uganda or any other person lawfully acting under the authority of either of them.

(4) Notwithstanding the other provisions of this section, in any case where concurrent bankruptcy proceedings have been instituted in Uganda the court may, after such inquiry and reference to such reciprocating courts as it deems fit, order that the property of the debtor situated in Uganda shall vest in or be administered by a trustee or receiver in Uganda or in some reciprocating territory other than that determined under the provisions of subsection (1) of this section if, upon an application by the official receiver or any creditor or other person interested, it appears that a majority of the creditors in number and value are resident in Uganda or such other reciprocating territory, and that from the situation of the property of the debtor or bankrupt or other causes his or her estate and effects may be more conveniently administered, managed and distributed in Uganda or such other reciprocating territory.

(5) The court shall not make an order under subsection (4) of this section unless it appears that a similar order has first been made by the reciprocating court of the territory wherein and according to the law of which the property of the debtor would have been administered under the provisions of subsection (1) of this section but for such order.

160. Power of official receiver, etc. to request an official receiver in a reciprocating territory to act as his or her agent.

(1) Where a receiving order or an order of adjudication is made in Uganda against a debtor or bankrupt having property situated in a reciprocating territory and where, under the provisions of this Act, the property of the debtor or bankrupt is administered by or vested in the official receiver or a trustee of or appointed in Uganda, it shall be the duty of such trustee and any interim receiver or special

manager appointed in pursuance of this Act to take all such steps as may be lawful in any reciprocating territory for the proper administration of any property of the debtor or bankrupt situated in such territory, and at his or her discretion and without further authority to request in the prescribed manner any bankruptcy official in such territory empowered in that behalf to act as his or her agent either generally or for any specific purpose, and to give such directions and to publish such notices and to do all such things in the reciprocating territory as may be lawful for the administration of the estate.

(2) Unless for any reason the contrary intention is expressed, every request sent to a bankruptcy official in a reciprocating territory requiring him or her to act as an agent as aforesaid shall contain a consent that he or she may assign the powers and duties vested in him or her as such agent to his or her deputy or any officer ordinarily authorised to act for him or her in the reciprocating territory.

(3) Where in any proceedings mentioned in subsection (1), the official receiver, interim receiver, special manager or trustee shall have completed and despatched to a reciprocating territory a request to a bankruptcy official therein to act as his or her agent as aforesaid and where the circumstances of the case so require, the court may, on the application of such official receiver, interim receiver, special manager or trustee and on an undertaking to indemnify against costs and charges being given, request the reciprocating court by telegram or otherwise to authorise the bankruptcy official of such court empowered in that behalf to act as agent until such time as the prescribed request shall arrive in the ordinary course of post.

161. Power to make special rules under this Part.

(1) The Chief Justice, with the approval of the Minister, may make rules for the purpose of carrying into effect all or any of the objects of this Part of this Act, and, in addition and for such purpose, shall have power to make rules extending or varying the time limited under this Act or any rules made under section 119 of this Act for the doing of any act or taking any proceeding, in so far as such limitation of time affects persons ordinarily resident or carrying on business in a reciprocating territory who are or may be interested in any bankruptcy proceedings in Uganda against a debtor having property in such reciprocating territory; no rules made under the powers conferred by this subsection shall come into force until the Chief Justice shall by statutory instrument declare himself or herself satisfied that the rule making authorities in all reciprocating territories have made rules having the like effect within their respective territories.

(2) Notwithstanding the provisions of subsection (1) of this section, the court may in respect of any particular matter exercise its general powers of extension of time under section 102 of this Act, in favour of a person ordinarily residing or carrying on business in a reciprocating territory, who is interested in bankruptcy proceedings instituted in Uganda against a debtor having property in such reciprocating territory.

PART X – GENERAL.

162. Bankruptcy Rules, 1915, applied.

Until the Chief Justice shall make general rules and prescribes fees under the powers conferred in sections 119 and 120 of this Act the Bankruptcy Rules, 1915, made under section 132 of the Bankruptcy Act, 1914, of the United Kingdom and the scale of fees prescribed under section 133 of the same Act are declared to be in force in Uganda and shall be read with and considered as part of this Act and it shall be lawful for the court to construe the said rules with such verbal alterations not affecting the substance as may be deemed expedient to render the same applicable to local circumstances and to any matters before the court; except that any such construction or alteration shall not be inconsistent with the provisions of this Act.

——————

SCHEDULES

First Schedule

RULES AS TO MEETING OF CREDITORS.

1. The first meeting of creditors shall be summoned for a day not later than twenty-eight days after the date of the receiving order, unless the court for any special reason deems it expedient that the meeting be summoned for a later day.
2. The official receiver shall summon the meeting by giving not less than six clear day's notice of the time and place thereof in the Gazette.
3. The official receiver shall also, as soon as practicable, send to each creditor mentioned in the debtor's statement of affairs a notice of the time and place of the first meeting of creditors, accompanied by a summary of the debtor's statement of affairs, including the cause of his or her failure, and any observations thereon, which the official receiver may think fit to make; but the proceedings at the first meeting shall not be invalidated by reason of any such notice or summary not having been sent or received before the meeting.
4. The meeting shall be held at such place as is in the opinion of the official receiver most convenient for the majority of the creditors.
5. The official receiver or the trustee may at any time summon a meeting of creditors, and shall do so whenever so directed by the court, or so requested by a creditor in accordance with the provisions of this Act.
6. Meetings subsequent to the first meeting shall be summoned by sending notice of the time and place thereof to each creditor at the address given in his or she proof, or if he or she has not proved, at the address given in the debtor's statement of affairs or at such other address as may be known to the person summoning the meeting.

7. The official receiver, or some person nominated by him or her, shall be the chairperson at the first meeting
8. The chairperson at subsequent meetings shall be such person as the meeting by resolution appoint.
9. A person shall not be entitled to vote as a creditor at the first or any other meeting of creditors unless he or she has duly proved a debt provable in bankruptcy to be due to him or her from the debtor, and the proof has been duly lodged before the time appointed for the meeting.
10. A creditor shall not vote at any such meeting in respect of any unliquidated or contingent debt, or any debt the value of which is not ascertained.
11. For the purpose of voting, a secured creditor shall, unless he or she surrenders his security, state in his or her proof the particulars of his security, the date when it was given, and the value at which he or she assesses it, and shall be entitled to vote only in respect of the balance, if any, due to him or her, after deducting the value of his or her security.
12. If a second creditor votes in respect of his or her whole debt he or she shall be deemed to have surrendered his or her security unless the court on application is satisfied that the omission to value his or her security has arisen from inadvertence.
13. A creditor shall not vote in respect of any debt on or secured by a current bill of exchange or promissory note held by him or her, unless he or she is willing to treat the liability to him or her thereon of every person who is liable thereon antecedently to the debtor, and against whom a receiving order has not been made, as a security in his or her hands, and to estimate the value thereof and for the purposes of voting, but not for the purposes of dividend, to deduct it from his or her proof.
14. It shall be competent to the trustee or to the official receiver, within twenty-eight days after a proof estimating the value of a security as aforesaid has been made use of in voting at any meeting, to require the creditor to give up the security for the benefit of the creditors generally on payment of the value so estimated with an addition thereto of twenty per centum; except that where a creditor has put a value on such security, he or she may, at any time before he has been required to give up such security as aforesaid, correct such valuation by a new proof and deduct such new value from his or her debt, but in that case such addition of twenty per centum shall not be made if the trustee requires the security to be given up.
15. If a receiving order is made against one partner of a firm, any creditor to whom that partner is indebted jointly with the other partners of the firm, or any of them, may prove his or her debt for the purposes of voting at any meeting of creditors, and shall be entitled to vote thereat.
16. The chairman of a meeting shall have power to admit or reject a proof for the purpose of voting, but his or her decision shall be subject to appeal to the court.
17. If the chairperson is in doubt whether the proof of a creditor should be admitted or rejected he or she shall mark the proof as objected to, and shall allow the creditor to vote, subject to the vote being declared invalid in the event of the objection being sustained.

18. A creditor may vote either in person or by proxy.

19. Every instrument of proxy shall be in the prescribed form, and shall be issued by the official receiver of the debtor's estate or by any deputy official receiver, or, after the appointment of a trustee, by the trustee, and every insertion therein shall be in the handwriting of the person giving the proxy, or of any manager or clerk, or other person in his or her regular employment or of any person authorised to administer oaths in the court.

20. General and special forms of proxy shall be sent to the creditors, together with a notice summoning a meeting of creditors, and neither the name nor the description of the official receiver, or of any other person, shall be printed or inserted in the body of any instrument of proxy before it is so sent.

21. A creditor may give a general proxy to his or her manager or clerk, or any other person in his or her regular employment.

22. In such case the instrument of proxy shall state the relation in which the person to act thereunder stands to the creditor.

23. A creditor may give a special proxy to any person to vote at any specified meeting or adjournment thereof on all or any of the following matters –

    (a) for or against any specific proposal for a composition or scheme of arrangement;

    (b) for or against the appointment of any specified person as trustee at a specified rate of remuneration, or as member of the committee of inspection, or for or against the continuance in office of any specified person as trustee or member of a committee of inspection;

    (c) on all questions relating to any matter other than those above referred to, arising at any specified meeting or adjournment thereof.

24. A proxy shall not be used unless it is deposited with the official receiver or trustee before the meeting at which it is to be used.

25. Where it appears to the satisfaction of the court that any solicitation has been used by or on behalf of a trustee or receiver in obtaining proxies, or in procuring the trusteeship or receivership, except by the direction of a meeting of creditors, the court shall have power, if it thinks fit, to order that no remuneration shall be allowed to the person by whom or on whose behalf such solicitation may have been exercised, notwithstanding any resolution of the committee of inspection or of the creditors to the contrary.

26. A creditor may appoint the official receiver to act in manner prescribed as his or her general or special proxy.

27. The chairperson of a meeting may, with the consent of the meeting, adjourn the meeting from time to time and from place to place.

28. A meeting shall not be competent to act for any purpose, except the election of a chairperson, the proving of debts, and the adjournment of the meeting, unless there are present, or represented thereat, at least three creditors, or all the creditors if their number does not exceed three.

29. If within half an hour from the time appointed for the meeting a quorum of creditors is not present or represented, the meeting shall be adjourned to such other day as the chairperson may appoint, being not less than three nor more than twenty-one days later.

30. The chairperson of every meeting shall cause minutes of the proceedings at the meeting to be drawn up and fairly entered in a book kept for that purpose, and the minutes shall be signed by him or her or by the chairperson of the next meeting.
31. No person acting either under a general or special proxy shall vote in favour of any resolution which would directly or indirectly place himself or herself, his or her partner or employer in a position to receive any remuneration out of the estate of the debtor otherwise than as a creditor rateably with the other creditors of the debtor; but where any person holds special proxies to vote for the appointment of himself or herself as trustee he or she may use the said proxies and vote accordingly.
32. The vote of the trustee, or of his or her partner, clerk, advocate, or advocate's clerk, either as creditor, or as proxy for a creditor, shall not be reckoned in the majority required for passing any resolution affecting the remuneration or conduct of the trustee.

SECOND SCHEDULE.

Rules as to proof of debts

Proof in ordinary cases

1. Every creditor shall prove his or her debt as soon as may be after the making of a receiving order.
2. A debt may be proved by delivering or sending through the post in a prepaid letter to the official receiver, or, if a trustee has been appointed, to the trustee, an affidavit verifying the debt.
3. The affidavit may be made by the creditor himself or herself, or by some person authorised by or on behalf of the creditor.
4. If made by a person so authorised it shall state his or her authority and means of knowledge.
5. The affidavit shall contain or refer to a statement of account showing the particulars of the debt, and shall specify the vouchers, if any, by which the same can be substantiated.
6. The official receiver or trustee may at any time call for the production of the vouchers.
7. The affidavit shall state whether the creditor is or is not a secured creditor, and if it is found at any time that the affidavit made by or on behalf of a secured creditor has omitted to state that he or she is a secured creditor, the secured creditor shall surrender his or her security to the official receiver or trustee for the general benefit of the creditors unless the court on application is satisfied that the omission has arisen from inadvertence, and in that case the court may allow the affidavit to be amended upon such terms as to the repayment of any dividends or otherwise as the court may consider to be just.
8. A creditor shall bear the cost of proving his or her debt, unless the court otherwise specially orders.

9. Every creditor who has lodged a proof shall be entitled to see and examine the proofs of other creditors before the first meeting, and at all reasonable times.

10. A creditor proving his or her debt shall deduct therefrom all trade discounts, but he or she shall not be compelled to deduct any discount, not exceeding 5 percent on the net amount of his or her claim, which he or she may have agreed to allow for payment in cash.

Proof by secured creditors

11. If a secured creditor realises his or her security, he or she may prove for the balance due to him or her, after deducting the net amount realised.

12. If a secured creditor surrenders his or her security to the official receiver or trustee for the general benefit of the creditors, he or she may prove for his or her whole debt.

13. If a secured creditor does not either realise or surrender his or her security, he or she shall, before ranking for dividend, state in his or her proof the particulars of his or her security, the date when it was given, and the value at which he or she assesses it, and shall be entitled to receive a dividend only in respect of the balance due to him or her after deducting the value so assessed.

14. (1) Where a security is so valued–

(a) the trustee may at any time redeem it on payment to the creditor of the assessed value;

(b) if the trustee is dissatisfied with the value at which a security is assessed, he or she may require that the property comprised in any security so valued be offered for sale at such times and on such terms and conditions as may be agreed on between the creditor and the trustee, or as, in default of such agreement, the court may direct.

(2) If the sale be by public auction, the creditor, or the trustee on behalf of the estate, may bid or purchase:

Notwithstanding subrule (1) the creditor may at any time, by notice in writing, require the trustee to elect whether he or she will or will not exercise his or her power of redeeming the security or requiring it to be realised, and if the trustee does not, within six months after receiving the notice, signify in writing to the creditor his or her election to exercise the power, he or she shall not be entitled to exercise it; and the equity of redemption, or any other interest in the property comprised in the security which is vested in the trustee, shall vest in the creditor and the amount of his or her debt shall be reduced by the amount at which the security has been valued.

15. Where a creditor has so valued his or her security, he may at any time amend the valuation and proof on showing to the satisfaction of the trustee, or the court, that the valuation and proof were made bona fide on a mistaken estimate or that the security has diminished or increased in value since its previous valuation; but every such amendment shall be made at the cost of the creditor, and upon such terms as the court shall order, unless the trustee shall allow the amendment without application to the court.

16. Where a valuation has been amended in accordance with rule 15, the creditor shall forthwith repay any surplus dividend which he or she may have received in

excess of that to which he or she would have been entitled on the amended valuation, or, as the case may be, shall be entitled to be paid out of any money, for the time being available for dividend, any dividend or share of dividend, which he or she may have failed to receive by reason of the inaccuracy of the original valuation, before that money is made applicable to the payment of any future dividend, but he or she shall not be entitled to disturb the distribution of any dividend declared before the date of the amendment.

17. If a creditor after having valued his or her security subsequently realises it, or if it is realised under the provisions of rule 14 of this Schedule, the net amount realised shall be substituted for the amount of any valuation previously made by the creditor and shall be treated in all respects as an amended valuation made by the creditor.

18. If a secured creditor does not comply with the foregoing rules he or she shall be excluded from all share in any dividend.

19. Subject to the provisions of rule 12 of this Schedule, a creditor shall in no case receive more than twenty shillings in the pound, and interest as provided by this Act.

Proof in respect of distinct contracts

20. If a debtor was, at the date of the receiving order, liable in respect of distinct contracts as a member of two or more distinct firms, or as a sole contractor, and also as a member of a firm, the circumstances that the firms are in whole or in part composed of the same individuals, or that the sole contractor is also one of the joint contractors, shall not prevent proof in respect of the contracts, against the properties respectively liable on the contracts.

Periodical payments

21. When any rent or other payment falls due at stated periods, and the receiving order is made at any time other than one of these periods, the persons entitled to the rent or payment may prove for a proportionate part thereof up to the date of the order as if the rent or payment grew due from day to day.

Interest

22. On any debt or sum certain, payable at a certain time or otherwise, whereon interest is not reserved or agreed for, and which is overdue at the date of the receiving order and provable in bankruptcy, the creditor may prove for interest at a rate not exceeding 6 percent per year to the date of the order from the time when the debt or sum was payable, if the debt or sum is payable by virtue of a written instrument at a certain time, and if payable otherwise, then from the time when a demand in writing has been made giving the debtor notice that interest will be claimed from the date of the demand until the time of payment.

Debt payable at a future time

23. A creditor may prove for a debt not payable when the debtor committed an act of bankruptcy as if it were payable presently, and may receive dividends equally

with the other creditors, deducting only thereout a rebate of interest at the rate of five per centum per annum computed from the declaration of a dividend to the time when the debt would have become payable, according to the terms on which it was contracted.

Admission or rejection of proofs

24. The trustee shall examine every proof and the grounds of the debt, and in writing admit or reject it, in whole or in part, or require further evidence in support of it.
25. If the trustee rejects a proof he or she shall state in writing to the creditor the grounds of the rejection.
26. If the trustee thinks that a proof has been improperly admitted, the court may, on the application of the trustee, after notice to the creditor who made the proof, expunge the proof or reduce its amount.
27. If a creditor is dissatisfied with the decision of the trustee in respect of a proof, the court may, on the application of the creditor, reverse or vary the decision.
28. The court may also expunge or reduce a proof upon the application of a creditor if the trustee declines to interfere in the matter, or, in the case of a composition or scheme, upon the application of the debtor.
29. For the purpose of any of his duties in relation to proofs, the trustee may administer oaths and take affidavits.
30. The official receiver, before the appointment of a trustee, shall have all the powers of a trustee with respect to the examination, admission, and rejection of proofs, and any of his or her act or decision in relation thereto shall be subject to the like appeal.

CHAPTER 342

THE STAMPS ACT

Arrangement of Sections

SECTION

Valuations for duty

Duty by whom payable

PART III – ADJUDICATIONS AS TO STAMPS

PART IV – INSTRUMENTS NOT DULY STAMPED

Part V – Allowances for Stamps in Certain cases

Part VI – Reference and Revision

Part VII – Criminal Offences and Procedure

Part VII I– Supplemental Provisions

Schedule

CHAPTER 342

THE STAMPS ACT

An act to provide for stamp duties **Commencement: 30 April 1915**

PART I – INTERPRETATION

1. Interpretation.

In this Act, unless there is something repugnant in the subject or context –

(a) "banker" includes a bank and any person acting a banker;

(b) "bill of exchange" means a bill of exchange as defined by section 27 of the Bills of Exchange Act and includes also a draft, order, cheque, letter of credit, and any other document, entitling or purporting to entitle any person, whether named in it or not, to payment by any other person of, or to draw upon any other person for, any sum of money;

(c) "bill of exchange payable on demand" includes –

(i) an order for the payment of any sum of money by a bill of exchange or promissory note, or for the delivery of any bill of exchange or promissory note in satisfaction of any sum of money, or for the payment of any sum of money out of any particular fund which may or may not be available, or upon any condition or contingency which may or may not be performed or happen;

(ii) an order for the payment of any sum of money weekly, monthly or at any other stated periods; and

(iii) a letter of credit, that is to say, any instrument by which one person authorises another to give credit to the person in whose favour it is drawn;

(d) "bill of lading" includes a "through bill of lading", but does not include a mate's receipt;

(e) "bond" includes –

(i) any instrument by which a person obliges himself or herself to pay money to another, on condition that the obligation shall be void if a specified act is performed, or is not performed, as the case may be;

(ii) any instrument attested by a witness and not payable to order or bearer, whereby a person obliges himself or herself to pay money to another; and

(iii) any instrument so attested, whereby a person obliges himself or herself to deliver grain or other agricultural produce to another;

(f) "chargeable" means, as applied to an instrument executed or first executed after the commencement of this Act, chargeable under this Act, and, as applied to any other instrument, chargeable under the law in force in Uganda when the instrument was executed or, where several persons executed the instrument at different times, first executed;

(g) "cheque" means a bill of exchange drawn on a specified banker and not expressed to be payable otherwise than on demand;

(h) "conveyance" includes a conveyance on sale and every instrument by which property, whether movable or immovable, is transferred *inter vivos* and which is not otherwise specifically provided for by the Schedule to this Act;

(i) "conveyance on sale" includes every instrument and every decree or order of a court by which any property, or any estate or interest in any property, upon the sale is transferred to or vested in a purchaser, or any other person on the purchaser's behalf or by his or her direction;

(j) "deed" includes any instrument which confers any right or passes any interest or gives any title or authority;

(k) "duly stamped", as applied to an instrument, means that the instrument bears an adhesive or impressed stamp of not less than the proper amount, and that such stamp has been affixed or used in accordance with the law for the time being in force in Uganda;

(l) "executed" and "execution", used with reference to instruments, mean "signed" and "signature",

(m) "impressed stamp" includes –

(i) labels affixed and impressed by the proper officer; and

(ii) stamps embossed or engraved on stamped paper;

(n) "instrument" includes every document by which any right or liability is, or purports to be, created, transferred, limited, extended, extinguished or recorded;

(o) "instrument of partition" means any instrument whereby co-owners of any property divide or agree to divide such property in severalty, and includes also a final order for effecting a partition passed by any civil court and an award by an arbitrator directing a partition;

(p) "lease" means a lease of immovable property, an under-lease or sub-lease, and any agreement to let or sub-let the same, and includes also –

(i) a grant for a term of the right to use and enjoy any easement, *profit a prendre,* or incorporeal right,

(ii) any instrument by which tolls of any description are let;

(iii) any writing on an application for a lease intended to signify that the application is granted;

(q) "marketable security" means a security of such a description as to be capable of being sold on a stock market;

(r) "mortgage deed" includes every instrument whereby, for the purpose of securing money advanced, or to be advanced, by way of loan, or an existing or future debt, or the performance of an engagement, one person transfers, or creates, to, or in favour of, another, a right over or in respect of specified property;

(s) "paper" includes vellum, parchment, or any other material on which an instrument may be written;

(t) "policy of insurance" includes –

(i) any instrument by which one person, in consideration of a premium, engages to indemnify another against loss, damage or liability arising form an unknown or contingent event;

(ii) a life-policy, and any policy insuring any person against accident or sickness, and any other personal insurance;

(u) "policy of sea-insurance" or "sea-policy" –

(i) means any insurance made upon any ship or vessel (whether for marine or inland navigation), or upon the machinery, tackle or furniture of any ship or vessel, or upon any goods, merchandise or property of any description on board of any ship or vessel, or upon the freight of, or any other interest which may be lawfully insured in, or relating to, any ship or vessel; and

(ii) includes any insurance of goods, merchandise or property for any transit which includes, not only a sea risk within the meaning of sub paragraph *(1)* but also any other risk incidental to the transit insured from the commencement of the transit to the ultimate destination covered by the insurance.

(iii) Where any person, in consideration of any sum of money paid or to be paid for additional freight or otherwise, agrees to take upon himself or herself any risk attending goods, merchandise or property of any description while on board of any ship or vessel, or engages to indemnify the owner of any such goods, merchandise or property from any risk, loss or damage, the agreement or engagement shall be deemed to be a contract for sea-insurance;

(v) "power of attorney" includes any instrument (not chargeable with a fee under the law relating to court fees for the time being in force) empowering a specified person to act for and in the name of the person executing it;

(w) "promissory note" means promissory note as defined by section 82 of the Bills of Exchange Act and includes a note promising the payment of any sum of money out of any particular fund which may or may not be available, or upon any condition or contingency which may or may not be performed or happen;

(x) "receipt" includes any note, memorandum or writing whether the same is or is not signed with the name of any person –

(i) by which any money, or any bill of exchange, cheque or promissory note is acknowledged to have been received; or

(ii) by which any other movable property is acknowledged to have been received in satisfaction of a debt; or

(iii) by which any debt or demand, or any part of a debt or demand, is acknowledged to have been satisfied or discharged; or

(iv) which signifies or imports any such acknowledgement;

(y) "Revenue Authority" means the officer appointed in that behalf by the Minister by statutory order;

(z) "settlement" means any non-testamentary disposition in writing of movable or immovable property made –

(i) in consideration of marriage;

(ii) for the purpose of distributing property of the settler among his or her family or those for whom he or she desires to provide, or for the purpose of providing for some person dependent on him or her; or

(iii) for any religious or charitable purpose, and includes an agreement in writing to make such a disposition, and where any such disposition has not been made in writing any instrument recording, whether by way of declaration of trust or otherwise, the terms of any such disposition.

PART II – STAMP DUTIES

Liability of instruments to duty

2. Instruments chargeable with duty.

(1) Subject to the provisions of this Act and the exemption contained in the Schedule to this Act, the following instruments shall be chargeable with duty of the amount indicated in that Schedule as the proper duty therefor respectively, –

(a) every instrument mentioned in that Schedule which, not having been previously executed by any person, is executed in Uganda after the commencement of this Act and relates to any property situate, or to any matter or thing done or to be done, in Uganda;

(b) every bill of exchange, cheque or promissory note drawn or made out of Uganda after the commencement of this Act and accepted or paid, or presented for acceptance or payment, or endorsed, transferred or otherwise negotiated, in Uganda; and

(c) every instrument (other than a bill of exchange, cheque or promissory note) mentioned in that Schedule, which, not having been previously executed by any person, is executed out of Uganda after the commencement of this Act, relates to any property situate, or to any matter or thing done or to be done, in Uganda and is received in Uganda.

(2) Notwithstanding subsection (1) –

(a) no duty shall be chargeable in respect of any instrument executed by, or on behalf of, or in favour of, the Government in cases where, but for this exemption, the Government would be liable to pay the duty chargeable in respect of the instrument; and

(b) every bill of exchange, cheque or promissory note drawn or made in Kenya or Tanzania and accepted and paid or presented for acceptance or payment, or endorsed, transferred or otherwise negotiated in Uganda, and which has previously been duly stamped in Kenya or Tanzania shall be deemed to be duly stamped in Uganda.

(3) For the purpose of subsection (2) (a), the expression "Government" shall be deemed to include the Uganda People's Defence Forces.

(4) The Minister may, by statutory instrument, amend the Schedule to this Act.

(5) An instrument made under subsection (4) shall be laid before Parliament and shall be subject to annulment by Parliament, and shall cease to have effect when so annulled, but without prejudice to anything contained in that instrument or the making of a further instrument.

3. Several instruments used in single transaction of sale, mortgate or settlement.

(1) Where, in the case of any sale, mortgage, or settlement, several instruments are employed for completing the transaction, the principal instrument only shall be chargeable with the duty prescribed in the Schedule to this Act for the conveyance, mortgage or settlement, and each of the other instruments shall be chargeable with a duty of two shillings instead of the duty, if any, prescribed for it in that Schedule; except that a power of attorney empowering a person to execute or to register such instrument or instruments shall be chargeable with the duty prescribed in the Schedule for such power of attorney.

(2) The parties may determine for themselves which of the instruments soemployed shall, for the purpose of subsection (1) of this section, be deemed to be the principal instrument; but the duty chargeable on the instrument so determined shall be the highest duty which would be chargeable in respect of any of the said instruments employed.

(3) Any instrument modifying the terms of a mortgage in respect of the reduction of principal or raising or reducing the rate of interest or varying the terms of repayment of principal shall be dutiable as an agreement.

4. Instruments relating to several distinct matters.

Any instrument comprising or relating to several distinct matters shall be chargeable with the aggregate amount of the duties with which separate instruments, each comprising or relating to one of such matters, would be chargeable under this Act.

5. Instruments coming within several descriptions in Schedule.

(1) Subject to section (4), an instrument so framed as to come within two or more of the descriptions in the Schedule to this Act shall, where the duties chargeable thereunder are different, be chargeable only with the highest of the duties:

(2) Notwithstanding subsection (1) nothing in this Act contained shall render chargeable with duty exceeding two shillings a counterpart or duplicate of any instrument chargeable with duty and in respect of which the proper duty has been paid.

6. Policies of sea-insurance.

(1) No contract for sea-insurance, other than such insurance as is referred to in section 506 of the Merchant Shipping Act, 1894, of the United Kingdom, shall be valid unless the same is expressed in a sea-policy.

(2) No sea-policy made for time shall be made for any time exceeding twelve months.

(3) No sea-policy shall be valid unless it specifies the particular risk or adventure, or the time, for which it is made, the names of the subscribers or underwriters, and the amount or amounts insured.

(4) Where any sea-insurance is made for or upon a voyage and also for time, or to extend to or cover any time beyond thirty days after the ship shall have arrived at her destination and been there moored at anchor, the policy shall be charged with duty as a policy for or upon a voyage, and also with duty as a policy for time.

7. Composition of stamp duty on policies of insurance against accident.

(1) Where any person issuing policies of insurance against accident shall, in the opinion of the Revenue Authority, so carry on the business of such insurance as to render it impracticable or inexpedient to require that the duty chargeable under Article 49 of the Schedule to this Act shall be paid upon the said policies, the Revenue Authority may, at the request of such person, enter into an agreement with such person for the delivery to him of quarterly accounts of all sums received in respect of premiums on such policies of insurance.

(2) The agreement shall be in such form and shall contain such terms and conditions as the Revenue Authority may think proper, and the person with whom the agreement is entered into shall observe the rules set out in the Second Part of the Schedule to this Act.

(3) After an agreement has been entered into, in accordance with the provisions of this section, between the Revenue Authority and any person, during the period for which the agreement is in force no policies of insurance against accident issued by that person shall be chargeable with any duty, but in lieu of and by way of composition for that duty there shall be charged on the aggregate amount of all sums received in respect of premiums on such policies a duty at the rate of five per centum as a stamp duty.

(4) If the duty charged is not paid upon the delivery of the account it shall be a debt due to the Revenue Authority from the person by or on whose behalf the account is delivered.

(5) In the case of neglect to deliver such an account as is hereby required or to pay the duty in conformity with this section the person shall be liable to pay to the Revenue Authority a sum equal to ten per centum upon the amount of duty payable, and a like penalty for every month after the first month during which the neglect continues.

8. Rules for the compounding of duty on cheques.

(1) Notwithstanding anything contained in any of the provisions of this Act, the Minister may, by statutory instrument, make rules respecting the compounding of duty on cheques by bankers and without restricting the generality of the foregoing provisions such rules may provide.

- (a) for the procedure to be adopted in, and the terms and conditions to be observed in, the compounding of stamp duty on cheques;
- (b) for the rendering of accounts to the Commissioner/Treasury Officer of Accounts in respect of cheques issued pursuant to the provisions of such rules;
- (c) the time within which such accounts shall be rendered, and the particulars which may be given together with the accounts; and
- (d) the penalty (which shall not in any case exceed a fine of one thousand shillings) and any interest to be charged on the duty due and not paid which may be imposed on any banker who makes default in delivering such accounts or on paying the duty payable on such accounts.

(2) When rules permitting the compounding of stamp duty on cheques have been made, any cheques issued by a banker in accordance with the provisions of such rules shall not be chargeable with stamp duty but the banker shall pay to the Commissioner/Treasury Officer of Accounts such sums as would, but for the provisions of such rules, have been chargeable by way of stamp duty on the cheques issued during the period specified in the rules.

9. Stamp duty on capital of companies.

(1) Where any company is to be incorporated in Uganda with limited liability, or where the nominal share capital of any company so incorporated is to be increased, there shall be delivered as the case may be to the Registrar of Companies –

(a) a statement of the amount which is to form the nominal share capital of the company to be incorporated; or

(b) a statement of the increase of the nominal share capital which may embody the notice of increased capital required by section 65 of the Companies Act.

(2) The statements referred to in subsection (1) of this section shall be charged with an *ad valorem* duty of five shillings for every one thousand shillings and for any fraction of one thousand shillings over any multiple of one thousand shillings of the amount of such capital or increase of capital as the case may be.

(3) The statement of the amount of any increase of nominal capital which is required to be delivered under paragraph *(b)* of subsection (1) of this section shall be delivered to the Registrar of Companies within thirty days after the passing of the resolution authorising the increase, and, in default of delivery, the duty, with interest thereon at the rate of five per centum per annum from the passing of the resolution, shall be recoverable summarily as a civil debt from the company.

10. Power to reduce, remit or compound duties.

The Minister, by statutory instrument, may –

(a) in relation to the whole or any part of Uganda, reduce or grant exemption from the payment of the duties with which any instruments or any particular class of instruments, or any of the instruments belonging to such class, of any instruments when executed by or in favour of any particular class or persons, or by or in favour of any members of such class, are chargeable; and

(b) provide for the composition or consolidation of duties in the case of issues by any incorporated company or other body corporate of debentures, bonds or other marketable securities.

11. Exemption of savings bank documents from stamp duty.

(1) Notwithstanding anything in this Act contained, no power, warrant, or letters of attorney granted or to be granted by the managing director of Post Bank Uganda Limited, nor any power, warrant or letters of attorney given by any depositor in the savings bank to any other person, authorising that person to make any deposit of any sum of money in the savings bank on behalf of the said depositor or to sign any document or instrument required by the rules or regulations of the

savings bank to be signed on making such deposit or to receive back any sum of money deposited in the savings bank, or the interest arising therefrom, nor any receipt nor any entry in any book of receipts nor money deposited in the savings bank, nor for any money received by any depositor, his or her executors or administrators, assigns, attorneys or agents, from the funds thereof, nor any draft or order, nor any appointment of any agent, nor any certificate, or other instrument or document required or authorised to be given, issued, signed, made or produced in pursuance of the Post Office Savings Bank Act, or of any Act amending or replacing it, shall be subject or charged with, any stamp duty or duties whatsoever.

(2) "Savings bank" in this section means the savings bank established under the provisions of the Post Office Savings Bank Act, or any Act amending or replacing it.

Stamps and the mode of using them

12. Duties, how to be paid.

(1) Except as otherwise expressly provided in this Act, all duties with which any instruments are chargeable shall be paid, and such payment shall be indicated on the instruments by means of stamps in such manner as the Minister may by rules direct.

(2) Rules made under subsection (1) of this section may among other matters regulate –

(a) in the case of each kind of instrument, the description of stamps which may be used;

(b) in the case of instruments stamped with impressed stamps, the number of stamps which may be used;

(c) in the case of bills of exchange or promissory notes, the size of the paper on which they are written.

13. Provisional use of stamps previously usable.

Until rules shall be made under section 12 hereof, any stamps which might lawfully be used immediately before the commencement of this Act for the payment of duties with which any instruments were chargeable may be used for the purpose of this Act.

14. Cancellation of adhesive stamps.

(1) Any person who –

(a) affixes any adhesive stamp to any instrument chargeable with duty which has been executed by any person shall, when affixing such stamp, cancel the same so that it cannot be used again; and

(b) executes any instrument on any paper bearing an adhesive stamp shall, at the time of execution, unless such stamp has been already cancelled in manner aforesaid, cancel it so that it cannot be used again.

(2) Any instrument bearing an adhesive stamp which has not been cancelled so that it cannot be used again shall, so far as such stamp is concerned, be deemed to be unstamped.

(3) The person required by subsection (1) of this section to cancel an adhesive stamp shall cancel it by writing on or across the stamp his or her name or initials or the name or initials of his or her firm with the true date of his or her so writing; but the Minister may by rule or statutory instrument prescribe any other mode of cancellation of adhesive stamps on any particular instrument or instruments or any particular class of instruments.

15. Instruments stamped with impressed stamps how to be written

Every instrument written upon paper stamped with an impressed stamp shall be written in such manner that the stamp may appear on the face of the instrument and cannot be used for or applied to any other instrument.

16. Only one instrument to be on same stamp.

(1) No second instrument chargeable with duty shall be written upon a piece of stamped paper upon which an instrument chargeable with duty has already been written:

(2) Nothing in this section shall prevent any endorsement which is duly stamped or is not chargeable with duty being made upon any instrument for the purpose of transferring any right created or evidenced the instrument, or of acknowledging the receipt of any money or goods, the payment or delivery of which is secured the instrument.

17. Instrument written contrary to section 15 or 16 deemed unstamped.

Every instrument written in contravention of section 15 or 16 of this Act shall be deemed to be unstamped.

18. Denoting duty.

Where the duty with which an instrument is chargeable, or its exemption from duty, depends in any manner upon the duty actually paid in respect of another instrument, the payment of such last mentioned duty shall, if application is made in writing to the Revenue Authority for that purpose, and on production of both the instruments, be denoted upon the first-mentioned instrument by endorsement under the hand of the Revenue Authority or in such other manner, if any, as the Minister may by rule prescribe.

19. Provisions as to duplicate and counterparts.

The duplicate or counterpart of an instrument chargeable with duty, except the counterpart of an instrument chargeable as a lease such counterpart not being executed by or on behalf of any lessor or grantor, is not to be deemed to be duly stamped unless it is stamped as an original instrument or unless it appears by some stamp impressed on it that the full and proper duty has been paid upon the original instrument of which it is the duplicate or counterpart.

Time of stamping instruments.

20. Instruments executed in Uganda.

Every instrument chargeable with duty which is executed by any person in Uganda shall be stamped within thirty days of execution:
except that any instrument chargeable with duty of ten cents or twenty cents and any promissory note and bill of exchange shall be stamped at or before the time of execution or the date of the instrument, whichever is the earlier.

21. Instruments executed out of Uganda.

Every instrument chargeable with duty which is wholly executed out of Uganda shall be stamped within thirty days of being received in Uganda:
Provided that a promissory note or bill of exchange payable on demand or at not more than thirty days from sight or date shall be stamped within seven days of being received in Uganda.

22. Bills, cheques and noted drawn out of Uganda.

(1) The first holder in Uganda of any bill of exchange, cheque or promissory note drawn or made out of Uganda shall, before he presents the same for acceptance or payment, or endorses, transfers or otherwise negotiates the same in Uganda, affix thereto the proper stamp and cancel the same:

(2) Notwithstanding subsection (1) if, at the time any such bill of exchange, cheque or note comes into the hands of any holder thereof in Uganda, the proper adhesive stamp is affixed to it and cancelled in manner prescribed by section 14 of this Act and such holder has no reason to believe that such stamp was affixed or cancelled otherwise than by the person and at the time required by this Act, such stamp shall, so far as relates to such holder, be deemed to have been duly affixed and cancelled; but nothing in this subsection shall relieve any person from any penalty incurred by him or her for omitting to affix or cancel a stamp.

Valuations for duty

23. Conversation of amount expressed in foreign currencies.

Where an instrument is chargeable with *ad valorem* duty in respect of any money expressed in any currency other than that of Uganda, such duty shall be calculated on the value of such money in the currency of Uganda according to the current rate of exchange on the day of the date of the instrument.

24. Stock and marketable securities, how to be valued.

(1) Where an instrument is chargeable with *ad valorem* duty in respect of any stock or of any marketable or other security, such duty shall be calculated on the value of such stock or security according to the average price or the value thereof on the day of the date of the instrument:

(2) Notwithstanding subsection (1) where the consideration for any conveyance or transfer of property is stock or any marketable or other security and in the opinion of the Revenue Authority the consideration is inadequate, having regard to the value of such stock or security calculated as aforesaid, *ad valorem* duty shall be charged on the value of the property to be conveyed or transferred.

25. Effect of statement of rate of exchange or average price.

Where an instrument contains a statement of current rate of exchange, or average price, as the case may require, and is stamped in accordance with such statement, it shall, so far as regards the subject-matter of such statement, be presumed, until the contrary is proved, to be duly stamped.

26. Instruments reserving interest.

Where interest is expressly made payable by the terms of an instrument, such instrument shall not be chargeable with duty higher than that with which it would have been chargeable had no mention of interest been made the instrument.

27. Certain instruments connected with mortgages of marketable securities to be chargeable as agreements.

(1) Where an instrument, not being a promissory note or bill of exchange –

(a) is given upon the occasion of the deposit of any marketable security by way of security for money advanced or to be advanced by way of loan, or for an existing or future debt; or

(b) makes redeemable or qualifies a duly stamped transfer intended as a security, of any marketable security, it shall be chargeable with duty as if it were an agreement or memorandum of an agreement chargeable with duty under Article 5 of the Schedule to this Act.

(2) A release or discharge of any such instrument shall be chargeable only with the like duty.

28. How transfer in consideration of debt or subject to future payment, etc, to be charged.

(1) Where any property is transferred to any person in consideration, wholly or in part, of any debt due to the person, or subject either certainly or contingently to the payment or transfer of any money or stock, whether being or constituting a charge or incumbrance upon the property or not, such debt, money or stock is to be deemed the whole or part, as the case may be, of the consideration in respect whereof the transfer is chargeable with *ad valorem* duty; except that nothing in this subsection shall apply to any such certificate of sale as is mentioned in Article 20 of the Schedule to this Act.

(2) In the case of a sale of property subject to a mortgage or other incumbrance, any unpaid mortgage-money or money charged, together with the interest, if any, due on the incumbrance, shall be deemed to be part of the consideration for the sale:

(3) Where property subject to a mortgage is transferred to the mortgagee, the mortgagee shall be entitled to deduct from the duty payable on the transfer the amount of any duty already paid in respect of the mortgage.

29. Valuation in case of annuity, etc.

Where an instrument is executed to secure the payment of an annuity or other sum payable periodically, or where the consideration for a conveyance is an annuity or other sum payable periodically, the amount secured by such instrument or the consideration for the conveyance, as the case may be, shall, for the purposes of this Act, be deemed to be –

(a) where the sum is payable for a definite period so that the total amount to be paid can be previously ascertained, such total amount;

(b) where the sum is payable in perpetuity or for an indefinite time not terminable with any life in being at the date of such instrument or conveyance, the total amount which, according to the terms of such instrument or conveyance, will or may be payable during the period of twenty years calculated from the date on which the first payment becomes due; and

(c) where the sum is payable for an indefinite time terminable with any life in being at the date of such instrument or conveyance, the maximum amount which will or may be payable as aforesaid during the period of twelve years calculated from the date on which the first payment becomes due.

30. Stamp where value of subject matter is indeterminate.

(1) Where the amount or value of the subject matter of any instrument chargeable with *ad valorem* duty cannot be, or, in the case of an instrument executed before the commencement of this Act, could not have been, ascertained at the date of its execution, or first execution; nothing shall be claimable under the instrument more than the highest amount or value for which, if stated in an instrument of the same description, the stamp actually used would, at the date of such execution, have been sufficient:

(2) Notwithstanding subsection (1) –

(a) in the case of the lease of a mine in which royalty or a share of the produce is received as the rent or part of the rent, it shall be sufficient to have estimated such royalty or the value of such share, for the purpose of stamp duty –

(i) when the lease has been granted by or on behalf of the Government at such amount or value as the Revenue Authority may, having regard to all the circumstances of the case, have estimated as likely to be payable by way of royalty or share to the Government under the lease; or

(ii) when the lease has been granted by any other person, at forty thousand shillings a year; and the whole amount of such royalty or share, whatever it may be, shall be claimable under such lease; and

(b) where proceedings have been taken in respect of an instrument under section 38 or 48 of this Act, the amount certified by the Revenue Authority shall be deemed to be the stamp actually used at the date of execution.

31. Facts affecting duty to be set forth in instrument.

(1) The consideration, if any, and other facts and circumstances affecting the chargeability of any instrument with duty, or the amount of the duty with which it is chargeable, shall be fully and truly set forth therein.

(2) The Revenue Authority may require any person executing or any person employed or concerned in the preparation of any such instrument to give evidence on oath or by affidavit that the facts and circumstances the instrument are fully and truthfully set forth and for such purpose the Revenue Authority may administer an oath.

32. Direction as to duty in case of certain conveyances.

(1) Where any property has been contracted to be sold for one consideration for the whole, and is conveyed to the purchaser in separate parts by different instruments, the consideration shall be apportioned in such manner as the parties think fit; provided that a distinct consideration for each separate part is set forth in the conveyance relating thereto, and such conveyance shall be chargeable with *ad valorem* duty in respect of such distinct consideration.

(2) Where property contracted to be purchased for one consideration for the whole by two or more persons jointly, or by any person for himself or herself and others, or wholly for others, is conveyed in parts by separate instruments to the persons by or for whom the same was purchased, for distinct parts of the consideration, the conveyance of each separate part shall be chargeable with *ad valorem* duty in respect of the distinct part of the consideration specified in the instrument.

(3) Where a person, having contracted for the purchase of any property but not having obtained a conveyance thereof, contracts to sell the same to any other person and the property is in consequence conveyed immediately to the sub-purchaser, the conveyance shall be chargeable with *ad valorem* duty in respect of the consideration for the sale by the original purchaser to the sub-purchaser.

(4) Where a person, having contracted for the purchase of any property but not having obtained a conveyance, the property contracts to sell the whole, or any part of it, to any other person or persons and the property is in consequence conveyed by the original seller to different persons in parts the consideration paid by such sub-purchaser, without regard to the amount or value of the original consideration; and the conveyance of the residue, if any, of such property to the original purchaser shall be chargeable with *ad valorem* duty in respect only of the excess of the original consideration over the aggregate of the consideration over the aggregate of the considerations paid by the sub-purchasers; but the duty on the last-mentioned conveyance shall in no case be less than two shillings.

(5) Where a sub-purchaser takes an actual conveyance of the interest of the person immediately selling to him or her, which is chargeable with *ad valorem* duty in respect of the consideration paid by him or her and is duly stamped accordingly, any conveyance to be afterwards made to him or her of the same property by the original seller shall be chargeable with a duty equal to that which would be chargeable on a conveyance for the consideration obtained by such original seller, or, where such duty would exceed ten shillings with a duty of ten shillings.

33. Reconstruction or amalgamation of companies.

(1) If in connection with a scheme for the reconstruction of any companies it is shown to the satisfaction of the Revenue Authority that there exist the conditions mentioned in subsection (2) of this section then, subject to the provisions of this section –

(a) The nominal share capital of the transferee company, or the amount by which the capital of the transferee company has been increased, as the case may be, shall, for the purpose of computing the stamp duty chargeable in respect of that capital, be treated as being reduced by either –

(i) an amount equal to the amount of the share capital of the existing company, or, in the case of the acquisition of a part of an undertaking, equal to such proportion of the said share capital as the value of that part of the undertaking bears to the whole value of the undertaking; or

(ii) the amount to be credited as paid up on the shares to be issued as such consideration as aforesaid and on the shares, if any, to be issued to creditors of the existing company in consideration of the release of debts (whether secured or unsecured) due or accruing due to them from the existing company or of the assignment of the debts to the transferee company, whichever amount is the less; and

(b) stamp duty under the headings of "CONVEYANCE" and "TRANSFER" in the Schedule to this Act shall not be chargeable on any instrument made for the purposes of or in connection with the transfer of the undertaking or shares, or on any instrument made for the purpose of or in connection with the assignment to the transferee company of any debts, secured or unsecured, of the existing company, nor shall any such duty be chargeable on any instrument vesting, or relating to the vesting of, the undertaking or shares in the transferee company; but

(i) no such instrument shall be deemed to be duly stamped unless either it is stamped with the duty to which it would but for this section be liable, or it has, in accordance with the provisions of section 38 of this Act, been submitted to the Revenue Authority for the adjudication and the Revenue Authority has certified it by endorsement pursuant to the provisions of section 39 of this Act that the document is not chargeable with any duty or that the full duty with which it is chargeable has been paid; and

(ii) in the case of an instrument made for the purposes of or in connection with a transfer to a company within the meaning of the Companies Act, paragraph (b) of this subsection shall not apply unless the instrument is either –

(A) executed within a period of twelve months from the date of the registration of the transferee company or the date of the resolution for the increase of the nominal share capital of the transferee company, as the case may be; or

(B) made for the purpose of effecting a conveyance or transfer in pursuance of an agreement which has been filed, or particulars of which have been filed, with the Registrar of Companies within the said period of twelve months specified in sub paragraph (ii) (A) of this paragraph; and

(iii) the foregoing provision with respect to the release and assignment of debts of the existing company shall not, except in the case of debts due to banks or to trade creditors apply to debts which were incurred less than two years before the proper time for making claim for exemption under this section.

(2) The conditions referred to in subsection (1) of this section are –

(a) that a company with a limited liability is to be registered, or that since the 30th August, 1956, a company has been incorporated by Letters Patent, or Act of Parliament of the United Kingdom or Uganda, or the nominal share capital of a company has been increased;

(b) that the company (in this section referred to as "the transferee company") is to be registered or has been incorporated or has increased its capital with a view to the acquisition either of the undertaking of, or of not less than ninety per centum of the issued share capital of, any particular existing company;

(c) that the consideration for the acquisition (except such part it as consists in the transfer to or discharge by the transferee company of liabilities of the existing company) consists as to not less than ninety per centum thereof –

(i) where an undertaking is to be acquired, in the issue of shares in the transferee company to the existing company or to holders of shares in the existing company; or

(ii) where shares are to be acquired, in the issue of shares in the transferee company to the holders of shares in the existing company in exchange for the shares held by them in the existing company.

(3) For the purposes of a claim for exemption under paragraph (b) of subsection (1) of this section, a company which has, in connection with a scheme of reconstruction or amalgamation, issued any un-issued share capital shall be treated as if it had increased its nominal share capital.

(4) A company shall not be deemed to be a particular existing company within the meaning of this section unless it is provided by the memorandum of association of, or the Letters Patent, or the Act of Parliament of the United Kingdom or Uganda incorporating the transferee company that one of the objects for which the company is established is the acquisition of the undertaking of, or shares in, the existing company, or unless it appears from the resolution, Act of Parliament, or other authority for the increase of the capital of the transferee company that the increase is authorised for the purpose of acquiring the undertaking of, or shares in, the existing company.

(5) In a case where the undertakings of or shares in two or more companies are to be acquired, the amount of the reduction to be allowed under this section in respect of the stamp duty chargeable in respect of the nominal share capital or the increase of the capital of a company shall be computed separately in relation to each of those companies.

(6) Where a claim is made for exemption under this section, the Revenue Authority may require the delivery to him or her of a statutory declaration in such form as he or she may direct, made by an advocate, and of such further evidence, if any, as the Revenue Authority may reasonably require.

(7) If–

(a) where any claim for exemption from duty under this section has been allowed, it is subsequently found that any declaration or other evidence furnished in support of the claim was untrue in any material particular, or that the conditions specified in subsection (2) of this section are not fulfilled in the reconstruction or amalgamation as actually carried out;

(b) where shares in the transferee company have been issued to the existing company in consideration of the acquisition, the existing company within a period of two years from the date, as the case may be, of the registration or incorporation, or of the authority for the increase of the capital of the transferee company, ceases, otherwise than in consequence of reconstruction, amalgamation, or liquidation, to be the beneficial owner of the shares so issued to it; or

(c) where any such exemption has been allowed in connection with the acquisition by the transferee company of shares in another company, the transferee company within a period of two years from the date of its registration or incorporation or of the authority for the increase of its capital, as the case may be, ceases, otherwise than in consequence of reconstruction, amalgamation or liquidation, to be the beneficial owner of the shares so acquired, the exemption shall be deemed not to have been allowed and an amount equal to the duty remitted shall become payable forthwith, and shall be recoverable from the transferee company as a debt due to the Government, together with interest the debt at the rate of five per centum per annum in the case of duty remitted under subsection (1) (a) of this section from the date of the registration of incorporation of the transferee company or the increase of its capital, as the case may be, and in the case of duty remitted under subsection (1) (b) from the date on which it would have become chargeable but for the provisions of this section.

(8) If in the case of any scheme of reconstruction or amalgamation the Revenue Authority is satisfied that at the proper time for making a claim for exemption from duty under subsection (1) of this section there were in existence all the necessary conditions for such exemption other than the condition that not less than ninety per centum of the issued share capital of the existing company would be acquired by the transferee company, the Revenue Authority may, if it is proved to his or her satisfaction that not less than ninety per centum of the issued capital of the existing company has under the scheme been acquired within a period of six months from he earlier of the two following dates, –

(a) the last day of the period of thirty days after the first allotment of shares made for the purposes of the acquisition ; or

(b) the date on which an invitation was issued to the shareholders of the existing company to accept shares in the transferee company, and on production of the instruments on which duty paid has been impressed, direct repayment to be made of such an amount of duty as would have been remitted if the said condition had been originally fulfilled.

(9) In this section, unless the context otherwise requires–

(a) references to the undertaking of an existing company include references to a part of the undertaking of an existing company;

(b) "shares" include stock.

34. Transfers between associated companies.

(1) Stamp duty under the headings "CONVEYANCE" and "TRANSFER" in the Schedule to this Act shall not be chargeable on an instrument to which this section applies; but no such instrument shall be deemed to be duly stamped unless either it is stamped with the duty to which it would, but for this section, be liable, or it has, in accordance with the provisions of section 38 of this Act, been submitted to the Revenue Authority for adjudication and the Revenue Authority has certified thereon by endorsement pursuant to the provisions of section 39 of this Act, that the document is not chargeable with any duty or that the full duty with which it is chargeable has been paid.

(2) This section applies to any instrument in respect of which it is shown to the satisfaction of the Revenue Authority –

(a) that the effect of the instrument is to convey or transfer a beneficial interest in property from one company with limited liability (hereinafter called "the transferor") to another such company (hereinafter called "the transferee"); and

(b) that either–

(i) one of such companies is beneficial owner of not less than ninety per centum of the issued share capital of the other company; or

(ii) not less than ninety per centum of the issued share capital of each of the companies is in the beneficial ownership of a third company with limited liability; and

(c) that the instrument was not executed in pursuance of or in connection with an arrangement under which–

(i) the consideration for the conveyance or transfer was to be provided directly or indirectly by a person other than a company which at the time of the execution of the instrument was associated with either the transferor or the transferee; or

(ii) the beneficial interest in the property was previously conveyed or transferred directly or indirectly by such a person as aforesaid.

35. Transfers inter vivos.

(1) Any conveyance or transfer operating as a voluntary disposition *inter vivos* shall be chargeable with the like stamp duty as if it were a conveyance or transfer on sale with the substitution in each case of the value of the property conveyed or transferred for the amount or value of the consideration for the sale.

(2) Notwithstanding anything in section 38 of this Act, the opinion of the Revenue Authority shall be required under that section on any conveyance or transfer operating as a voluntary disposition *inter vivos,* and no such conveyance or transfer shall be deemed to be duly stamped unless the Revenue Authority has expressed his or her opinion thereon in accordance with this section.

(3) Where any instrument is chargeable with duty both as a conveyance or transfer under this section and as a settlement under the heading "SETTLEMENT" in the Schedule to this Act the instrument shall be charged with duty as a conveyance or transfer under this section but not as a settlement.

(4) Any conveyance or transfer, not being a disposition made in favour of a purchaser or incumbrancer or other person in good faith and for valuable consideration, shall for the purpose of this section be deemed to be a conveyance or transfer operating as a voluntary disposition *inter vivos*, and, except where marriage is the consideration, for any conveyance or transfer shall not for this purpose be deemed to be valuable consideration where the Revenue Authority is of the opinion that by reason of the inadequacy of the sum paid as consideration or other circumstances the conveyance or transfer confers a substantial benefit on the person to whom the property is conveyed or transferred.

(5) Section (1) to (4) shall not apply to a conveyance or transfer made for nominal consideration for the purpose of securing the repayment of an advance or loan or made for effecting the appointment of a new trustee or the retirement of a trustee, whether the trust is expressed or implied, or under which no beneficial interest passes in the property conveyed or transferred, or made to a beneficiary by a trustee or other person in a fiduciary capacity under any trust, whether expressed or implied, and this subsection shall have effect notwithstanding that the circumstances exempting the conveyance or transfer from charge under this section are not set forth in the conveyance or transfer.

Duty by whom payable

36. Duties by whom payable.

In the absence of an agreement to the contrary, the expense of providing the proper stamp shall be borne–

(a) in the case of any instrument described in any of the following Articles of the Schedule to this Act. Namely–

(i) No. 2 (Administration - Bond)
(ii) No. 6 (Agreement relating to Deposit of Title-Deeds, Pawnor Pledge)
(iii) No. 13 (Bill of Exchange)
(iv) No 16 (Bond)
(v) No. 27 (Debenture)
(vi) No. 34 (Further Charge)
(vii) No. 37 (Indemnity Bond)
(viii) No. 42 (Mortgage Deed)
(ix) No. 51 (Promissory Note)
(x) No. 55 (Release)

(xi) No. 56 (Respondentia Bond)
(xii) No. 57 (Security Bond or Mortgage Deed)
(xiii) No. 58 (Settlement), by the person drawing, making or executing the instrument:

(b) in the case of a policy of insurance other than fire insurance, by the person effecting the insurance;
(c) in the case of policy of fire insurance, by the person effecting the insurance;
(d) in the case of a conveyance, including a reconveyance of mortgaged property, by the grantee;
(e) in the case of a lease or agreement to lease, by the lessee or intended lessee;
(f) in the case of a counterpart of a lease, by the lessor;
(g) in the case of an instrument of exchange, by the parties in equal shares;
(h) in the case of a certificate of sale, by the purchaser of the property to which such certificate relates;
(i) in the case of an instrument of partition, by the parties it in proportion to their respective shares in the whole property partitioned, or, when the partition is made in execution of an order passed by a civil court or arbitrator, in such proportion as the court or arbitrator directs;
(j) in the case of a transfer of shares in an incorporated company or other body corporate, by the purchaser or transferee;
(k) in the case of a transfer of debentures, being marketable securities, whether the debenture is liable to duty or not, by the purchaser or transferee; and
(l) in the case of a transfer of any interest secured by bond, mortgage, deed or policy of insurance, by the purchaser or transferee.

37. Obligation to give receipt in certain cases.

(1) Any person receiving any money exceeding forty shillings in amount, or any bill of exchange, cheques or promissory note for an amount exceeding forty shillings, or receiving in satisfaction or part satisfaction of a debt any movable property exceeding forty shillings in value, shall, on demand by the person paying or delivering such money, bill, cheques, note or property give a duly stamped receipt for the same.

(2) Any person receiving or taking credit for any premium or consideration for any renewal of any contract of fire insurance shall, within one month after receiving or taking credit for such premium or consideration, give a duly stamped receipt for the same.

Part III – Adjudicating as to stamps

38. Adjudication as to proper stamp.

(1) When any instrument, whether executed or not and whether previously stamped or not, is brought to the Revenue Authority, and the person bringing it applies to have the opinion of that officer as to the duty, if any, with which it is chargeable,

and pays a fee of such amount, not exceeding one hundred shillings and not less than one shilling as that officer may in each case direct, that officer shall determine the duty, if any, with which, in his or her judgment, the instrument is chargeable.

(2) For this purpose the Revenue Authority may require to be furnished with an abstract of the instrument, and also with such affidavit or other evidence as he or she may deem necessary to prove that all the facts and circumstances affecting the chargeability of the instrument with duty, or the amount of the duty with which it is chargeable, are fully and truly set forth in it, and may refuse to proceed upon any such application until the abstract and evidence have been furnished accordingly; but

(a) no evidence furnished in pursuance of this section shall be used against any person in any civil proceedings, except in an inquiry as to the duty with which the instrument to which it relates is chargeable; and

(b) every person by whom any such evidence is furnished shall, on payment of the full duty with which the instrument to which it relates is chargeable, be relieved from any penalty which he or she may have incurred under this Act by reason of the omission to state truly in the instrument any of the facts or circumstances aforesaid.

39. Certificate by revenue authority.

(1) When an instrument brought to the Revenue Authority under the last section 38 is, in his or her opinion, one of a description chargeable with duty, and –

(a) that officer determines that it is already fully stamped; or

(b) the duty determined by that officer under the section 38 or such a sum as, with the duty already paid in respect of the instrument, is equal to the duty so determined, has been paid, that officer shall certify by endorsement on such instrument that the full duty, stating the amount, with which it is chargeable has been paid.

(2) When such instrument is, in his or her opinion, not chargeable with duty, the Revenue Authority shall certify in manner aforesaid that such instrument is not so chargeable.

(3) Any instrument upon which an endorsement has been made under this section shall be deemed to be duly stamped or not chargeable with duty, as the case may be; and, if chargeable with duty, shall be receivable in evidence or otherwise, and may be acted upon and registered as if it had been originally duly stamped:

(4) Nothing in this section shall authorise the Revenue Authority to endorse –

(a) any instrument executed or first executed in Uganda and brought to him or her after the expiration of one month from the date of its execution or first execution, as the case may be;

(b) any instrument executed or first executed out of Uganda and brought to him or her after the expiration of three months after it has been first received in Uganda; or

(c) any instrument chargeable with the duty of twenty cents or under or any bill of exchange or promissory note, when brought to him, after the drawing or execution thereof, not duly stamped.

Part IV – Instruments not duly stamped

40. Examination and impounding of instruments.

(1) Every person having by law or consent of parties authority to receive evidence, and every person in charge of a public office, except an officer of police, before whom any instrument chargeable, in his or her opinion, with duty, is produced or comes in the performance of his or her functions, shall, if it appears to him or her that such instrument is not duly stamped, impound it.

(2) For that purpose every such person shall examine every instrument so chargeable and so produced or coming before him, in order to ascertain whether it is stamped with a stamp of the value and description required by the law in force in Uganda when such instrument was executed or first executed; but

(a) nothing in this section contained shall be deemed to require any judge or magistrate of a criminal court to examine or impound, if he does not think fit so to do, any instrument coming before him or her in the course of any proceeding;

(b) nothing in this section contained shall be deemed to require any magistrate or justice of the peace to examine or impound any document coming before him or her in the course of taking an affidavit or exercising or performing any of the other powers or duties of a notary public or commissioner for oaths;

(c) in the case of a Judge of the High Court the duty of examining and impounding any instrument under this section may be delegated to such officer a the court appoints in this behalf.

(3) for the purposes of this section, in case of doubt, the Minister may determine what offices shall be deemed to be public offices, and who shall be deemed to be persons in charge of public offices.

41. Special provision as to unstamped receipts.

Where any receipt chargeable with a duty of ten cents is tendered to or produced before any officer unstamped in the course of the audit of any public account, the officer may in his or her discretion, instead of impounding the instrument, require a duly stamped receipt to be substituted thereof.

42. Instruments not duly stamped inadmissible in evidence, etc.

No instrument chargeable with duty shall be admitted in evidence for any purpose by any person having by law or consent of parties authority to receive evidence, or shall be acted upon, registered or authenticated by any such person or by any public officer, unless such instrument is duly stamped; but

(a) any such instrument, not being an instrument chargeable with duty of ten cents or twenty cents only, other than a cheques, or a bill of exchange, other than a bill of exchange presented for acceptance, accepted or payable elsewhere than in Uganda, or a promissory note, shall subject to all just exceptions be admitted in evidence on payment of the duty with which the same is chargeable, or, in the case of an instrument insufficiently stamped, of the amount required to make up such duty, together with a penalty of ten shillings, or, when ten times the amount of the proper duty or deficient portion thereof exceeds ten shillings, of a sum equal to ten times such duty or portion;

(b) where any person from whom a stamped receipt could have been demanded has given an unstamped receipt, and such receipt, if stamped, would be admissible in evidence against him, then such receipt shall be admitted in evidence against him or her on payment of a penalty of two shillings by the person tendering it;

(c) where a contract or agreement of any kind is effected by correspondence consisting of two or more letters and any one of the letters bears the proper stamp, the contract or agreement shall be deemed to be duly stamped.

(d) nothing in this section shall prevent the admission of any instrument in evidence in any proceeding in a criminal court;

(e) nothing in this section shall prevent the admission of any instrument in any court when the instrument has been executed by or on behalf of the Government, or where it bears the certificate of the Revenue Authority as provided by section 39 or any other provision of this Act.

43. Admission of instrument where not to be questioned.

Where an instrument has been admitted in evidence, the admission shall not, except as provided in section 68 of this Act, be called in question at any stage of the same suit or proceeding on the ground that the instrument has not been duly stamped.

44. Admission of improperly stamped instruments.

The Minster may make rules providing that, where an instrument bears a stamp of sufficient amount but of improper description, it may, on payment of the duty with which the same is chargeable, be certified to be duly stamped, and any instrument so certified shall then be deemed to have been duly stamped as from the date of its execution.

45. Instruments impounded, how dealt with.

(1) When the person impounding an instrument under section 36 of this Act has by law or consent of parties authority to receive evidence and admits the instrument in evidence upon payment of the duty with which the instrument is chargeable, or in the case of an instrument insufficiently stamped of the amount required to make up such duty together with a penalty as provided by section 42 of this Act, or of duty as provided by section 44 of this Act, he or she shall send to the Revenue Authority an authenticated copy of such instrument, together with a certificate in writing, stating the amount of duty and penalty levied in respect the instrument, and shall send such amount to the Revenue Authority; or to such person as he or she may appoint in this behalf.

(2) In every other case, the person so impounding an instrument shall send it in original to the Revenue Authority.

46. Revenue authority's power to refund penalty paid under section 45 (1).

(1) When a copy of an instrument is sent to the Revenue Authority under subsection (1) of section 45, he or she may, if he or she thinks fit, refund any portion of the penalty in excess of ten shillings which has been paid in respect of such instrument.

(2) When such instrument has been impounded only because it has been written in contravention of section 15 or 16 of this Act the Revenue Authority may refund the whole penalty so paid.

47. Revenue authority's Power to Stamp Instruments impunded.

(1) When the Revenue Authority impounds any instrument under section 40 of this Act or receives any instrument sent to him or her under subsection (2) of section 45 of this Act, not being an instrument chargeable with a duty of twenty cents or under only or a bill of exchange or promissory note, he or she shall adopt the following procedure–

(a) if the revenue authority is of opinion that such instrument is duly stamped, or is not chargeable with duty, he or she shall certify by endorsement thereon that it is duly stamped, or that it is not so chargeable, as the case may be;

(b) if the revenue authority is of opinion that the instrument is chargeable with duty and is not duly stamped, he or she shall require the payment of the proper duty or the amount required to make up the same, together with a penalty of ten shillings; or if he or she thinks fit, an amount not exceeding ten times the amount of the proper duty or of the deficient portion of that duty, whether such amount exceeds or falls short of ten shillings, but, when such instrument has been impounded only because it has been written in contravention of section 15 or 16 of this Act, the Revenue Authority may, if he or she thinks fit, remit the whole penalty prescribed by this section.

(2) Every certificate under paragraph *(a)* of subsection (1) of this section shall, for the purposes of this Act, be conclusive evidence of the matters stated the certificate.

(3) Where an instrument has been sent to the Revenue Authority under subsection (2) of section 45 of this Act the Revenue Authority shall, when he or she has dealt with it as provided by this section, return it to the impounding officer.

48. Instruments unduly stamped by accident.

If any instrument chargeable with duty and not duly stamped, not being an instrument chargeable with a duty of twenty cents or under only, or a bill of exchange or promissory note, is produced by any person of his or her own motion before the Revenue Authority within one year from the date of its execution or first execution, and such person brings to the notice of the Revenue Authority the fact that such instrument is not duly stamped and offers to pay to the Revenue Authority the amount required to make up the same, and the Revenue Authority is satisfied that the omission duly to stamp such instrument has been occasioned by accident, mistake or urgent necessity, he or she may instead of proceeding under sections 40 and 47 of this Act, receive such amount and proceed as next hereinafter prescribed.

49. Endorsement of instruments on which duty has been paid under section 42, 47 or 48.

(1) When the duty and penalty, if any, leviable in respect of any instrument have been paid under section 38,43 or 44 of this Act, the person admitting such instrument in evidencement or the Revenue Authority, as the case may be, shall certify by endorsement thereon that the proper duty or, as the case may be, the proper duty and penalty (stating the amount of each) have been levied in respect thereof, and the name and residence of the person paying it or them.

(2) Every instrument so endorsed shall thereupon be admissible in evidence, and may be registered and acted upon and authenticated as if it had been duly stamped, and shall be delivered on his or her application in this behalf to the person from whose possession it came into the hands of the officer impounding it, or as such person may direct; but –

(a) no instrument which has been admitted in evidence upon payment of duty and a penalty under section 42 of this Act shall be so delivered before the expiration of one month from the date of such impounding, or if the Revenue Authority has certified that its further detention is necessary and has not cancelled such certificate;

(b) nothing in this section shall affect Order 12, Rule 5, of the Civil Procedure Rules.

50. Prosecution for offence against stamp law.

The taking of proceedings or the payment of a penalty under this Part of this Act in respect of any instrument shall not bar the prosecution of any person who appears to have committed an offence against the stamp law in respect of the instrument; but no such prosecution shall be instituted in the case of any instrument in respect of which such a penalty has been paid, unless it appears to the Revenue Authority that the offence was committed with an intention of evading payment of the proper duty.

51. Persons paying duty or penalty may recover same in certain cases.

(1) When any duty or penalty has been paid under section 42, 44 , or 47 of 48 of this Act by any person in respect of an instrument, and, by agreement or under the provisions of section 36 of this Act or any other enactment in force at the time such instrument was executed, some other person was bound to bear the expense of providing the proper stamp for such instrument, the first-mentioned person shall be entitled to recover from such other person the amount of the duty or penalty so paid.

(2) For the purpose of such recovery any certificate granted in respect of such instrument under this Act shall be conclusive evidence of the matters certified in it.

(3) Such amount may, if the court thinks fit, be included in any order as to costs in any suit or proceedings to which such persons are parties and in which such instrument has been tendered in evidence, but if the court does not include the amount in such order, no further proceedings for the recovery of the amount shall be maintainable.

52. Power of revenue authority to refund penalty of excess duty in certain cases.

(1) Where any penalty is paid under section 42 or 47 of this Act, the Revenue Authority may, upon application in writing made within one year from the date of the payment, refund such penalty wholly or in part.

(2) Where, in the opinion of the Revenue Authority, stamp duty in excess of that which is legally chargeable has been charged and paid under section 42 of this Act, such Authority may, upon application in writing made within three months of the order charging the same, refund the excess.

53. Non-liability for loss of instruments sent under section 45.

(1) If any instrument sent to the Revenue Authority under subsection (2) of section 45 of this Act is lost, destroyed or damaged during transmission, the person sending the same shall not be liable for such loss, destruction or damage.

(2) When any instrument is about to be so sent, the person from whose possession it came into the hands of the person impounding the same, may require a copy of the instrument to be made at the expense of such first-mentioned person and authenticated by the person impounding such instrument.

54. Power to stamp bills, promisory notes and cheques received unstamped.

When any bill of exchange, promissory note or cheque chargeable with the duty of twenty cents is presented for payment unstamped, the person to whom it is so presented may affix thereto the necessary adhesive stamp, and, upon cancelling the same in manner hereinbefore provided, may pay the sum payable upon such bill, note or cheques, and may charge the duty against the person who ought to have paid the same, or deduct it from the sum payable as aforesaid, and such bill, note or cheque shall, so far as respects the duty, be deemed good and valid; but nothing herein contained shall relieve any person from any penalty or proceeding to which he or

55. Recovery of duties and penalties.

All duties, penalties and other sums required to be paid under this Part of this Act may be recovered by the Revenue Authority by distress and sale of the movable property of the person from whom the same are due.

PART V – ALLOWANCES FOR STAMPS IN CERTAIN CASES

56. Allowances for spoiled stamps.

(1) Subject to such rules as may be made by the Minister as to the evidence to be required, or the inquiry to be made, the Revenue Authority may, on application made within the period prescribed in section 57 of this Act, and if he or she is satisfied as to the facts, make allowance for stamps spoiled in the following cases–

(a) the stamp on any paper inadvertently and undesignedly spoiled, obliterated or by error in writing or any other means rendered unfit for the purpose intended before any instrument written thereon is executed by any person;

(b) the stamp on any document which is written out wholly or in part, but which is not signed or executed by any party to the documents;

(c) in the case of bills of exchange, cheques or promissory notes–

(i) the stamp on any bill of exchange or cheque signed by or on behalf of the drawer which has not been accepted or made use of in any manner whatever or delivered out of his hands for any purpose other than by way of tender for acceptance; if paper on which any such stamp is impressed does not bear any signature intended as or for the acceptance of any bill of exchange or cheque to be afterwards written on it;

(ii) the stamp on any promissory note signed by or on behalf of the maker which has not been made use of in any manner whatever or delivered out of the maker's hands;

(iii) the stamp used or intended to be used for any bill of exchange, cheque or promissory note signed by, or on behalf of, the drawer thereof, but which from any omission or error has been spoiled or rendered useless, although the same, being a bill of exchange or cheque, may have been presented for acceptance or accepted or endorsed, or, being a promissory note, may have been delivered to the payee; if another completed and duly stamped bill of exchange, cheque or promissory note is produced identical in every a particular, except in the correction of such omission or error as aforesaid, with the spoiled bill, cheque or note;

(d) the stamp used for an instrument executed by any party thereto which–

(i) has been afterwards found to be absolutely void in law from the beginning;

(ii) has been afterwards found unfit by reason of any error or mistake therein, for the purpose originally intended;

(iii) by reason of the death of any person by whom it is necessary that it should be executed without having executed the same, or of the refusal of any such person to execute the same, cannot be completed so as to effect the intended transaction in the form proposed;

(iv) for want of the execution thereof by some material party, and his inability or refusal to sign the same, is in fact incomplete and insufficient for the purpose for which it was intended.

(v) by reason of the refusal of any person to act under the same, or to advance any money intended to be thereby secured, or by the refusal or non-acceptance of any office thereby granted, totally fails of the intended purpose;

(vi) becomes useless in consequence of the transaction intended to be thereby effected being effected by some other instrument between the same parties and bearing a stamp of not less value;

(vii) is deficient in value and the transaction intended to be thereby effected has been effected by some other instrument between the same parties and bearing a stamp of not less value;

(viii) is inadvertently and undesignedly spoiled, and in lieu whereof another instrument made between the same parties and for the same purpose is executed and duly stamped; if in the case of an executed instrument, no legal proceeding has been commenced in which the instrument could or would have been given or offered in evidence, and that the instrument is given up to be cancelled.

(2) The certificate of the Revenue Authority under section 39 of this Act that the full duty with which an instrument is chargeable, has been paid, is a stamp within the meaning of this section.

57. Application for relief under section 56, when to be made.

The application for relief under the last preceding section shall be made within the following periods, that is to say–

(a) in the cases mentioned in paragraph *(d)*, (v) of subsection (1) of the section 56, within two months of the date of the instrument;

(b) in the case of a stamped paper on which no instrument has been executed by any of the parties thereto, within six months after the stamp has been spoiled;

(c) In the case of a stamped paper on which an instrument has been executed by any of the parties thereto, within six months after the date of the instrument, or, if it is not dated, within six months after the execution thereof by the person by whom it was first or alone executed:

(2) Notwithstanding subsection

(i) when the spoiled instrument has been for sufficient reasons sent out of Uganda, the application may be made within six months after it has been received back in Uganda;

(ii) when, from unavoidable circumstances, any instrument for which another instrument has been substituted, cannot be given up to be cancelled within the aforesaid period, the application may be made within six months after the date of execution of the substituted instrument.

58. Allowance in case of printed forms no longer required by corporations.

The Revenue Authority may, without limit of time, make allowance for stamped papers used for printed forms of instruments by any banker or by any incorporated company or other body corporate, if for any sufficient reason such forms have ceased to be required by the said banker, company or body corporate if Authority is satisfied that the duty in respect of the stamped papers has been duly paid.

59. Allowance for misused stamps.

When–

(a) any person has inadvertently used for an instrument chargeable with duty a stamp of a description other than that prescribed for the instrument by the rules made under this Act, or a stamp of greater value than was necessary, or has inadvertently used any stamp for an instrument not chargeable with any duty; or

(b) any stamp used for an instrument has been inadvertently rendered useless under section 17 of this Act owing to such instrument having been written in contravention of the provisions of section 15 of this Act, the Revenue Authority may, on application made within six months after the date of the instrument, or, if it is not dated, within six months after the execution thereof by the person by whom it was first or alone executed, and upon the instrument, if chargeable with duty, being re-stamped with the proper duty, cancel and allow as spoiled the stamp so misused or rendered useless.

60. Allowance for spoiled or misused stamps, how to be made.

In any case in which allowance is made for spoiled or misused stamps, the Revenue Authority may give in lieu thereof–

(a) other stamps of the same description and value; or

(b) if required and he or she thinks fit, stamps of any other description to the same amount in value; or

(c) at his or her discretion, the same value in money, deducting six cents for each shilling or fraction of a shilling.

61. Allowance for stamps not required for use.

When any person is possessed of stamps which have not been spoiled or rendered unfit or useless for the purpose intended, but for which he or she has no immediate use, the Revenue Authority shall repay to such person the value of such stamps in money, deducting six cents for each shilling or portion of a shilling, upon such person delivering up the same to be cancelled, and proving to the Revenue Authority's satisfaction–

(a) that such stamp or stamps were purchased by such person with a *bona fide* intention to use them; and

(b) that he or she has paid the full price of the stamps; and

(c) that they were so purchased within the period of six months before the date on which they were so delivered; but, where the person is a licensed vendor of stamps the Revenue Authority may, if he or she thinks fit, repay the sum actually paid by the vendor without any such deduction.

62. Allowance on renewal of certain debentures.

(1) When any duly stamped debenture is renewed by the issue of a new debenture in the same terms, the Revenue Authority shall, upon application made within one month, repay to the person issuing the debenture the value of the stamp on the original or on the new debenture, whichever shall be less; if the original debenture is produced before the Revenue Authority and cancelled by him or her in such manner as the Minister may direct –

(2) A debenture shall be deemed to be renewed in the same terms within the meaning of this section notwithstanding the following changes –

(a) the issue of two or more debentures in place of one original debenture, the total amount secured being the same;

(b) the issue of one debenture in place of two or more original debentures, the total amount secured being the same;
(c) the substitution of the name of the holder at the time of renewal for the name of the original holder; and
(d) the alteration of the rate of interest or the dates of payment of the debenture.

PART VI – REFERENCE AND REVISION

63. Statement of case by revenue authority to High Court.

The Revenue Authority may state any case coming to his or her notice, and refer such case, with his own opinion thereon, to the High Court.

64. Appeal from revenue authority to High Court.

Any person considering himself or herself aggrieved by any decision of the Revenue Authority may appeal from it to the High Court and may require the Revenue Authority to draw up a statement of the case, with his or her own opinion thereon, for reference to the High Court.

65. Power of High Court to call for further particulars as to case stated.

If the High Court, is not satisfied that the statements contained in any case referred to it under sections 63 or 64 are sufficient to enable it to determine the questions raised thereby, the Court may refer the case back to the Revenue Authority, to make such additions thereto or alterations therein as the Court may direct in that behalf.

66. Procedure in disposing of case stated.

(1) The High Court, upon the hearing of any such case, shall decide the questions raised by it, and shall deliver its judgment on it containing the ground on which such decision is founded.
(2) The Court shall send to the Revenue Authority a copy of its judgment under the seal of the Court; and the Revenue Authority shall, on receiving such copy, dispose of the case conformably to such judgment.

67. Statement of case by other courts to High Court

(1) If any court, other than the High Court, feels doubt as to the amount of duty to be paid in respect of any instrument under section 42 (a) the magistrate may draw up a statement of the case and refer it, with his or her own opinion thereon, for the decision of the High Court.
(2) The High Court shall deal with the case as if it had been referred under section 63 of this Act, and send a copy of its judgment under the seal of the Court to the Revenue Authority and another like copy to the magistrate making the reference, who shall, on receiving such copy dispose of the case conformably to the judgment.

68. Revision of certain decisions of courts regarding the sufficiency of stamps.

(1) When any court in the exercise of its civil jurisdiction makes any order admitting any instrument in evidence as duly stamped or as not requiring a stamp, or upon payment of duty and a penalty under section 42 of this Act, the court to which appeals lie from, or references are made by, such first-mentioned court may, of its own motion or on the application of the Revenue Authority, take such order into consideration.

(2) If such court, after such consideration, is of opinion that such instrument should not have been admitted in evidence without the payment of duty and penalty under section 42 of this Act, or without the payment of a higher duty and penalty than those paid, it may record a declaration to that effect, and determine the amount of duty with which such instrument is chargeable, and may require any person in whose possession or power such instrument then is to produce the same, and may impound it when produced.

(3) When any declaration has been recorded under subsection (2) of this section, the court recording it shall send a copy of the declaration to the Revenue Authority, and where the instrument to which it relates has been impounded or is otherwise in the possession of such court, shall also send the revenue authority him the instrument.

(4) The Revenue Authority may thereupon, notwithstanding anything contained in the order admitting the instrument in evidence, or in any certificate granted under section 49 or under section 50 of this Act, prosecute any person for any offence against the stamp law which the Revenue Authority considers him to have committed in respect of the instrument; except that –

(a) no such prosecution shall be instituted where the amount (including duty and penalty) which, according to the determination of such court, was payable in respect of the instrument under section 42 of this Act, is paid to the Revenue Authority, unless he or she thinks that the offence was committed with an intention of evading payment of the proper duty;

(b) except for the purposes of such prosecution, no declaration made under this section shall affect the validity of any order admitting any instrument in evidence, or of any certificate granted under section 49 of this Act.

PART VII – CRIMINAL OFFENCES AND PROCEDURE

69. Penalty for executing, etc. instrument not duly stamped.

(1) Any person–

(a) drawing, making, issuing, endorsing or transferring, or signing, otherwise than as a witness, or presenting for acceptance or payment, or accepting, paying or receiving payment of, or in any manner negotiating any bill of exchange, cheque or promissory note without the same being duly stamped; or

(b) executing or signing, otherwise than as a witness, any other instrument chargeable with duty without it being duly stamped; or

(c) voting or attempting to vote under any proxy not duly stamped, shall for every such offence be punishable with a fine not exceeding one thousand shillings; but when any penalty has been paid in respect of any instrument under section 42, 47 or 68 of this Act, the amount of such penalty shall be allowed in reduction of the fine, if any, subsequently imposed under this section in respect of the same instrument upon the person who paid that penalty.

(2) If a share-warrant is issued without being duly stamped, the company issuing it, and also every person who, at the time when it is issued, is the managing director or secretary or other principal officer of the company, shall be punishable with a fine not exceeding one thousand shillings.

70. Penalty for failure to cancel adhesive stamp.

Any person required by section 14 of this Act to cancel an adhesive stamp and failing to cancel the stamp in manner prescribed by that section shall be punishable with a fine not exceeding two hundred shillings.

71. Penalty for failure to comply with provisions of section 31, etc.

Any person who, with intent to defraud the Government–

(a) executes any instrument in which all the facts and circumstances required by section 31 of this Act to be set forth in such instrument are not fully and truly set forth; or

(b) being employed or concerned in or about the preparation of any instrument, neglects or omits fully and truly to set forth therein all such facts and circumstances; or

(c) does any other act calculated to deprive the Government of any duty or penalty under this Act, shall be punishable with a fine not exceeding ten thousand shillings.

72. Penalty for refusal to give receipt, and for devices to evade duty on receipts.

Any person who–

(a) being required under section 37 of this Act to give a receipt, refuses or neglects to give the same; or

(b) with intent to defraud the Government of any duty, upon a payment of money or delivery of property exceeding forty shillings in amount or value, gives a receipt for an amount or value not exceeding forty shillings, or separates or divides the money or property paid or delivered, shall be punishable with a fine not exceeding two hundred shillings.

73. Penalty for not making out policy, or making one not duly stamped.

(1) Any person who –

(a) receives or takes credit for, any premium or consideration for any contract of insurance and does not, within one month after receiving, or taking credit for, such premium or consideration, make out and execute a duly stamped policy of such insurance; or

(b) makes, executes or delivers out any policy which is not duly stamped, or pays or allows in account, or agrees to pay or allow in account, any money upon, or in respect of, any such policy, shall be punishable with a fine not exceeding four hundred shillings.

(2) Subsection (1) shall not apply to policies of insurance against accident in respect of which an agreement for the composition of stamp duty has been entered into under section 7 of this Act.

74. Penalty for not drawing full number of bills or marine policies purporting to be in sets.

Any person drawing or executing a policy of marine insurance purporting to be drawn or executed in a set of two or more, and not at the same time drawing or executing on paper duly stamped the whole number of policies of which such policy purports the set to consist, shall be punishable with a fine not exceeding two thousand shillings.

75. Penalty for post-dating bills, and for other devices to defraud the revenue.

Any person who–

(a) *with* intent to defraud the Government of duty, draws, makes or issues any bill of exchange or promissory note, bearing a date subsequent to that on which such bill or note is actually drawn or made;

(b) knowing that such bill or note has been so postdated, endorses, transfers, presents for acceptance or payment, or accepts, pays or receives payment of, such bill note, or in any manner negotiates the same;

(c) with the like intent, practises has been so postdated, endorses, transfers, presents for acceptance or payment, or accepts, pays or receives payment of, such bill or note or is concerned in any act, contrivance or device not specially provided for by this Act or any other law for the time being in force, shall be punishable with a fine not exceeding two thousand shillings.

76. Penalty for breach of rule relating to sale of stamps and for unauthorised sale.

Any person–

(a) appointed to sell stamps who disobeys any rule made under section 81 of this Act; and

(b) not so appointed, who sells or offers for sale any stamp (other than adhesive stamps of the value of twenty cents or under) shall be punishable with imprisonment for a period not exceeding six months, or with a fine not exceeding one thousand shillings or with both.

77. Institution and conduct of prosecutions.

(1) Subject to article 120 of the Constitution, no prosecution in respect of any offence punishable under this Act shall be instituted without the sanction of the Revenue Authority or such other officer as the Revenue Authority specially authorises in that behalf.

(2) The Revenue Authority, or any officer specially authorised by him or her in this behalf, may, with the consent of the Director of Public Prosecutions, stay any such prosecution or compound any such offence.

(3) The amount of any such composition shall be recoverable in the manner provided by section 55 of this Act.

78. Jurisdication of magistrates.

No magistrate grade III shall try any offence under this Act.

79. Place of trial.

Every offence committed in respect of any instrument may be tried in any district or area in which such instrument is found as well as in any district or area in which such offence might be tried under the Criminal Procedure Code.

PART VIII – SUPPLEMENTAL PROVISIONS

80. Books, etc. to be open to inspection.

Every public officer having in his or her custody any registers, books, records, papers, documents, or proceedings, the inspection whereof may tend to secure any duty or to prove or lead to the discovery of any fraud or omission in relation to any duty, shall at all reasonable times permit any person authorised in writing by the Revenue Authority to inspect for such purpose the registers, books, papers, documents and proceedings, and to take such notes and extracts as he or she may deem necessary, without fee or charge.

81. Power to make rules relating to sale of stamps.

The Minister may make rules for regulating–

(a) the supply and sale of stamps and stamped papers;

(b) the persons by whom alone such sale is to be conducted; and

(c) the duties and remuneration of such persons; but the rules shall not restrict the sale of adhesive stamps of the value of twenty cents or under.

82. Power to make rules generally to carry out Act.

The Minister may make rules to carry out generally the purposes of this Act, and may by such rules prescribe the fines, which shall in no case exceed one thousand shillings, to be incurred on breach if a rule.

83. Savings as to court fees.

Nothing in this Act shall be deemed to affect the duties chargeable under any enactment for the time being in force relating to court fees.

SCHEDULE

Stamp duty on instruments.

FIRST PART.

	Instrument	Proper stamp duty (in shillings)
1.	Acknowledgment of a debt exceeding shs. 100,000	5,000
2.	Administration bond	5,000
3.	Adoption deed	5,000
4.	Affidavit including an affirmation or declaration	5,000
5.	Agreement or memorandum of an agreement	5,000
6.	Agreement relating to deposit of title deeds, pawn or pledge – of the total value	1%
7.	Appointment in execution of a power, whether of trustees or of property	5,000
8.	Appraisement or valuation made otherwise than under an order of court – of the total value	1%
9.	Apprenticeship deed	5,000
10.	Articles of association of a company	10,000
11.	Assent to bequest whether under hand or seal	5,000
12.	Award by arbitrator or umpire	5,000
13.	Bill of exchange [as defined in section 2] not being a BOND, bank note or currency note	5,000
14.	Bill of lading (including a thorough bill of lading)	5,000
15.	Bill of sale	5,000
16.	Bond (not being a debenture)	5,000
17.	Cancellation – instrument of	5,000
18.	Capital duty –	
	(i) on nominal share capital or any increase thereof of any company incorporated in Uganda with limited liability – of the total value.	0.5%
	(ii) on increase of share capital of any company when the increase is a condition precedent for disbursement of loan funds of a development project	Nil
	(iii) on becoming public through the operation of the stock exchange	Nil
19.	Caveat (under the Registration of Titles Act or any other law relating to the registration of title to land)	5,000
20.	Certificate of sale (in respect of each property put up as a separate lot and sold)	5,000

	Instrument	Proper stamp duty (in shillings)
21.	Charter party (instrument for charter hire or vessel or part thereof)	5,000
22.	Cheque	
23.	Composition deed (instrument of conveyance of property by a debtor for the benefit of his or her creditors) – of the total value	1%
24.	Conveyance (not being transfer) – of the total value	1%
25.	Copy of extract	5,000
26.	Counterpart or duplicate of an instrument chargeable with duty and in respect of which the proper duty has been paid	5,000
27.	Debenture – whether a mortgage debenture or not, being of a marketable security – of the total value	0.5%
28.	Deed	5,000
29.	Delivery – order in respect of goods	5,000
30.	Divorce – (any instrument by which any person effects the dissolution of his or her marriage)	5,000
30.	Equitable mortgage – of the total value	0.5%
32.	Exchange of property – of the total value	1%
33.	Extract	5,000
34.	Further charge – any instrument imposing a further charge on] mortgaged property – of the total value	0.5%
35.	Gift – instrument not being a settlement or will or transfer – of the total value	1%
36.	Hire purchase agreement – of the total value	1%
37.	Indemnity bond	5,000
38.	Lease – of the total value	1%
39.	Letter of credit – any instrument by which one person authorises another to give credit to the person in whose favour it is drawn	5,000
40.	Letter of licence – any agreement between a debtor and his or her creditors that the latter shall for a specified time, suspend their claims and allow the debtor to carry on business at his or her own discretion.	5,000
41.	Memorandum of association of a company	10,000
42.	(a) Mortgage deed of the total value	0.5%
	A mortgagor who gives a power of attorney to collect rents of a lease of the property mortgaged is deemed to give possession within the meaning of this item	
	(b) Where a collateral or auxiliary or additional or substituted security is given by way of further assurance where the principal or primary security is duly stamped	5,000
43.	Mortgage of a crop – including any instrument, endorsement, note, attestation, certificate or entry not being protest of a bill or note, made or signed by a notary public in the execution of the duties of his or her office or by any other person lawfully acting as a notary public.	5,000

	Instrument	Proper stamp duty (in shillings)
44.	Notarial act – made or signed by a notary public in the execution of the duties of his or her office or by any other person lawfully acting as a notary public	5,000
45.	Note or memorandum – sent by a broker or agent to his or her principal intimating the purchase or sale on account of that principal of any goods, stock or marketable security	5,000
46.	Note of protest by the master of ship	5,000
47.	Partition	5,000
48.	(1) Partnership	5,000
	(2) Dissolution of partnership	5,000
49.	(1) Policy of insurance	
	(2) Life insurance	5,000
50.	Power of attorney	5,000
51.	Promissory note	5,000
52.	Protest of bill or note – any declaration in writing made by a notary public, attesting the dishonour of a bill of exchange or promissory note	5,000
53.	Receipt – as defined by section 1 for any money or other property the amount of value of which exceeds shs. 50,000	5,000
54.	Reconveyance of mortgaged property – of the total value	1%
55.	Release – any instrument not being such a release as is provided for by section 27 (2) by which a person renounces a claim upon another person or against any specified property.	5,000
56.	Respondetia bond – any instrument securing a loan on the cargo laden on board a ship and making repayment contingent on the arrival of the cargo at the port of destination.	5,000
57.	Security bond or mortgage deed – executed by way of security for the due execution of an office, or to account for money or other property received by virtue thereof or executed by a surety to secure the due performance of a contract – of the total value	1%
58.	Settlement –	
	(a) Instrument of – (including a deed of dower)	5,000
	(b) Revocation of 5,000	
59.	Share warrants – to bearer issued under the Companies Act – of the total value	1%
60.	Shipping order – for or relating to the conveyance of goods on board any vessel	5,000
61.	Solemn or statutory declaration	5,000
62.	Surrender of lease	5,000
63.	(i) Transfer – of the total value	1%
	(ii) The transfer of shares in an incorporated company listed on the stock exchange, arising from the trading of those shares on the stock exchange	

	Instrument	Proper stamp duty (in shillings)
	(iii) Of debt securities listed on the stock exchange arising from trading on the stock exchange	Nil.
64.	Trust – concerning any property made by any writing not being a will	5,000
65.	Any instrument if attested not otherwise provided for	5,000

Second Part.

Rules as to composition for stamp duties.

1. Every account shall be made in such form and shall contain all such particulars as the revenue authority shall require.
2. Every account shall be a full and true account of all unstamped aviation personal accident policies of insurance issued during the quarter of a year ending on the quarterly day next preceding the delivery of the account, and of all sums of money received for or in respect of those policies so issued during that quarter, and of all sums of money received and not already accounted for in respect of any other unstamped aviation personal accident policies of insurance issued at any time before the commencement of the quarter.
3. Accounts shall be delivered to the revenue authority within twenty days after the 1st January, the 1st April, the 1st July and the 1st October in each year.
4. The duty shall be paid upon the delivery of the account.

History: Cap. 172; Act 16/1966; s.3; S.I 7/1967; S.I. 77/1967; S.I. 105/1967; Act 27/1969; S.I. 2/1975; Statute 6/1991; s. 20; Statute 1/1992, s.34; Statute 1/1993, ss. 19, 20; Statute 9/1994, s. 39; Act 3/1996, s. 6; S.I. 27/2000.

Commissioner's note: Under section 86 of the Uganda Communications Act, the Post Bank Uganda Limited has assumed the service of the Post Office Savings Bank, referred to in section 11 of this Act.

Cross References

Bills of Exchange Act, Cap. 68.
Civil Procedure Rules, S.I. 71-1.
Companies Act, Cap. 110.
Constitution of 1995.
Criminal Procedure Code Act, Cap. 116.
Merchant Shipping Act, 1894, of the United Kingdom, 57 & 58 Vict. c. 60.
Post Office Savings Bank Act, 1964 Revision, Cap. 89.
Registration of Titles Act, Cap. 230.

Statutory Instruments

1967 No. 7

The Stamps (Amendment) Instrument, 1967

IN EXERCISE of the powers conferred upon the Minister by subsection (3) of section 3 of the Stamps Act, this Instrument is hereby made this 10th day of January, 1967.

1. The Schedule to the Act is hereby amended by substituting for the First Part thereof, the Part set out in the Schedule to this Instrument.
2. This Instrument may be cited as the Stamps (Amendment) Instrument, 1967.

L. KALULE-SETTALA
Minister of Finance

Schedule
"First Part"
Stamp duty on instruments

Description of Instrument	*Proper Stamp Duty (in shillings)*
1. ACKNOWLEDGEMENT of a debt exceeding Shs.100000	1000
2. ADMINISTRATION-BOND–	
(1) where the amount does not exceed Shs. 100,000	Shs 1000

Statutory Instruments

1967 No. 77

The Stamps (Amendment) (No. 2) Instrument, 1967

IN EXERCISE of the powers conferred upon the Minister by subsection (3) of section 3 of the Stamps Act, this Instrument is hereby made this 8th day of July, 1967.

1. The Schedule to the Act is hereby amended by substituting for the First Part thereof, the Part set out in the Schedule to this Instrument.
2. This Instrument may be cited as the Stamps (Amendment) (No.2) Instrument, 1967.

L. KALULE- SETTALA
Minister of Finance

Schedule

"First Part"

Stamp duty on instruments

Description of Instrument	*Proper Stamp Duty*

1. ACKNOWLEDGEMENT of a debt exceeding Shs. 40 in amount or, value, written, signed by, or on behalf of, a debtor in order to supply evidence of such debt in any book (other than a banker's passbook) or on a separate piece of paper when such book or paper is left in the creditor's possession:

Provided that such acknowledgment does not contain any promise to pay the debt or any stipulation to pay interest or to deliver any goods or other property.

Cents 30.

2. ADMINISTRATION-BOND–

(1)	where the amount does not exceed Shs. 5,000	Shs 5.
(2)	where the amount exceeds shs 5000 but does not exceed 10,000	Shs 10.

Statutory Instruments

1967 No. 105

Corrigendum

Statutory Instrument 1967 No. 77

The Stamps (Amendment) (No. 2) Instrument, 1967

In the Schedule,

(a) in item 47. H *substitute* the expression "(No. 47F)" for the expression "(No. 47E)" occurring in column 2 thereof;

(b) in item 62 under the heading "Exemptions" *substitute* the expression "(iii)" for the expression "(ii)" occurring at the beginning of the last subparagraph of paragraph (b) thereof.

Date of publication: 20th October, 1967

Statutory Instruments 1970 No. 58

1970 No. 58
The Stamps (Compounding of Duty) Rules, 1970

IN EXERCISE of the powers conferred upon the Minister by section 8A of the Stamps Act, these Rules are hereby made this 8th day of April, 1970.[463]

1. Compounding of duty.

(1) Every bank shall compound duty on all bank cheques issued by it from the date of commencement of these Rules.

(2) The provisions of sub-rule (1) of this rule shall not apply to cheques specially printed for specific customers, travellers' cheques, drafts or any other commercial paper which is required by law to bear a revenue stamp.

2. Mode of compounding.

Every compounded cheque shall have the expression "Stamp duty paid" prominently printed and encircled at the top right-hand corner of the cheque.

3. When duty due and payable.

(1) Duty on cheques subject to compounding shall become due and payable on the issue of cheques at the time of issue to customers.

(2) Notwithstanding the provisions of sub-rule (1) of this rule, the Commissioner may permit the payment of duty to be deferred to a date not later than the fifteenth day of the month next following the month on which it became due.

(3) Notwithstanding the provisions of sub-rules (1) and (2) of this rule, the Commissioner may require the head office of each bank to deposit a sum of money which in the opinion would be sufficient to cover the duty payable under these Rules by the bank and its branches during the ensuing six months.

4. Returns. Schedule 1.

(1) Every bank shall submit to the Commissioner so as the reach him by the fifteenth day of each month, a return in the form prescribed in Schedule 1 to these Rules, giving details of the receipt, issue and duty payable in respect of cheques compounded during the previous month.

(2) Cheques subject to compounding of duty under these Rules which become spoilt or unusable prior to issue must be shown separately in the return submitted under this rule and such cheques must be attached to that return.

5. Duty payable.

(1) Where a deposit has been made in accordance with the provisions of sub-rule (3) of rule 3 of these Rules the Commissioner shall, on receipt of the return referred to in rule 4 of these Rules, charge that deposit account with the amount of duty payable.

(2) The Commissioner shall notify the head office of each bank the total amount charged to that bank's deposit account each month in respect of duty payable by that bank and its branches.

6. Refund of duty on compounded spoil cheques. Schedule 2.

(1) Any bank may submit an application to the Commissioner in the form prescribed in Schedule 2 to these Rules for the refund of compounded duty on cheques issued to customers which have become spoilt or unusable.

(2) Applications made under sub-rule (1) of this rule must be submitted so as to reach the Commissioner within twelve months of the date on which the duty on such cheques became due and payable.

(3) No refund shall be granted under this rule if the amount of refund claimed at any one time is less than fifty shillings.

(4) All refunds made under this rule shall be subject to the provisions of section 56 of the Stamps Act.

7. Persons exempted from duty.

A bank shall not issue cheques subject to compounding of duty to any person exempted from the payment of stamp duty on cheques, but such persons shall be issued with cheques specially printed for exempted persons.

8. Keeping of records.

Every bank shall keep the following records relating to cheques subject to compounding of duty, that is to say,

(a) an inventory suitably analysed to facilitate reconciliation with

(b) physical stocks containing particulars as to,

(i) the date of receipt of cheque books;

(ii) the quantity received and the serial numbers thereof;

(iii) the date, quantity and serial numbers of cheques issued; and

(iv) the balance of unissued quantity of cheques;

(a) a suitable daily record showing issues of cheques to customers and the charges made therefor;

(b) a separate ledger account in which all charges made to customers for cheques issued must be entered; and

(c) any other records which the Commissioner may from time to time, in writing, require.

9. Inspection of books and records.

The Commissioner, or an officer authorised by him in writing, may, from time to time, inspect any bank's books and records and may require officials of the bank to give him any information or explanation he may require in the performance of his duties.

10. Auditor's certificate.

Within one month after the end of its accounting year, every bank shall submit to the Commissioner an auditor's certificate certifying that all the records and returns required under these Rules have been properly kept or accurately submitted as the case may be.

11. Offences.

Any bank which,

(a) fails to pay duty or deposit a sum of money on account thereof, as the case may be, on due dates as provided under these Rules;

(b) fails or refuses to produce any information document, account or return required under the provisions of these Rules, or, as the case may be, produces such document, account or return later than the time specified in the provisions of these Rules or later than the date specified in a written notice from the Commissioner;

(c) pays any cheque on which duty has not been paid or exempted;

(d) commits an act in order to evade payment of duty payable on cheques issued by it; or

(e) contravenes any of the provisions of these Rules, commits an offence and shall be liable to a fine not exceeding one thousand shillings.

12. Transitional arrangements.

(1) Stocks of unembossed cheques held by any bank at the date of commencement of these Rules and which do not conform to rule 2 of these Rules shall continue to be embossed by the Commissioner as at present until exhausted.

(2) Every bank shall submit to the Commissioner within twenty-one days of commencement of these Rules a return of all the cheques referred to in sub-rule (1) of this rule containing the following particulars, that is to say,

(a) total number of unembossed cheques held; and

(b) serial numbers of those cheques.

(3) Every bank shall notify the Commissioner on each occasion unembossed cheques referred to in this rule are submitted for embossing and must give the following particulars, that is to say,

(a) total number of unembossed cheques submitted for embossing;

(b) serial number for the amount of duty paid in respect of those cheques;

(c) receipt number for the amount of duty paid in respect of those cheques.

13. Interpretation Act 16 of 1969.

In these Rules, unless the context otherwise requires, "bank" has the same meaning as in the Banking Act, 1969; "Commissioner" means the Commissioner Treasury Officer of Accounts.

14. Commencement.

These Rules shall come into force on the 1st day of July, 1970.

15. Citation.

These Rules may be cited as the Stamps (Compounding of Duty) Rules, 1970.

L. KALULE-SETTALA
Minister of Finance

Schedules

SCHEDULE 1

The stamps (compounding of duty) rules, 1970
Return in respect of cheques subject to compounding of duty for the month of .... 19 ....
To: The Commissioner /Treasury Officer of Accounts, *From:*..
(Name and address of bank)

We submit herewith a return in respect of bank cheques subject to compounding of duty for the months of....................19...........

We declare that to the best of our knowledge and belief the particulars contained herein are true and accurate.

	Quantity	*Serial Nos.*
(a) Balance of unissued cheques at the beginning of the month		
(b) Cheques received during the months		(1) *See details* overleaf
(c) Total of *(a)* and *(b)*		

	Quantity	Serial Nos.
(d) Less: (i) Unissued cheques spoilt during the month *(attached)*		(2) *See details overleaf*
(ii) Balance of unissued cheques at the end of the month		(3) *See details overleaf*

(iii) Total of (i) and (ii) .. ..

(e) Number of cheques on which duty is due and payable .. ..

(f) Amount of duty payable on *(e)* at the rate of 30cts. Per cheque Shs. ....

(g) Cheques for Shs. .... attached hereto. *(N.B)* – No. cheques should be sent where the head office of the bank has been required to pay a deposit under sub-rule (3) of rule (3).

Date.., 19............ ....

Signature of bank manager and official stamp

Schedule 2

THE STAMPS (COMPOUNDING OF DUTY) RULES, 1970

APPLICATION FOR REFUND OF COMPOUND DUTY ON CHEQUES

From…………………………………………………………………………………..
(Name and address of bank)

To: The Commissioner / Treasury Officer of Accounts, Kampala
Application is hereby made for refund of duty which was compounded on …………………….. *(quantity)*
Cheques (*attached)* which have become spoilt/ unusable, the particulars of which are as follows:-

Serial No.	Date duty became due and payable	Serial No.	Date duty became due and payable
…………	…………………………	…………	…………………………
…………	…………………………	…………	…………………………
…………	…………………………	…………	…………………………
…………	…………………………	…………	…………………………
…………	…………………………	…………	…………………………

……………………………………………………

Date ………………………… *Signature of bank manager and official stamp*

For Official Use	
Checked and verified by………………………. Amount of refund payable Shs……………………	Refund authorised by…………………… Date……………………

Date of publication: 17th April, 1970

Statutory Instruments

1970 No. 64
The Stamps (Exemption) (No. 2) Instrument, 1970

IN EXERCISE of the powers conferred upon the Minister by section 10 of the Stamps Act, this Instrument is hereby made this 11th day of April, 1970.

1. The instruments specified in the Schedule to this Instrument are hereby exempted from the payment of stamp duty.
2. This Instrument may be cited as the Stamps (Exemption) (No. 2) Instrument, 1970.

L. KALULE-SETTALA
Minister of Finance

Schedule

The original, counterparts and duplicates of,

(a) the Agreement (which relates to the transfer to the Housing Finance Company of Uganda Limited of the undertaking in Uganda of the First Permanent (East Africa Limited) made between the Government, the National Housing Corporation and the Commonwealth Development Corporation and dated 18th April, 1968; and

(b) every Note or Instrument executed pursuant to paragraph *(h)* of clause 10 of the said Agreement.

Date of publication: 30th April, 1970.

Statutory Instruments

1970 No. 94
The Stamps (Exemption From Stamp Duty) (No. 2) Instrument, 1970

IN EXERCISE of the powers conferred upon the Minister by section 10 of the Stamps Act, this Instrument is hereby made this 14th day of May, 1970.

1. Any instrument executed after the date set out in column 1 of the Schedule to this Instrument by a person named in column 2 thereof whereby any movable or immovable property or any estate or interest therein or any debenture, mortgage, charge, interest therein held by or vested in him on 1st November 1969, is by such person assigned or memorandum of deposit, letter of hypothecation, pledge, lien, agreement, bill of sale, policy of insurance, indemnity or guarantee or any other security whatsoever or any transferred to or vested in the person named opposite to such first named person in column 3 of the Schedule hereto is hereby exempted from the payment of stamp duty.

2. This Instrument may be cited as the Stamps (Exemption from Stamp Duty) (No. 2) Instrument, 1970.

L. KALULE-SETTALA
Minister of Finance

Schedule

1st November, 1969.	National and Grindlays Bank Limited	Grindlays Bank (Uganda) Limited
1st November, 1969.	Barclays Bank D.C.O.	Barclays Bank of Uganda Limited
1st November, 1969.	The Standard Bank Limited	Standard Bank (Uganda) Limited
1st January 1970	Algemene Bank Nederland N.V.	Grindlays Bank Uganda Limited
1st February, 1970	Commercial Bank of Africa Limited	Barclays Bank of Uganda Limited
1st November 1969	Ottoman Bank	Grindlays Bank (Uganda) Limited
1st November 1969	The Bank of India Limited	Bank of India (Uganda) Limited
1st November 1969	The Bank of Baroda Limited	Bank of Baroda (Uganda) Limited

Date of publication: 12th June, 1970

Statutory Instruments

1970 No. 131
The Stamps (Exemption) (No. 3) Instrument, 1970

IN EXERCISE of the powers conferred upon the Minister by section 10 of the Stamps Act, this Instrument is hereby made this 19th day of June, 1970.

1. Any instrument executed between the Government and any person for the purpose of providing financial assistance to that person in relation to his studies, or other training undertaken within or outside East Africa, is hereby exempted from the payment of stamp duty.

2. This Instrument may be cited as the Stamps (Exemption) (No. 3) Instrument, 1970.

L. KALULE-SETTALA
Minister of Finance

Date of publication: 24th July, 1970

Statutory Instruments

1970 No. 204
The Stamps (Exemption From Stamp Duty) (No. 6) Instrument, 1970

IN EXERCISE of the powers conferred upon the Minister by section 10 of the Stamps Act, this Instrument is hereby made this 7th day of December, 1970.

1. The Uganda American Insurance Company Limited is hereby exempted from the payment of stamp duty.

2. This Instrument may be cited as the Stamps (Exemption from Stamp Duty) (No. 6) Instrument, 1970.

L. KALULE-SETTALA
Minister of Finance

Date of publication: 11th December, 1970

Statutory Instruments

1971 No. 67
The Stamps (Exemption) Instrument, 1971

IN EXERCISE of the powers conferred upon the Minister by section 10 of the Stamps Act, this Instrument is hereby made this 8th day of May, 1971.

1. All statutory leases granted to urban authorities by Uganda Land Commission are hereby exempted from payment of stamp duty.

2. This Instrument may be cited as the Stamps (Exemption) Instrument, 1971.

E. B. WAKHWEYA
Minister of Finance

Date of publication: 21st May, 1971

Statutory Instruments

1972 No. 63
The Stamps (Exemption) Instrument, 1972

IN EXERCISE of the powers conferred upon the Minister by section 10 of the Stamps Act, this Instrument is hereby made this 11th day of April, 1972.

1. Any cheque issued by and bearing the name of the United Nations High Commission for refugees is hereby exempted from stamp duty.

2. This Instrument may be cited as the Stamps (Exemption) Instrument, 1972.

E. B. WAKHWEYA
Minister of Finance

Date of publication: 21st April, 1972.

Statutory Instruments

1972 No. 103
The Stamps (Exemption) (No. 2) Instrument, 1972

IN EXERCISE of the powers conferred upon the Minister by section 10 of the Stamps Act, this Instrument is hereby made this 21st day of June, 1972.

1. Any instrument executed by the Produce Marketing Board with any bank for the purpose of obtaining a bank overdraft is hereby exempted from stamp duty.
2. This Instrument may be cited as the Stamps (Exemption) (No. 2) Instrument, 1972.

E. B. WAKHWEYA
Minister of Finance, Planning & Economic Development

Date of publication: 30th June, 1972.

Statutory Instruments

1972 No. 133
The Stamps (Exemption From Stamp Duty) (No. 3) Instrument, 1972

IN EXERCISE of the powers conferred upon the Minister by section 10 of the Stamps Act, this Instrument is hereby made this 9th day of August, 1972.

1. Any instrument executed after the 30th day of June, 1972, by Bank of India (Uganda) Limited, whereby any moveable or immovable property or any estate or interest therein or any debenture, mortgage, charge, memorandum of deposit, letter of hypothecation, pledge, lien, agreement, bill of sale, policy of insurance, indemnity or guarantee or any other security whatsoever or any interest therein held by or vested in Bank of India (Uganda) Limited assigned conveyed or transferred to or vested in Bank of Baroda (Uganda) Limited, is hereby exempted from the payment of stamp duty.
2. This Instrument may be cited as the Stamps (Exemption from Stamp Duty) (No. 3) Instrument, 1972.

E. B. WAKHWEYA
Minister of Finance, Planning & Economic Development

Date of publication: 18th August, 1972.

Statutory Instruments

1972 No. 145
The Stamps (Exemption) (No. 4) Instrument, 1972

IN EXERCISE of the powers conferred upon the Minister by section 10 of the Stamps Act, this Instrument is hereby made this 4th day of September, 1972.

1. Any cheque issued or any instrument executed by and bearing the name of United Nations International Children's Education Fund is hereby exempted from stamp duty.
2. This Instrument may be cited as the Stamps (Exemption) (No. 4) Instrument, 1972.

E. B. WAKHWEYA
Minister of Finance, Planning & Economic Development

Date of publication: 15th September, 1972.

Statutory Instruments

1972 No. 178
The Stamps (Exemption) (No. 4) (Amendment) Instrument, 1972

IN EXERCISE of the powers conferred upon the Minister by section 10 of the Stamps Act, this Instrument is hereby made this 20th day of November, 1972.

1. The Stamps (Exemption) (No. 4) Instrument, 1972, is hereby amended by substituting for the expression "United Nations International Children's Education Fund" occurring in paragraph 1 thereof, the expression "United Nations Children's Fund".
2. This instrument may be cited as the Stamps (Exemption) (No. 4) (Amendment) Instrument, 1972.

E. B. WAKHWEYA
Minister of Finance, Planning & Economic Development

Date of publication: 24th November, 1972.

Statutory Instruments

1975 No. 20

The Stamps (Amendment) Instrument, 1975

IN EXERCISE of the powers conferred upon the Minister by subsection (3) of section 3 of the Stamps Act, this Instrument is hereby made this 5th day of March, 1975.

1. Item 48 of the Schedule of the Act is hereby amended,

(a) by inserting immediately after paragraph (i) thereof, the following new paragraph and the corresponding proper stamp duty therefore,

"(ii)when authorising one person to act in more than one transaction or generally Shs. 15";

(b) by renumbering the existing paragraphs (ii) to (v) as paragraphs (iii) to (vi), respectively.

2. This Instrument may be cited as the Stamps (Amendment) Instrument, 1975.

A.C.K. OBOTH- OFUMBI,

Minister of Internal Affairs (holding the portfolio of Minister of Finance)

Date of publication: 27th March, 1975.

Statutory Instruments

1978 No. 52

The Stamps (Exemption) Instrument, 1978

IN EXERCISE of the powers conferred upon the Minister by section 10 of the Stamps Act, this Instrument is hereby made this 12th day of June, 1978.

1. The co-operative unions specified in the schedule to this Instrument are hereby exempted from the payment of stamp duty in respect of bank loans secured for purposes of crop finance.

2. This Instrument may be cited as the Stamps (Exemption) Instrument, 1978.

BRIG. MOSES ALI,

Minister of Finance, Planning & Economic Development

Schedule

Name of Union	Address
East Mengo Growers Co-operative Union Ltd.	P.O. Box 7092, Kampala
West Mengo Growers Co-operative Union Ltd.	P.O. Box 7039, Kampala
Wamala Growers Co-operative Union Ltd	P.O. Box 99, Mityana
Buruli Growers Co-operative Union Ltd	P.O. Luwero, Nakasongola
Masaka District Co-operative Union Ltd	P.O. Box 284, Masaka
Banyankore Kweterana Co-operative Union Ltd	P.O. Box 324, Mbarara
Kigezi District Co-operative Union Ltd	P.O. Box 45, Rukungiri
Kigezi Vegetable Co-operative Union Ltd	P.O. Box 195, Kabale
North Kigezi Tobacco Co-operative Union Ltd	P.O. Box 61, Rukungiri
Nyakatonzi Growers Co-operative Union Ltd	P.O. Box 32, Kasese
Bwamba Rwenzori Co-operative Union Ltd	P.O. Box 1100, Bundibugyo
Toro Tea Growers Co-operative Union Ltd	P.O. Box 496, Fort Portal
Kakumiro Growers Co-operative Union Ltd	P.O. Box 511, Kakumiro
Bunyoro Growers Co-operative Union Ltd	P.O. Box 1, Masindi
West Acholi Growers Co-operative Union Ltd	P.O. Box 225, Gulu
East Acholi Growers Co-operative Union Ltd	P.O. Box 112, Kitgum

Date of publication: 22nd June, 1978.

Statutory Instruments

1979 No. 8
The Stamps (Exemption) (Amendment) Instrument, 1979

IN EXERCISE of the powers conferred upon the Minister by section 10 of the Stamps Act, this Instrument is hereby made this 12th day of September, 1979.

1. The schedule to the Stamps (Exemption) Instrument, 1978, is hereby amended by adding at the end thereof, the following,

Name of Union	Address
Madi Co-operative Union	P.O. Box 52, Adjumani
Central West Nile Union	P.O. Box 33, Arua
South West Nile Union	P.O. Box 33, Pakwach
Lango Co-operative Union	P.O. Box 59, Lira
Teso Co-operative Union	P.O. Box 231, Soroti
North Mbale Co-operative Union	P.O. Box 447, Mbale
Bugisu Co-operative Union	Private Bag, Mbale
Masaaba Co-operative Union	P.O. Box 991, Mbale
Sebei Elgon Co-operative Union	P.O. Box 12, Kapchwora
South Bukedi Co-operative Union	P.O. Box 101, Jinja
Busoga Growers Co-operative Union	Private Bag, Jinja
Okoro Coffee Co-operative Union	P.O. Box 22, Nebbi
Middle North Tobacco Co-operative Union	P.O. Box 186, Gulu

Statutory Instruments

1980 No. 22
The Stamps Duty (Exemption of Duty) (No. 1) Instrument, 1980

IN EXERCISE of the powers conferred upon the Minister by section 10 of the Stamps Act, this Instrument is hereby made this 18th day of August, 1980.

1. The enterprises specified in the Schedule to this Instrument are hereby exempted from the payment of stamp duty in respect of all instruments by them or on their behalf.

2. This Instrument shall be deemed to have come into force on the 10th day of March, 1980, and shall remain in force for a period of five years.

3. This Instrument may be cited as the Stamps Duty (Exemption of Duty) (No. 1) Instrument, 1980.

LAWRENCE SEBALU,
Minister of Finance

Schedule

1. Messrs. Continental Sugar Corporation Limited.
2. EMCO Glass (East Africa) Limited.
3. East Africa Steel Corporation Limited.
4. EMCO Oil Refineries Limited.
5. Madhvani Soap Industries Limited.
6. Madhvani Confectioners Limited.

Date of publication: 31st October, 1980

Statutory Instruments

1981 No. 16
The Stamps Duty (Exemption of Duty) (No. 1) Instrument, 1981

IN EXERCISE of the powers conferred upon the Minister by section 10 of the Stamps Act, this Instrument is hereby made this 31st day of March, 1981.

1. The enterprises specified in the schedule to this Instrument are hereby exempted from the payment of Stamp Duty in respect of all transactions and transfers of assets carried on by them or on their behalf.

2. This Order shall be deemed to have come into force on the 1st day of March 1980, and shall remain in force for a period of five years.

3. This Instrument may be cited as The Stamps Duty (Exemption of Duty) (No. 1) Instrument, 1981.

APOLO MILTON OBOTE,
President (holding the portfolio of the Minister of Finance).

Schedule

1. The Uganda Sugar Corporation limited
2. Ugma Engineering Corporation.
3. Cable Corporation Limited.

Date of publication : 8th March, 1981

STATUTORY INSTRUMENT
SUPPLEMENT No. 21 29th July, 1994

STATUTORY INSTRUMENTS SUPPLEMENT
to the Uganda Gazette No. 32 Volume LXXXVII dated 29th July, 1994
printed by UPPC, Entebbe by Order of Government.

Statutory Instruments

1994 No. 240

The Stamps Duty (Exemption from Stamp Duty) (No. 2) Instruments, 1994

IN EXERCISE of the powers conferred upon the Minister by section 10 of the Stamps Act, this Instrument is hereby made this 19th day of April, 1994.

1. This Instrument may be cited as the Stamps (Exemption from Stamp Duty) (No. 2) Instrument, 1994.

2. Any instrument executed by Agricultural Enterprises Limited or its subsidiaries on the one hand and Rwenzori Highlands Tea Company Limited on the other hand whereby any movable or immovable property or any estate or interest therein held by or vested in Agricultural Enterprises Limited or its subsidiaries assigned, conveyed or transferred to or vested in Rwenzori Highlands Tea Company Limited is exempted from the payment of Stamp Duty.

J.S MAYANJA-NKANGI
Minister of Finance and Economic Planning

Statutory Instrument

SUPPLEMENT No. 21 4th April, 1996

STATUTORY INSTRUMENTS SUPPLEMENT
to the Uganda Gazette No. 21 Volume LXXXVII dated 4th April, 1996
printed by UPPC, Entebbe by Order of Government.

Statutory Instruments

1996 No. 15
The Stamps (Exemption from Stamp Duty) Instrument, 1996

IN EXERCISE of the powers conferred upon the Minister by section 10 of the Stamps Act, this Instrument is hereby made this 21st day of March, 1996.

1. This Instrument may be cited as the Stamps (Exemption from Stamp Duty) Instrument, 1996.

2. The Stamp duty chargeable under the provisions of the Act on Instruments specified in the first column of the Schedule to this Order in favour of persons specified in the second column of the Schedule to this Order is exempted.

CHAPTER 273

THE MONEY-LENDERS ACT

Arrangement of Sections

Section

SCHEDULE

CHAPTER 273

THE MONEY-LENDER'S ACT

[Commencement 1ST January, 1952.]

An Act to make provision for the regulation of money-lending.

1. Interpretation.

(1) In this Act, unless the context otherwise requires–

(a) "authorised name" and "authorised address" mean respectively the name under which and the address at which a money-lender is authorised by a certificate granted under this Act to carry on business as a money-lender;

(b) "business name" means the name or style under which any business is carried on, whether in partnership or otherwise;

(c) "certificate" means a certificate granted under section 3;

(d) "chattels transfer" means a bill of sale, a letter of hypothecation, or a hire purchase agreement;

(e) "firm" mens an unincorporated body of two or more individuals, or one or more individuals and one or more corporations, or two or more corporations, who have entered into partnership with one another with a view to carrying on business for profit;

(f) "interest" includes any amount, by whatsoever name called, in excess of the principal, paid or payable to a money-lender in consideration of or otherwise in respect of loan;

(g) "magistrate" means a chief magistrate, a magistrate grade I or grade II and a magistrate of the first or second class;

(h) "money-lender" includes every person whose business is that of money-lending or who advertises or announces himself or holds himself out in any way as carrying on that business whether or not that person also possesses or earns property or money derived from sources other than the lending of money and whether or not that person carries on the business as a principal or agent; but shall not include–

  (a) any person *bona fide* carrying on the business of banking or insurance or *bona fide* carrying on any business not having for its primary object the lending of money, in the course of which and for the purposes whereof he lends money;

  (b) any society registered under the Co-operative Societies Act;

  (c) any body corporate, incorporated or empowered by special Act to lend money in accordance with that Act;

  (d) any person or body corporate exempted from the provisions of this Act by order of the Minister;

(i) "principal" means in relation to a loan the amount actually lent to the borrower.

(2) Where by a contract for the loan of money by a money-lender the interest charged on the loan is not expressed in terms of a rate, any amount paid or payable to the money-lender under the contract, other than simple interest charged in accordance with the proviso to section 8 of this Act, shall be appropriated to principle and interest in the proportion that the principal bears to the total amount of the interest, and the rate per centum per annum represented by the interest charged as calculated in accordance with the provisions of the schedule to this Act shall be deemed to be the rate of interest charged on the loan.

2. Licences to be taken out by money-lenders.

(1) Except as hereinafter provided, every money-lender shall take out annually in respect of every address at which he carries on his business as such, a licence (in this Act referred to as a "money-lender's licence") which shall expire on the thirty-first day of December in every year, and there shall be charged on every money-lender's licence a licence fee of one thousand shillings, or, if the licence be taken out not more than six months before the expiration thereof, of five hundred shillings:

(2) Provided that if one partner in a firm of money-lenders has duly taken out a money-lender's licence, every other partner in the firm shall, subject to the provisions of section 4 of this Act, be issued with a money-lender's licence free of charge for the business of the firm for such time as he shall remain a member of the firm.

(3) A money-lender's licence shall be taken out by a money-lender in his true name, and shall be void if it be taken out in any other name, but every money-lender's licence shall also show the money-lender's authorised name and authorised address.

(4) If any person–

(a) takes out a money-lender's licence in any name other than his true name; or

(b) carries on business as a money-lender without having in force a proper money-lender's licence authorising him so to do so, or being licensed as a money-lender, carries on business as such in any name other than his authorised address or addresses; or

(c) enters into any agreement in the course of his business as a money-lender with respect to the advance or repayment of money, or takes any security for money in the course of his business as a money-lender, otherwise than in his authorised name, he shall be guilty of a contravention of the provisions of this Act and shall for each offence be liable on conviction to a penalty of two thousand shillings, provided that, on a second or subsequent conviction of any person, other than a company, for an offence under this subsection, the court may, in lieu of or in addition to ordering the offender to pay the penalty aforesaid, order him to be imprisoned for a term not exceeding three months, and an offender being a company shall on a second or subsequent conviction be liable to a penalty of ten thousand shillings.

3. Certificate required for grant of money-lender's licence.

(1) A money-lender's licence shall not be granted except to a person who holds a certificate granted in accordance with the provisions of this section authorising the grant of the licence to that person, and a separate certificate shall be required in respect of every separate licence.

(2) Any money-lender's licence granted in contravention of this section shall be void.

(3) Certificates under this section (in this Act referred to as "certificates") shall be granted by a magistrate having jurisdiction in the place in which the money-lender's business is to be carried on.

(4) Every certificate granted to a money-lender shall show his true name and the name under which, and the address at which, he is authorised by the certificate to carry on business as such, and a certificate shall not authorise a money-lender to carry on business at more than one address or under more than one name, or under any name which includes the word "bank", or otherwise implies that he carries on banking business, and no certificate shall authorise a money-lender to carry on business under any name except–

(a) his true name; or

(b) the name of a firm in which he is a partner, not being a farm required by the Business Names Registration Act to be registered; or

(c) a business name, whether of an individual or of a firm in which he is a partner, under which he or the firm has, at the commencement of this Act, been registered for not less than three years under the Business Names Registration Act.

(5) A certificate shall come into force on the date specified therein, and shall expire on the next following thirty-first day of December.

(6) A certificate shall not be refused except on one or more of the following grounds–

(a) that satisfactory evidence has not been produced of the good character of the applicant, and, in the case of a company, of the persons responsible for the management thereof;

(b) that satisfactory evidence has been produced that the applicant, or any person responsible or proposed to be responsible for the management of his business as a money-lender, is not a fit and proper person to hold a certificate;

(c) that the applicant, or any person responsible or proposed to be responsible for the management of his business as a money-lender, is by order of a court disqualified from holding a certificate;

(d) that the applicant has not complied with the provisions of any rules made under this Act with respect to applications for certificates.

(7) Any person aggrieved by the refusal of a magistrate to grant a certificate may appeal to the High Court.

4. Suspension and forfeiture of money-lender's certificate.

(1) Where any person, being the holder of a certificate, is convicted of any offence under this Act, the court–

(a) may order that any certificate held by that person and in the case of a partner in a firm by any other partner in the firm, shall either be suspended for such time as it thinks fit, or shall be forfeited, and may also, if it thinks fit, declare any such person, or any person responsible for the management of the money-lending business carried on by the person convicted, to be disqualified from obtaining a certificate for such time as it thinks fit; and

(b) shall cause particulars of the convicted and of any order made by it under this section to be endorsed on every certificate held by the person convicted or by any other person affected by the order, and shall cause copies of those particulars to be sent to the authority by whom any certificate so endorsed was granted.

(2) Where by order of a court a certificate held by any person is suspended or forfeited, or any person is disqualified from obtaining a certificate, he may, whether or not he is the person convicted, appeal against the order in the same manner as any person convicted may appeal against his conviction, and the court may, if it thinks fit, pending the appeal, defer the operation of the order:

(3) Any certificate required by a court for endorsement in accordance with the foregoing provisions of this section shall be produced in such manner and within such time as may be directed by the court, by the person by whom it is held, and any person who, without reasonable cause, makes default in producing any certificate so required shall be guilty of an offence and shall, in respect of each offence, be liable on conviction by a magistrate to a penalty not exceeding one hundred shillings for each day during which the default continues.

(4) Where a certificate held by any person is ordered to be suspended or to be forfeited under the foregoing provisions of this section, any money-lender's licences granted to that person, whether in pursuance of that or any other certificate, shall be suspended or become void, as the case may be.

5. Names to be stated on documents issued by money-lenders.

(1) Without prejudice to the provisions of section 21 of the Business Names Registration Act, a money-lenders shall not, for the purposes of his business as such, issue or publish, or cause to be issued or published, any advertisement, circular, business letter or other similar document which does not show in such manner as to be not less conspicuous than any other name, the authorised name of the money-lender, and any money-lender who acts in contravention of this subsection shall be guilty of an offence and liable on conviction by a magistrate to a fine not exceeding four hundred shillings in respect of each offence.

(2) If a money-lender, for the purposes of his business as such, issues or publishes, or causes to be issued or published, any advertisement, circular or document of any kind whatsoever containing expressions which might reasonably be held to imply that he carries on banking business, he shall be guilty of an offence and shall on conviction by a magistrate be liable to a fine not exceeding two thousand shillings, and on a second or subsequent conviction, in lieu of or in addition to such a fine as aforesaid, to imprisonment for a term not exceeding three months, or, in the case of a second or subsequent conviction of an offender being a company, to a fine not exceeding ten thousand shillings.

6. Form of money-lender's contracts.

(1) No contract for the repayment by a borrower of money lent to him or to any agent on his behalf by a money lender or for the payment by him of interest on money so lent, and no security given by the borrower or by any such agent as aforesaid in respect of any such contract shall be enforceable, unless a note or memorandum in writing of the contract is made and signed personally by the borrower, and unless a copy thereof is delivered or sent to the borrower within seven days of the making of the contract; and no such contract or security shall be enforceable if it is proved that the note or memorandum aforesaid was not signed by the borrower before the money was lent or before the security was given, as the case may be.

(2) The note or memorandum aforesaid shall contain all the terms of the contract, and in particular shall show the date on which the loan is made, the amount of the principal of the loan, and either the interest charged on the loan expressed in terms of a rate per centum per annum, or the rate per centum per annum represented by the interest charged as calculated in accordance with the provisions of the Schedule to this Act.

7. Prohibition of compound interest and provisions as to defaults.

(1) Subject as hereinafter provided, any contract made after the commencement of this Act for the loan of money by a money-lender shall be illegal in so far as it provides directly or indirectly for the payment of compound interest or for the rate or amount of interest being increased by reason of any default in the payment of sums due under the contract:

(2) Provided that provision may be made by any such contract that if default is made in the payment upon the due date of any sum payable to the money-lender under the contract, whether in respect of principal or interest, the money-lender shall be entitled to charge simple interest on that sum from the date of the default until the sum is paid, at a rate not exceeding the rate payable in respect of the principal apart from any default, and any interest so charged shall not be reckoned for the purposes of this Act as part of the interest charged in respect of the loan.

8. Obligation to supply information to borrower.

(1) In respect of every contract for the repayment of money lent by a month-lender, whether made before or after the commencement of this Act, the money-lender shall, on any reasonable demand in writing being made by the borrower at any time during the continuance of the contract and on tender by the borrower of the sum of one shilling for expenses, supply to the borrower or, if the borrower so requires, to any person specified in that behalf in the demand, a statement signed by the money-lender or his agent showing–

(a) the date on which the loan was made, the amount of the principal of the loan and the rate per centum per annum of interest charged;

(b) the amount of any payment already received by the money-lender in respect of the loan and the date on which it was made; and

(c) the amount of every sum due to the money-lender but unpaid and the date upon which it became due, and the amount of interest accrued due and unpaid in respect of every such sum; and

(d) the amount of every sum not yet due which remains outstanding, and the date upon which it will become due.

(2) A money-lender shall, on any reasonable demand in writing by the borrower, and on tender of a reasonable sum for expenses, supply a copy of any document relating to a loan made by him or any security therefor to the borrower, or, if the borrower so requires, to any person specified in that behalf in the demand.

(3) If a money-lender to whom a demand has been made under this section fails without reasonable excuse to comply therewith one month after the demand has been made, he shall not, so long as the default continues, be entitled to sue for or recover any sum due under the contract on account either of principal or interest, and interest shall not be chargeable in respect of the period of the default, and if such default is made or continued after proceedings have ceased to lie in respect of the loan, the money-lender shall be guilty of an offence and shall be liable on conviction by a magistrate to a fine not exceeding one hundred shillings for every day on which the default continues.

9. Money-lenders to give receipts and keep records.

(1) Every money-lender shall give a receipt for every payment made to him on account of a loan or of interest thereon; every such receipt shall be given immediately the payment is made.

(2) Every money-lender shall keep a book which shall be securely bound and paged so that leaves cannot be removed or inserted without apparent damage, in which he shall enter in connection with every loan made by him–

(a) the date on which the loan was made;

(b) the amount of the principal;

(c) the rate of interest;

(d) all sums received in respect of the loan or the interest thereon, with the dates of payment thereof and shall produce such book when required to do so by any court.

(3) The entries in the said books hall be made forthwith on the making of the loan or the receipt of sums paid in respect thereof, as the case may be.

(4) Any money-lender who fails to comply with any of the requirements of this section shall not be entitled to enforce any claim in respect of any transaction in relation to which the default shall have been made, and shall be guilty of an offence under this Act and shall be liable on conviction to a fine not exceeding two hundred shillings or in the case of a continuing offence to a fine not exceeding one hundred shillings for each day or part of a day during which such offence continues.

10. Powers of court.

(1) Where proceedings are taken in any court by any person for the recovery of any money lent, or the enforcement of any agreement or security made or taken in respect of money lent, the plaintiff shall produce a statement of this account as prescribed in section 9 of this Act.

(2) Where in any such proceedings there is evidence which satisfies the court that default in payment of any sum due to the plaintiff under a contract for the loan of money has been made by the borrower and it is proved that any further amount is outstanding under the contract but not yet due, the court may determine the contract and order the principal outstanding to be paid to the plaintiff with such interest thereon, if any, as the court may allow up to the date of payment.

(3) The foregoing provisions of this section shall apply to any transaction which, whatever its form may be, is substantially one of money-lending.

(4) Nothing in the foregoing provisions of this section shall affect the rights of any *bona fide* assignee or holder for value without notice.

(5) Nothing in this section shall be construed as derogating from the existing powers or jurisdiction of any court.

11. Reopening transactions of money-lenders.

(1) Where proceedings are taken in any court by a money-lender for the recovery of any money lent after the commencement of this Act, or the enforcement of any agreement or security made or taken after the commencement of this Act, in respect of money lent either before or after the commencement of this Act, and there is evidence which satisfies the court that the interest charged in respect of the sum actually lent is excessive, or that the amounts charged for expenses, inquiries, fines, bonus, premium, renewals or any other charges are excessive, and that, in either case, the transaction is harsh and unconscionable, or is otherwise such that the court of equity would give relief, the court may reopen the transaction, and take an account between the money-lender and the person sued, and may, notwithstanding any statement or settlement of account or any agreement purporting to close previous dealings and create a new obligation reopen any account already taken between them, and relieve the person sued from payment of any sum in excess of the sum adjudged by the court to be fairly due in respect of such principal, interest and charges, as the court, having regard to the risk and all the circumstances, may adjudge to be reasonable; and if any such excess has been paid, or allowed in account, by the debtor, may order the creditor to repay it; and may set aside, either wholly or in part, or revise or alter any security given or agreement made in respect of money lent by the money-lender, and if the money-lender has parted with the security may order him to indemnify the borrower or other person sued.

(2) Any court in which proceedings might be taken for the recovery of money lent by a money-lender shall have and may, at the instance of the borrower or surety or other person liable, exercise the like powers as may be exercised under this section, where proceedings are taken for the recovery of the money lent, and the court shall have power, notwithstanding any provision or agreement to the

contrary, to entertain any application under this Act by the borrower or surety, or other person liable, notwithstanding that the time for repayment of the loan, or any instalment thereof, may not have arrived.

(3) Where a court reopens a transaction of a money-lender under subsection (1) of this section, the court may require the money-lender to produce any certificate granted to him in accordance with the provisions of this Act, and may cause such particulars as the court thinks desirable to be endorsed on any such certificate, and a copy of the particulars to be sent to the authority by whom the certificate was granted.

(4) On any application relating to the admission or amount of a proof by a money-lender in any bankruptcy proceedings, the court may exercise the like powers as may be exercised under this section when proceedings are taken for the recovery of money.

(5) The foregoing provisions of this section shall apply to any transaction which, whatever its form may be, is substantially one of money-lending by a money-lender.

(6) Nothing in the foregoing provisions of this section shall affect the rights of any *bona fide* assignee or holder for value without notice.

(7) Nothing in this section shall be construed as derogating from the existing powers or jurisdiction of any court.

12. Harsh and unconscionable interest rates.

(1) Where, in any proceedings in respect of any money lent by a money-lender after the commencement of this Act or in respect of any agreement or security made or taken after the commencement of this Act in respect of money lent either before or after the commencement of this Act, it is found that the interest charged exceeds the rate of twenty-four per centum per annum, or the corresponding rate in respect of any other period , the court shall presume for the purposes of section 12 of this Act, that the interest charged is excessive and that the transaction is harsh and unconscionable, but this provision shall be without prejudice to the powers of the court under that section where the court is satisfied that the interest charged, although not exceeding twenty-four per centum per annum, is excessive.

(2) The powers of a court under subsection (2) of section 12 of this Act, may, in the event of the bankruptcy of the borrower be exercised at the instance of the trustee in bankruptcy, notwithstanding that he may not be a person liable in respect of the transaction.

(3) The powers of a court under subsection (2) of section 12 of this Act may be exercised notwithstanding that the money-lender's right of action for the recovery of the money lent is barred.

13. Restriction on money-lending advertisements.

(1) No person shall knowingly send or deliver or cause to be sent or delivered to any person except in response to his written request any circular or other document advertising the name, address or telephone number of a money-lender, or containing an invitation–

(a) to borrow money from a money-lender;

(b) to enter into any transaction involving the borrowing of money from a money-lender;

(c) to apply to any place with a view to obtaining information or advice as to borrowing any money from a money-lender.

(2) Subject as hereinafter provided, no person shall publish or cause to be published in any newspaper or other printed paper issued periodically for public circulation, or by means of any poster or placard, an advertisement advertising any such particulars, or containing any such invitation, as aforesaid,

(3) An advertisement in conformity with the requirements of this Act relating to the use of names on money-lenders' documents may be published by or on behalf of a money-lender in any newspaper or in any such paper as aforesaid or by means of a poster or placard exhibited at any authorised address of the money-lender, if it contains no addition to the particulars necessary to comply with the said requirements, except any of the following particulars, that is to say, any authorised address at which he carries on business as a money-lender, and the telegraphic address and telephone number thereof, any address at which he formerly carried on business, a statement that he lends money with or without security, and of the highest and lowest sums that he is prepared to lend, and a statement of the date on which the business carried on by him was first established.

(4) No money-lender or any person on his behalf shall employ any agent or canvasser for the purpose of inviting any person to borrow money or to enter into any transaction involving the borrowing of money from a money-lender, and no person shall act as such agent or canvasser, or demand or receive, directly or indirectly, any sum or other valuable consideration by way of commissioner or otherwise for introduction or undertaking to introduce to a money-lender any person desiring to borrow money.

(5) Where any document issued or published by or on behalf of a money-lender purports to indicate the terms of interest upon which he is willing to make loans or any particular loan, the document shall express the interest proposed to be charged in terms of a rate per centum per annum or show the rate per centum per annum represented by the interest proposed to be charged as calculated in accordance with the provisions of the Schedule to this Act.

(6) Any person acting in contravention of any of the provisions of this section shall be guilty of an offence and shall in respect of each offence be liable on conviction to imprisonment for a term not exceeding three months or a fine not exceeding two thousand shillings or to both such imprisonment and fine.

(7) Where it is shown that a money-lending transaction was brought about by a contravention of any of the provisions of this section, the transaction shall, notwithstanding that the money-lender was duly licensed under this Act, be illegal unless the money-lender proves that the contravention occurred without his consent or connivance.

14. Penalties for false statements and representations.

If any money-lender, or any manager, agent or clerk of a money-lender, or if any person being a director, manager or other officer or any corporation carrying on the business of a money-lender, by any false, misleading, or deceptive statement, representation or promise, or by any dishonest concealment of material facts, fraudulently induces or attempts to induce any person to borrow money or to agree to the terms on which money is or is to be borrowed, he shall be guilty of an offence and shall be liable on conviction to imprisonment for a term not exceeding two years, or to a fine not exceeding ten thousand shillings or to both such imprisonment and fine.

15. Notice and information on assignment of money-lenders' debts.

(1) Where any debt in respect of money lent by a money-lender whether before or after the commencement of this Act or in respect of interest on any such debt or the benefit of any agreement made or security taken in respect of any such debt or interest is assigned to any assignee, the assignor, whether he is the money-lender by whom the money was lent or any person to whom the debt has been previously assigned, shall, before the assignment is made–

(a) give to the assignee notice in writing that the debt, agreement or security is affected by the operation of this Act; and

(b) supply to the assignee all information necessary to enable him to comply with the provisions of this Act relating to the obligation to supply information as to the state of loans and copies of documents relating thereto, and any person acting in contravention of any of the provisions of this section shall be liable to indemnify any other person who is prejudiced by the contravention, and shall also be guilty of an offence, and shall in respect of each offence be liable on conviction to imprisonment for a term not exceeding two years, or to a fine not exceeding ten thousand shillings or to both such imprisonment and fine.

(2) In this section "assigned" means assigned by any assignment *inter vivos* other than an assignment by operation of law, and "assignor" and "assignee" have corresponding meanings.

16. Application in respect of assignees.

(1) Subject as hereinafter provided, the provisions of this Act shall continue to apply in respect of any debt to a money-lender in respect of money lent by him after the commencement of this Act or in respect of interest on money so lent or of the benefit of any agreement made or security taken in respect of any such debt or interest, notwithstanding that the debt or the benefit of the agreement or security may have been assigned to any assignee, and, except where the context otherwise requires, references in this Act to a money-lender shall, accordingly, be construed as including any such assignee as aforesaid provided that

(2) Notwithstanding anything in this Act–

(a) any agreement with, or security taken by, a money-lender in respect of money lent by him after the commencement of this Act shall be valid in favour of any *bona fide* assignee or holder for value without notice of any defect due to the operation of this Act and of any person deriving title under him; and

(b) any payment or transfer of money or property made *bona fide* by any person, whether acting in a fiduciary capacity or otherwise, on the faith of the validity of any such agreement or security, without notice of any such defect shall, in favour of that person, be as valid as it would have been if the agreement or security had been valid; and

(c) the provisions of this Act limiting the time for proceedings in respect of money lent shall not apply to any proceedings in respect of any such agreement or security commenced by a *bona fide* assignee or holder for value without notice that the agreement or security was affected by the operation of this Act, or by any person driving title under him, but in every such case the money-lender shall be liable to indemnify the borrower or any person who is prejudiced by virtue of this section, and nothing in this proviso shall render valid an agreement or security in favour of, or apply to proceedings commenced by, an assignee or holder for value who is himself a money-lender.

(3) Nothing in this section shall render valid for any purpose any agreement, security, or other transaction which would, apart from the provisions of this Act, have been void or unenforceable.

17. Provisions as to bankruptcy proceedings for money-lenders' loans.

(1) Where a debt due to a money-lender in respect of a loan made by him after the commencement of this Act includes interest, that interest shall, for the purposes of the provisions of the Bankruptcy Act relating to the presentation of a bankruptcy petition, voting at meetings, compositions and schemes of arrangement and dividend, be calculated at a rate not exceeding five per centum per annum, but nothing in the foregoing provision shall prejudice the right of the creditor to receive out of the estate, after all the debts proved in the estate have been paid in full, any higher rate of interest to which he may be entitled.

(2) The provisions of this subsection shall, in relation to such a debt as aforesaid, have effect in substitution for the provisions of subsection (1) of section 69 of the Bankruptcy Act.

(3) No proof of a debt due to a money-lender in respect of a loan made by him shall be admitted for any of the purposes of the Bankruptcy Act, unless the affidavit verifying the debt is accompanied by a statement showing in detail–

(a) the amount of the sums actually lent to the debtor and the dates on which they were lent, and the amount of every payment already received by the money-lender in respect of the loan and the date on which every such payment was made; and

(b) the amount of the balance which remains unpaid, distinguishing the amount of the principal from the amount of interest included therein, the appropriation between principal and interest being made in accordance with the provisions of this Act where the iinterest is not expressed by the contract for the loan in terms of a rate; and

(c) where the amount of interest included in the unpaid balance represents a rate per centum per annum exceeding five per centum, the amount of interest which would be so included if it were calculated at the rate of five per centum per annum.

(4) General rules may be made under section 120 of the Bankruptcy Act for the purpose of carrying into effect the objects of this section.

18. Prohibition of charge for expenses on loans.

Any agreement between a money-lender and a borrower or intending borrower for the payment by the borrower or intending borrower to the money-lender of any sum on account of costs, charges or expenses incidental to or relating to the negotiations for or the granting of the loan or proposed loan shall be illegal; and if any sum is paid to a money-lender by a borrower or intending borrower as for or on account of any such costs, charges or expenses, that sum shall be recoverable as a debt due to the borrower or intending borrower, or, in the event of the loan being completed, shall, if not so recovered, be set off against the amount actually lent and that amount shall be deemed to be reduced accordingly.

19. Limitation of time for proceedings.

(1) No proceedings shall lie for the recovery by a money-lender of any money lent by him after the commencement of this Act or of any interest in respect thereof, or of the enforcement of any agreement made or security taken after the commencement of this Act in respect of any loan made by him, unless the proceedings are commenced before the expiration of twelve months from the date which the cause of action accrued:

(2) Notwithstanding subsection (1) –

(a) if during the period of twelve months aforesaid or at any time within any subsequent period during which proceedings may by virtue of this proviso be brought, the debtor acknowledges in writing the amount due and gives a written undertaking to the money-lender to pay that amount, proceedings for the recovery of the amount due may be brought at any time within a period of twelve months from the date of the acknowledgement and undertaking;

(b) the time limited by the foregoing provisions of this section for the commencement of proceedings shall not begin to run in respect of any payments from time to time becoming due to a money-lender under a contract for the loan of money until a cause of action accrues in respect of the last payment becoming due under the contract;

(c) if at the date on which the cause of action accrues or on which any such acknowledgement and undertaking as aforesaid is given by the debtor, the person entitled to take the proceedings is *non compos mentis,* the time limited by the foregoing provisions of this section for the commencement of proceedings shall not begin to run until that person ceases to be *non compos memntis* or dies, whichever first occurs; and

(d) if at the date of which the cause of action accrues or on which any such acknowledgement and undertaking as aforesaid is given by the debtor, the debtor is out of Uganda, the time limited by the foregoing provisions of this section for the commencement of proceedings shall not begin to run until he returns to Uganda.

(3) Without prejudice to the powers of a court under section 12 of this Act, if at the time when proceedings are taken by a money-lender in respect of a default in the payment of any sum due to him under a contract for the loan of money, any further amount is outstanding under the contract but not yet due, the court may determine the contract and order the principal outstanding to be paid to the money-lender with such interest thereon, if any, as the court may allow up to the date of payment.

20. Penalty for taking promisory note in which amount left blank or not truly stated.

Any money-lender who takes, as security for any loan, a promissory note or other contract for the repayment of money lent in which the principal is to the knowledge of the lender not truly stated, or is left blank, shall be guilty of an offence and shall be liable on conviction to a fine not exceeding one thousand shillings or, in the event of a second or subsequent offence, either to a fine not exceeding three thousand shillings or to imprisonment for a term not exceeding six months.

21. Saving.

(1) The provisions of this Act shall not apply–

(a) to any money-lender transactions where the security for repayment of the loan and interest thereon is effected by execution of a chattels transfer in which the interest provided for is not in excess of nine per centum per annum;

(b) to any transaction where a bill of exchange is discounted at a rate of interest not exceeding nine per centum per annum;

(c) to any money-lending transaction where the security for repayment of the loan and interest thereon is effected by execution of a legal or equitable mortgage upon immovable property or of a charge upon immovable property or of any *bona fide* transaction of money-lending upon such mortgage or charge.

(2) The exemption provided for in this section shall apply whether the transactions referred to are effected by a money-lender or not.

(3) Any person who lends money only by means of the type of transaction set out in subsection (1) of this section and by means of no other type of transaction shall be deemed not to be a money-lender for the purpose of this Act.

22. Rules.

The Ministry may by rule prescribe –

(a) the form of a money-lender's licence;

(b) the officers entitled to issue money-lender's licences;

(c) the procedure to be followed and forms to be completed by applicants for money-lender's licences and for certificates under section 4 of this Act;

(d) any other matter necessary for the better carrying out of this Act.

Schedule

Calculation of interest where the interest charged on a loan is not expressed in terms of a rate

1. The amount of principal outstanding at any time shall be taken to be the balance remaining after deducting from the principal the total of the portions of any payments appropriated to principal in accordance with the provisions of this Act.
2. The several amounts taken to be outstanding by way of principal during the several periods ending on the dates on which payments are made shall be multiplied in each case by the number of calendar months during which those amounts are taken to be respectively outstanding and there shall be ascertained the aggregate amount of the sum so produced.
3. The total amount of the interest shall be divided by one-twelfth part of the aggregate amount mentioned in paragraph 2 of this Schedule, and the quotient, multiplied by one hundred, shall be taken to be the rate of interest per centum per annum.
4. If having regard to the intervals between successive payments it is desired so to do, the calculation of interest may be made by reference to weeks instead of months, and in such a case the foregoing paragraphs shall have effect as though in paragraph 2 of this Schedule the word "weeks" were substituted for the words "calendar months", and in paragraph 3 thereof the words "one fifty-second" were substituted for the words "one-twelfth".
5. Where any interval between successive payments is not a number of complete weeks or complete months, the foregoing paragraphs shall have effect as though one day were one-seventh part of a week or one-thirtieth part of a month, as the case may be.

Statutory Instruments

1966 No. 57
The Money Lenders (Exemption) Order, 1966

IN EXERCISE of the powers conferred upon the Minister by paragraph *(d)* of subsection (1) of section 2 of the Money-Lenders Ordinance, 1951, this Order is hereby made this 4th day of May, 1966.

1. The Development Finance Company of Uganda Limited, whose registered office is at 9/11, Obote Avenue (Ralli House), Kampala, is hereby exempted from the provisions of the Money-Lenders Ordinances, 1951.

2. This Order may be cited as the Money-Lenders (Exemption) Order, 1966.

L. KALULE-SETTALA
Minister of Finance

Date of publication: 13th May, 1966.

Statutory Instruments

1971 No. 49
The Money-Lenders (Exemption) Order, 1971

IN EXERCISE of the powers conferred upon the Minister by paragraph *(d)* of subsection (1) of section 2 of the Money-Lenders Ordinance, 1951, this Order is hereby made this 22nd day of March, 1971.

1. The National and Grindlays Finance and Developme`nt Corporation Limited and the Standard Bank Finance and Development Corporation Limited are hereby exempted from the provisions of the Money-Lenders Act.
2. This Order may be cited as the Money-Lenders (Exemption) Order, 1971.

F.B WAKHWEYA,
Minister of Finance

Date of publication: 30th March, 1971.

www.ingramcontent.com/pod-product-compliance
Lightning Source LLC
LaVergne TN
LVHW080043210926
848481LV00011B/3265
9789970023615